WOMEN IN HOLLYWOOD

DAWN B. SOVA

WOMEN IN HOLLYWOOD

FROM VAMP TO STUDIO HEAD

ALLSTON BRANCH LIBRARY

FROMM INTERNATIONAL · NEW YORK

First Fromm International Edition, 1998

LIBRARY OF CONGRESS CATALOGING-IN-PUBLICATION DATA

Sova, Dawn B.
   Women in Hollywood / Dawn B. Sova. -- 1st Fromm International ed.
      p. cm.
   Includes bibliographical references and index.
   ISBN 0-88064-232-7
   1. Women in the motion picture industry--California--Los Angeles.
 I. Title.
PN1995.9.W6S68 1998   98-8793
384'.8'0820979494--dc21   CIP

10 9 8 7 6 5 4 3 2 1

This book is dedicated to my son, Rob Gregor.

•

C O N T E N T S

•

Acknowledgments   ix

Introduction   xi

1 Pre-Hollywood Pioneers   1

2 Inventing Hollywood in the 1920s   25

3 Creating Stars in the 1930s   45

4 Glamour and Growth in the Golden Age:
   The Late 1930s and the 1940s   75

5 A Decade of Transition: The 1950s   106

6 Sex and Tumult: The 1960s   138

7 The Slow Climb Back: The 1970s   153

8 Women at the Top: The 1980s   168

9 The Limitless Decade: The 1990s   181

   Epilogue   197

   Appendix A: Academy Awards for Acting, 1928–1994   198

   Appendix B: Academy Awards in Other Categories   203

   Appendix C: Top Moneymaking Female Stars, 1933–1992   207

   Select Bibliography   210

   Index   217

•

A BOOK OF THIS SORT makes contact with many people in many capacities necessary. For them all, a simple "thank you" seems less than adequate.

I am grateful to my agent, Bert Holtje of James Peter Associates, Inc., for working the magic that knowledgeable agents work, and especially for the patience he has shown, a patience that lesser mortals could not possibly have.

I feel fortunate to have worked on this project with Jim Ellison, editor at Carol Publishing. His experience and skill were invaluable in maintaining the focus of the book, even when deadlines pressed a little too closely. I admire him for taking a previously committed work and handling it like a true gentleman, with style, grace, and patience.

Once again, I appreciate the invaluable assistance provided by the Garfield (N.J.) Free Public Library, whose director, I. MacArthur Nickles; two reference experts, Kathleen Zalenski and Karen Calandriello; and wonderful staff continue to perform near-miracles in locating materials throughout the state and throughout the nation, no matter what my latest topic.

The deepest appreciation of all, however, is given to my family. My son, Rob Gregor, is my most honest and most valued critic; he is also my most trusted researcher. My parents, Emil and Violet Sova, gave me life, and their love for and confidence in me sustain that life.

●

NINETEEN NINETY-FIVE marked the one-hundredth anniversary of the American film industry. Over the years, thousands of books have covered nearly every aspect of the business. Books that deal with the history of the industry have also been numerous but incomplete, because their focus has most commonly been on the accomplishments and contributions of men as studio heads, producers, directors, screenwriters, and actors, while women's accomplishments in only the last category have been of interest.

Unless dealt with in isolation, perhaps, in a history of women screenwriters, discussions of the contributions of women have been restricted to their roles on-screen, playing glamour girls, mothers, B-girls, sidekicks, and dowagers. Despite evidence of its existence, their influence in other areas has been ignored, played down, or even buried in collaborations with men. Yet, even the most naive of film students must realize that the history of film in Hollywood is also a history of women working in the industry—writing, directing, producing, and making highly successful films, behind as well as in front of the camera.

Despite the lack of credit given for their efforts—aside from their more visible on-screen roles—women have a Hollywood film history. Female film pioneers cofounded studios, directed and wrote many early screenplays, and edited numerous box office blockbusters. In 1918, director Lois Weber commanded the queenly sum of $5,000 weekly, a top Hollywood salary of the time for a director of either sex. Writer Anita Loos sold hundreds of story ideas to D. W. Griffith for the silent screen, then continued producing numerous scripts for talkies. Jeanne Macpherson collaborated with Cecil B. De Mille for more than three decades and throughout the years of production of the epic films that carved De Mille's name into American cinematic history but left hers in obscurity. Former studio secretary Anne Bauchens edited De Mille's The Ten Commandments and most of his other films past 1925, which accomplishment added to his fame but not to hers.

Despite their strong start in the silent era, women lost ground once the sound era began, and their limited behind-the-camera participation remained hidden for the following five decades. As the film industry grew larger and entered the Golden Age of the 1930s and 1940s, many women were pushed out of the high-power jobs of producer, director, and studio executives, although some fought tenaciously to remain in an industry that sought to exclude them. Only two female directors, Dorothy Arzner in the 1930s and former actress Ida Lupino in the 1950s, stand out in the five decades following the end of the silent era. From 1949 through 1979, women directed only one-fifth of 1 percent of all films put out by the major studios. Not only did the proportion of women directors drop sharply after the 1920s ended and female-headed studios went out of business, so did the number of scripts written by women. In 1928, 52 of 238 screenplays were written by women, but the percentage decreased sharply by 1940 when women accounted for only 64 of a total of 608 screenplays.

The 1960s and 1970s provided little improvement in opportunities for female directors, aside from 1976 when Lina Wertmuller became the first woman to earn the Academy Award nomination for Best

Director for Seven Beauties. Women behind the camera made important progress when film editor Dede Allen became one of the first editors to negotiate a cut of film profits. Only a few other women emerged to prominence in these two decades.

Real change became evident in the 1980s, the beginning of a restoration to power for women in the American film industry, as women scored several of the top box office successes of the decade, notably the production of Ghost by Lisa Weinstein and the production of Pretty Woman by Laura Ziskin. Commercial success led to a greater visibility of women in other male bastions of the industry. Women also began to occupy power positions with decision-making responsibility, as Sherry Lansing was named to head 20th Century–Fox, Dawn Steel headed Columbia Pictures, and actresses such as Jessica Lange, Goldie Hawn, and Sally Field formed their own production companies and used their star power to make deals. Dissatisfied with the quality of roles written for women, actresses who were proven winners at the box office produced, cowrote, directed, and starred in their own creations. New faces also emerged to make names for themselves as directors.

Halfway through the 1990s, women have created a strong place for themselves in Hollywood, and their influence is strongly felt in all facets of the business. The "old boy" network that formerly excluded women from the charmed circle of power has also suffered, because women are forming their own networks and aiding newcomers to the business. Unlike female film pioneers who occupied a tenuous position in an industry that only grudgingly tolerated their influence, contemporary women in the American film industry are not asking permission of their male counterparts, nor are they walking gingerly around male egos. They have learned that money is power in Hollywood, and they are using that power to exert their influence on the industry as a whole.

Pre-Hollywood Pioneers

•

THE STORY OF WOMEN in the American film industry begins nearly a century ago shortly after Thomas A. Edison introduced the Kinetoscope, in 1893, as a peep show novelty; the public loved it. Edison had little idea of the industry that would follow, but he did realize that the public needed moving pictures to view in its Kinetoscopes, so he built the first movie studio in 1893 in West Orange, New Jersey, and nicknamed it the "Black Maria" because of its dark, claustrophobic structure that resembled police vans of the period, known by that name. Edison later bought the rights to an invention that would project pictures on a large surface, renamed it the Edison Vitascope, and began his filmmaking venture, the Edison Company. The first film was a one-half-minute feature entitled *The Execution of Mary, Queen of Scots*, made in 1895, in which a male plays Mary, is led to a block, pushed onto it, then beheaded. The first Edison film to costar a woman was *John Rice–May Irwin Kiss*, originally created for Kinetoscopes in 1896. It was also the first film to feel the ire of censors. When projected on the big screen, the large mouths of these two romantic leads, who were appearing in a current Broadway play, provoked a deluge of letters to newspapers from moralists and reformers.

Edison failed to apply for patents, so other companies with similar aims and equipment also emerged, among them Selig, Vitagraph, Biograph, Kalem, and Essanay. And this is where the story of women in American film begins, for the many actresses who supplied these early screens with images also took a strong hand in the business. Because Edison wisely contacted the competing studios and created with them the Motion Picture Patents Company—a group that effectively destroyed competitors until 1917, when the monopoly was broken—there existed a network that inadvertently allowed women in one studio to become familiar with leaders in another studio and to more easily cross studio boundary lines.

Filmmaking before the movies began to "talk" is divided into two eras. The first, beginning in 1895, was a period of making and projecting films by trial and error, while the second can truly be called the actual silent era of film, beginning in about 1910 and continuing into the 1920s. A great deal of experimentation in film processes and development of equipment characterized these early years, as the business moved slowly toward Hollywood and what would become a strong studio system.

Women had a major role in the early days of the American film industry because no rigid role distinctions had yet been set. Both men and women learned as they went, and there were no "experts" to establish rules and regulations in the filmmaking business—whoever could achieve a desired effect or result, male or female, got the job. The availability of start-up money determined who might become a studio head, and wise and solvent women sought the advantage. Actresses such as Florence Lawrence, Clara Kimball Young, and Mary Pickford, for the most part anonymous in the early films, parlayed their familiarity with the business into the creation of their own studios. Because film making was learned through hands-on experience, and also because no one had as yet perceived of film making as a profession with any status, women found many opportunities available in directing, screenwriting, film editing, and other areas of production.

Florence Lawrence (National Archives)

The pre-Hollywood film pioneers were based in the northeast portion of the United States, and several later Hollywood stars had their first acting experiences in New Jersey studios. The list includes Tallulah Bankhead, Theda Bara, Ethel Barrymore, Billie Burke, Dorothy Gish, Lillian Gish, Mae Marsh, Alla Nazimova, Mary Pickford, Blanche Sweet, and Norma Talmadge.

The first woman to head a movie studio in America was French-born Alice Guy Blaché, also the first female director in the history of world cinema. She would be followed by other women—among them Lule Warrenton, Florence Lawrence, Dorothy Davenport, and Lois Weber—as studio heads. Blaché began working as a secretary with the Gaumont Company in France in 1896, until Leon Gaumont instructed Alice to establish the filmmaking division. She produced nearly all of the films released by Gaumont over the following decade and wrote many of the scripts. After working with the company in various capacities for a decade, she married head cameraman Herbert Blaché in 1907, and they were sent to the United States to set up the Gaumont Talking Pictures Company.

As Alice became more involved in the commercial as well as the creative aspects of the business, she realized that films had to be made that were specific to America and to the interests of Americans. In 1910, she and Herbert, with partner George Magie, founded the Solax Company in Flushing, New York, and they moved their operation to Fort Lee, New Jersey, in 1912. In France, Alice had acted in and directed films for the Gaumont Talking Pictures company. In the United States, she served as the production head and directed the more than 300 films produced by Solax—largely the comedies, melodramas, and adventure stories that were popular with American audiences. As Solax concentrated on feature-length films, the Blachés organized a new company to produce the longer movies, and they began to release their works through larger companies, such as Pathé Exchange and Metro Pictures. They produced films that starred actresses Bessie Love, Dolores Cassinelli, Claire Whitney, Olga Petrova, and Mary Miles Minter. When they weren't using their studios, they leased them to other production companies, most notably the Goldwyn production company. The studio dissolved when the Blachés ended their marriage. Alice Blaché returned to France in 1922.

During its existence, the Gaumont Talking Pictures Company provided opportunity to director Lois Weber, who later went to Hollywood, where Universal Studios hired her in 1916 at a salary of $5,000 per week, thus making her one of the top-salaried directors of the time. She had begun her show-business career by touring in 1905 with a road company that performed the melodrama *Why Girls Leave Home*. Soon after beginning the tour, she married the manager of the company, Phillips Smalley, who demanded that she be a stay-at-home wife. In 1908, while her husband was on tour with another show, Lois applied for and obtained a job with the Gaumont studios, newly begun by the Blachés, where she took on a variety of tasks. She started by acting, but her writing and directing skills were in greater need. She has the distinction of being the first woman to write, direct, produce, and star in a movie, seven decades before Barbra Streisand performed a similar feat in the 1983 *Yentl*.

Unlike other writer-directors of the day, who stayed safely in the realm of adventure or comedy entertainment, Weber was willing to take risks; she wrote films that tackled women's problems and addressed such issues as birth control in *The Hand That Rocks the Cradle* (1917), ethnic bias in *The Jew's Christmas* (1913), and capital punishment in *The People vs. John Doe* (1916). She also has the distinction of being one of the earliest of filmmakers to confront the censor, with the 1914 film *Hypocrites*, in which a minister is stoned to death for displaying a statue titled "The Naked Truth." The thirty-three-year-old Weber played the statue in the movie, because no actress was willing to disrobe on screen. The film was banned by the mayor of Boston until clothes were painted onto the statue, while crowds rioted at New York theaters when it was shown. The Ohio Board of Censors, choosing to risk nothing, banned the film with no qualification. Needless to say, *Hypocrites* was a huge commercial success because of all the free publicity. Weber also got on the wrong side of the censors—and produced another commercial success—in her most famous film, *Where Are My Children?* It told the story of a young working-class girl who is seduced and impregnated by a wealthy young man, who then coerces her into an abortion, during which she dies. Philadelphia first banned *Children*, then censorship trials ensued in cities throughout the nation, and the film made the then-fabulous sum of $3 million in profits for Universal Studios.

Florence Lawrence became an early studio head, as well as the first popular screen actress, when she and her husband formed the Victor Film Company in 1912 in Fort Lee, New Jersey. She had acted in movies for the Biograph Company studios earlier, but few people knew her name. The names of movie actors who worked for the companies that belonged to the Motion Picture Patents Company were kept from the public so that they would not become too well known and demand higher salaries. Therefore, the leading performer of a studio would be known under the studio name, as "The Vitagraph Girl" or, in Lawrence's case, "The Biograph Girl." Lawrence left Biograph in 1910 to join an independent studio, IMP Company, which publicized her by name, thus making her a star as an individual rather than as simply a company property. In 1912, she was recruited to found the Victor Film Company. Lawrence was the star of all the films made by her company during the first year, and her regular leading man was Mary Pickford's first husband, Owen Moore. The films were short by today's standards, usually one, two, or three reels, each running about ten minutes. They included comedies, adventure stories, and melodramas. Soon after its founding, the Victor Film Company joined Universal Film Manu-facturing Company, and Universal took major control of the enterprise by 1914. That same year, Lawrence suffered extensive injuries in a studio fire, requiring a two-year recuperation period. When she attempted a comeback, a physical relapse forced her into retirement. She emerged once again in 1921, but by then the industry had changed, and most of it had moved west to Hollywood. For the next seventeen years, Lawrence played bit parts and took what extra work she could get. She committed suicide in 1938.

Technical personnel of the pre-Hollywood studios remain nameless, and some doubled in various capacities, especially as actors. Alice Joyce and Marguerite Courtot were both actresses with the Kalem Company, founded in 1907 in New York City, with later studios in Cliffside Park, New Jersey, and Jacksonville, Florida. In addition to its short (one- or two-reel) adventure films, the company featured the demure and lady-like Joyce and Courtot in serials bearing their names. *The Alice Joyce Series* ran from 1913 through 1914, while *The Ventures of Marguerite* appeared in 1915. Both stars were paired with handsome leading men, and their characters were forced to contend with and to triumph over the forces of evil.

The growing film industry soon began to focus on the commercial possibilities in promoting specific stars. Clara Kimball Young was a leading actress with Vitagraph Company when, in 1914, Lewis Selznick, the general manager of Universal, joined with mail order merchant Arthur Spiegel to lure her away to their new enterprise, Equitable Pictures, a Fort Lee, New Jersey–based production company cofounded by the Shubert Theatrical Company. Young became the principal star, and Equitable was bought by World Pictures the following year. Young made eleven pictures in her two years with World, including the 1915 *Camille*. She then left when Selznick formed the Clara Kimball Young Film Company, with her as the star. She made thirteen pictures over the following three years, all financial successes.

Many women writers for these early studios went on to write for Hollywood studios. Clair Beranger, who in 1928 married William De Mille, the producer-director brother of Cecil B. De Mille, was a writer for Edison, Kalem, Fox, Pathé, and World before going in 1922 to Hollywood, where she continued to write screenplays throughout the 1920s. Her husband depended upon her for most of his films. Bess Meredyth started with Biograph in 1911 as an actress, and by 1917, she was writing scripts and turned out over ninety features by 1919. In 1912, Anita Loos sold her first story to D. W. Griffith at the Biograph Company. She was paid fifteen dollars. Griffith filmed it in Fort Lee, New Jersey, turning it into *The New York Hat*. She wrote for Griffith

Anita Loos (MoMA/Film Stills)

while he remained with Biograph, then joined him when he made his move to Hollywood, where she was assigned to write scripts for Douglas Fairbanks in 1916. Thanks to Loos's witty and exuberant dialogue, Fairbanks exuded charm and personality on screen and became a success, thus increasing her value—and salary—as a screenwriter. Throughout the silent era and into the 1930s, she continued a steady stream of female-oriented films, as well as the occasional melodrama. Loos is probably best known for her novel and play *Gentlemen Prefer Blondes*, filmed first in 1928 with Ruth Taylor, then in 1953 with Marilyn Monroe and Jane Russell.

Frances Marion, a cub reporter on her hometown paper and later a prolific Hollywood screenwriter, began her career when Lois Weber gave her a break in the fledgling Hollywood film industry in 1915.

Frances Marion with Mary Pickford (MoMA/Film Stills)

Weber trained Marion in all aspects of the production business, from editing and costuming through set design and maintenance. Her first work was supplying the extras in mob scenes with the correct responses to mouth in case deaf viewers in the silent movie house audiences were reading lips. Although such training was exhausting, it prepared her to be aware of all aspects of the production when writing, thus making her later screenplays easier to produce.

Marion left for New York in 1916 and persuaded Louis Selznick to hire her at World Pictures; the next year, she moved to the newly created Fox Film Corporation. She wrote nineteen screenplays for the two companies in 1916 and 1917, but her move back to Hollywood in 1922 sealed her success. Marion became a frequent writer for Mary Pickford, then went on to write the scripts for *Stella Dallas* (1925), *The Son of the Sheik* (1926), *Anna Christie* (1926), and other star vehicles. She continued to write, turning out numerous successful movies in the 1930s and winning Oscars for *The Big House* and *The Champ*.

Quite a few women worked as directors during the silent era, and they were successful both in the pre-Hollywood and the early Hollywood periods. All of the pre-Hollywood studios employed women directors, and Universal Pictures of the late 1910s had nine women in charge of direction at one time. Lois Weber, Ida May Park, Margery Wilson, and Dorothy Davenport wielded considerable directorial power and turned out numerous productions. Actresses also moved freely from in front of the camera to behind the camera with the aim of providing themselves with the type of direction that would exhibit their talents on screen to the greatest advantage. Film history has generally omitted their names, and the directorial efforts of early actresses such as Margery Wilson, Ruth Stonehouse, Kathlyn Williams, and Lucille McVey have been lost with the records of the pre-Hollywood studios. Such famous actresses as Lillian Gish, Alla Nazimova, Mabel Normand, and Dorothy Gish made it a point to direct or write their early films as a means of controlling the quality of the productions.

Gene Gauntier was one early actress who found success as a screenwriter and a director after starting her career acting with the Kalem Film Company in New York in 1906. But perhaps more important for the future of the movie industry, she was the woman who first recognized and encouraged the directing talents of a young unknown named D. W. Griffith.

Within the year she was lured away by the Biograph Company, but after a short stint there, Gauntier decided to return to Kalem in 1908. By 1910, she had begun her own production company, Gene Gauntier Features Players Company, based in New York and specializing in action/adventure films.

Gauntier also holds the dubious distinction of being the person whose indiscretion resulted in a change in copyright law, related to screenwriting property rights. In 1912, the screenplay written by Gauntier for the 1907 Kalem production of *Ben-Hur* became the subject of a test case which eventually resulted in a court decision that films produced in the United States must be registered for copyright. Gauntier had adapted the Lew Wallace novel without seeking permission from the author's estate. Kalem lost the suit, and Gauntier entered copyright law history.

Jeanne Macpherson, who enjoyed a three-decades-long personal and professional collaboration with Cecil B. De Mille, began her career in film as an actress with the Biograph Company, then moved to the Edison Company after two years. When she moved west to Hollywood in 1914, she was given her own unit at Universal and wrote, directed, and acted in a large number of two-reel films. Her break into directing came when the negative of a film she had written was destroyed in a fire and the original director was no longer available for the remake. She successfully shepherded the film through to completion and established herself as both a leading lady and director, a dual role that led the studio to overwork her. In 1915, she joined De Mille and became his writing collaborator on such films as *Male and Female* (1919), *The Ten Commandments* (1923), and *The King of Kings* (1926), as well as early and trendy comedies that starred a young Gloria Swanson and that poked fun at society.

Women also found success as film editors, once movies progressed beyond the simple one-reel affairs of the very early productions. A good film editor then, as now, worked closely with the producer or director to combine individual scenes from the footage shot by the director. In some cases, a skillful editor could save a mediocre film from obscurity. Early editors were simply called cutters, because their job was not to create a vision but to eliminate excess film from the beginning or end of one reel and splice the pieces together. However, the films of D. W. Griffith demanded a great deal of the film editor, who had to blend together shifts in camera angles, chase sequences, and a variety of reaction shots. Anne Bauchens began to work early with Cecil B. De Mille, editing his monumental epics. Her value in the industry, in common with that of other film editors, was not recognized until the Academy Awards were created and the "film editing" category was added in 1934. That year she was nominated for editing

Gloria Swanson, 1919 (National Archives)

De Mille's *Cleopatra*. Over the decades, Bauchens won the Academy Award for editing once and received two additional Academy Award nominations for her editing. In 1940, Bauchens won an Oscar for her work on De Mille's *North West Mounted Police*. She was later nominated in 1952 for *The Greatest Show on Earth*, and in 1956 for her work on *The Ten Commandments*.

From its beginnings, the American film industry courted female viewers, and early films included many female characters whose behavior was carefully orchestrated as part of the industry's effort to reach middle-class female viewers. Before the advent of film, public entertainment had a shady reputation, and "respectable" middle-class ladies and families rarely attended stage shows. Although the rich had always had access to private performances, affordable entertainment for the middle class was limited to either dramas presented in church or to traveling shows. However, in their effort to appeal to the gender that controlled the money (men), traveling shows tailored their material and presentation to bring in males, not women and families. Minstrel shows and traveling theater could be very bawdy, and such entertainment was considered too immoral for the delicate natures of "respectable" women.

Early filmmakers were clever enough to target a huge, untapped market of spectators with moderate financial means but a great desire to be entertained. Once the feature film had become somewhat refined and the large movie theaters were built to show this new entertainment, film entrepreneurs began to tailor their product to appeal to middle-class women. If they could bring that target audience into their theaters, their success would be ensured because women would not go to the theater alone. Families, other women, and men would be there with them, enjoying the spectacle and spending money.

In order to appeal to female audiences, the filmmakers demanded that their screenplays reflect the nature and concerns of society. In the early years of film, the virginal heroine who reflected the moral values of small-town America was symbolic of the way in which society had determined that middle-class women were expected to think of themselves, and that was how middle-class men preferred their mothers, wives, and daughters to act.

Serial heroines captured the attention of viewers, and filmmakers created their story installments to keep people returning to the theater to learn what would happen next. The first commercially successful serial was *The Perils of Pauline*, a twenty-part serial produced by the Pathé Company in 1914. Employing dangerous stunts, outdoor sites, and cliff-hanger endings to each installment, this serial created a model that was heavily imitated. The "Queen of the Serials," Pearl White, was placed in a series of life- and virtue-threatening situations. Unlike earlier heroines of melodrama who swooned, wept, and pleaded with the villain, their eyes large and tearful and hands clasped in supplication, Pauline was intelligent, shrewd, and tough, and she always managed to emerge from each episode with her virtue—and everything else—intact.

Pearl White began acting in traveling stock companies at age six, then left to become the secretary at a small film company where in 1910 she was given a lead role in *The Life of Buffalo Bill*. She later worked for the Pathé Company which placed her first in the "Pauline" serial, then in later serials such as *The Exploits of Elaine* in 1915, *Pearl of the Army* (1916), and *The Fatal Ring* (1917), all with White as a plucky and daring heroine. When she grew tired of the serials, she left Pathé for Fox, where she made several films, with none of her earlier success. Few other actresses achieved such fame in the serials, but Ruth Roland made a respectable number of Western serials in which she played the tomboy cowgirl. She frequently wrote the scripts as well.

Mary Pickford, with her demure, ruffled dresses, lacy anklets, Mary Jane shoes, and long sausage curls, was another of the early film heroines. She parlayed her image as "America's Sweetheart" not only into a good income but also into substantial power behind the scenes. Pickford began life as Gladys Smith in Ontario, Canada, and started acting in a traveling theater company at the age of five. When she was thirteen, she appeared on Broadway in David Belasco's *The Warrens of*

Mary Pickford (National Archives)

Virginia, and changed her name to Mary Pickford. Three years later, in 1909, she began a film career at the Biograph Company under the direction of D. W. Griffith with *Her First Biscuits*. In 1912, Pickford made *The New York Hat* for Biograph, a movie based on Anita Loos's first filmed screenplay. The story focuses on a young woman's dreams of escaping her shabby existence, and of her longing for the stylish hat—the latest fashion from New York City—that she sees in a store window. Overcome with sympathy, the young minister in town buys her the hat, and the town gossips begin to whisper of a scandal. To save both of their reputations, the minister exhibits a letter that the girl's mother had written as she was dying, asking that he take care of her daughter. The movie culminates in the minister's proposal of marriage and the girl's acceptance.

As she moved from Biograph to IMP Studios, then to the Famous Players company in 1912, Pickford shrewdly negotiated salary increases until, by 1915, she was earning $10,000 weekly. Pickford played a variety of roles in her early films, including an Indian maiden, a young bride, and a coy coquette. Among the last films made in her pre-Hollywood days were *Madame Butterfly* (1915), *The Pride of the Clan* (1917), and *The Poor Little Rich Girl* (1917). By 1919, Pickford was in Hollywood where, with Charlie Chaplin, Douglas Fairbanks, and D. W. Griffith, she formed United Artists film studios.

Blanche Sweet succeeded Mary Pickford as D. W. Griffith's leading actress at Biograph, and she made her debut in 1911 as an independent-minded telegraph operator who outwits bandits in *The Lonedale Operator*. Unlike the coy, simpering little-girl characters played by Pickford, Sweet's characters have both brains and energy. In the movie, Sweet manages to fend off her attacker and telegraph her fiancé, a railroad engineer, for help. As he speeds his engine toward the station, Sweet gains the advantage over her attacker by tricking him into believing that her wrench is a pistol. Her startled fiancé enters the station to find Sweet keeping the man at bay with the disguised wrench. She plays similarly assertive roles in *The Battle* (1911) and *Judith of Bethulia* (1913), pushing her cowardly fiancé into a fight in the former film and, in the latter, playing the Jewish heroine who seduces and assassinates the brutal Assyrian leader Holofernes in order to save her people from destruction.

In 1914, Sweet moved to the Lasky Company, where she made nineteen films, including several that dealt with controversial topics. In *The Secret Sin* (1915), she plays poverty-stricken twin sisters whose lives are made a living hell by sweatshop labor and drug addiction, while in *Public Opinion* (1916), she is a nurse who is accused falsely of murder and tried in the media before she can get a fair trial in court. Sweet continued to make films with Lasky until 1918, when she formed a partnership with director Marshall Neilan to coproduce their own films, which were distributed by Pathé, First National, and MGM.

Comedy actress Mabel Normand also directed her own films. She started at the Biograph Company in 1910, where first D. W. Griffith and then Mack Sennett guided her early career. Her early roles were created to exploit her comedic talents, and in rapid succession she appeared in *The Diving Girl* (1911), *Mabel's Adventures* (1911), *Mabel's Heroes* (1912), and *Mabel's Awful Mistakes* (1912). Normand left Biograph and went to Sennett's Keystone Studios in 1912, where she not only acted but also directed a number of her own films. In 1915 and 1916, she starred in several comedies with the extremely popular Roscoe "Fatty" Arbuckle, then left to sign with the Samuel Goldwyn Company. In 1922, Normand's career was in ruins when she became a suspect in the murder of her lover, William Desmond Taylor. The bad publicity killed her career, and her wild living destroyed her body. She died of pneumonia, complicated by tuberculosis, at the age of thirty-six.

Lillian Gish and her sister, Dorothy, also began their careers in pre-Hollywood films, and they owe their start to Mary Pickford, whom they knew from their child acting days in stock companies. Pickford convinced D. W. Griffith to employ the teenage Gish sisters for his movies, and Lillian appeared in *An Unseen Enemy*, a two-reel film made by the Biograph Company in 1912. She joined Griffith when he went to Hollywood and appeared in twenty films; Griffith cast her in the epic *Birth of a Nation* (1915). Her success impressed him so much

Lillian Gish (Evans Collection)

that he made her the star of his most important films until 1922, when a salary dispute ended their relationship. Once she had signed with MGM, Gish made *La Bohème* (1926), *The Scarlet Letter* (1926), and other films, but her looks worked against her as the Jazz Age intruded and made the feminine ideal outmoded. She made a few more film appearances in the 1920s through the 1940s, but none was successful. Instead, she turned to the stage, where she created numerous successful roles in the decades following her exit from film. She returned at intervals to act in such films as Robert Altman's *A Wedding* (1978) and *The Whales of August* (1987).

Other silent screen stars began their careers in pre-Hollywood film companies on the east coast. Norma Talmadge was born in Brooklyn, and she started her acting career by posing for photographic slides that were used to illustrate the songs on nickelodeon screens. She later worked as an extra at the Vitagraph film studios in Flatbush, then left for Hollywood to make films with D. W. Griffith. In Hollywood, Talmadge met movie mogul Joseph Schenck, whom she married in 1917 and who worked to turn her into a star. She exuded little of the distinctive personality of her contemporaries, (she is unknown to movie fans today), yet Talmadge is really representative of stars in this era because her career spans the silent years and ends when the sound films begin. She was beautiful and wore stunning clothes in her very emotional roles that were characterized by romance, suffering, and a faraway look of sadness that the camera caught in close-up shots of her pained face. In essence, she personified on-screen elegance with her ability to wear clothes and her carefully arranged hair. Although most of her films were instantly forgettable, several roles became central to the growth of film in the silent era. She made *New Moon* in 1919, followed by *Smilin' Through* in 1922. *Secrets* (1924) and *Kiki* (1926) were well received, but she earned real praise for *Camille* (1927) and *DuBarry, Woman of Passion* (1930). Although her films were box office successes, few have survived the years, and Talmadge remains one of the least-known of the successful players on the silent screen.

A more exotic product of the early film industry is Alla Nazimova,

Norma Talmadge (National Archives)

billed only as "Nazimova," who was born in the Crimea in Russia and began her career as a stage star. In 1916, after years of stage work, she filmed her first movie, *War Brides*, at Ideal Studios in Hudson Heights, New Jersey, for which she was paid $1,000 per day for thirty days. She returned to the stage for two more years, then headed west to Metro Studios in Hollywood and made *Revelation* (1918), *Toys of Fate* (1918), and *Eye for Eye* (1918) as well as a range of other soap operas that were topped by her tear-filled *Camille* in 1921. She was unable to maintain a thriving career in the Hollywood silent films and played occasional bit parts in later sound films, such as *Blood and Sand* (1941) and *The Bridge of San Luis Rey* (1944).

At the same time that the sweet and simpering heroine drew the approval of audiences, viewers also welcomed the sexy star who would heat up the screen—within the moral limits of the time, of course. The flip side of the virginal heroine was the "vamp," the exotic and wicked seductress who cast irresistible spells over men with her sexually aggressive behavior and intriguing, relatively unclothed body. Nazimova had made hesitant moves in this direction, but Theda Bara took the role to its limits as the movies' first female sex symbol. Born Theodosia Goodman in Cincinnati, Ohio, she slithered across pre-1920s screens in forty movies between 1916 and 1919 as "The Vamp," short for "vampire." The first twenty-two films were made in New Jersey studios. Still a movie extra at the age of twenty-six in 1916, she happened to be in the right place at the right time when movie-maker Frank J. Powell decided to film the play *A Fool There Was*. He decided that an unknown should be cast as the evil seductress of the film, and he planned a media blitz to excite future filmgoers. Powell first changed Goodman's name to Theda Bara, then manufactured a mysterious past for her, claiming that she was the daughter of an Egyptian ruler and that her name was an anagram of the words "Arab death." Publicity stunts were arranged in which the heavily made-up Bara assumed an evil persona and was rumored to perform unspeakable acts in black-draped hotel suites in which Eastern incenses burned constantly. As press releases "leaked" stories of macabre and unearthly behavior to the media, the public devoured every sinister detail. Viewers flocked to the film, famous for its line "... kiss me, my fool!" making it so successful that it provided the start-up money to establish the Fox Film Corporation in New Jersey.

On-screen, Bara exuded an evil sensuality that rendered men helpless, and she did so in a series of suggestively titled movies, among them *Sin* (1915), *The She-Devil* (1919), and *The Siren's Song* (1919). By 1919, there were so many imitation "vamps" on the screen that the concept became high camp. In these movies, virtue was rewarded, but seductive, sexually aggressive behavior represented a danger for both "the vamp" and the men who succumbed to her. Halfway through her career, Fox Film Corporation moved with Bara to Hollywood. Two years later, Bara was no longer a box-office attraction. She retired in 1926 with her husband, director Charles Brabin, and substantial investments, to become a Hollywood hostess who threw great dinner parties, but she never again acted.

Tallulah Bankhead and Ethel Barrymore had their start in the pre-Hollywood film studios, and both went on to careers in the later sound films. Bankhead, a society beauty and the daughter of a speaker of the House of Representatives, had her first role in *Thirty a Week*, a 1918 film made by Samuel Goldwyn in a leased studio in Fort Lee, New Jersey. Barrymore, as a member of the prominent stage dynasty, brought respectability to screen acting when she made movies for both the Famous Players film studios and Metro Pictures. Among these early films were *The Nightingale* (1914), *The Awakening of Helen Ritchie* (1916), and *The Divorcee* (1919).

Although the names of many of the pre-Hollywood women pioneers are no longer known, others went on to star in, direct, write, and place their personal imprint on the silent films that followed as women joined in inventing Hollywood. As the film industry expanded and became a full-fledged, multi-million-dollar business, the roles of both men and women became more strictly defined and limited. Women who were already in the industry learned that the increasing complexity of the business required that they choose between struggling to retain their

Theda Bara,1917 (Evans)

decision-making positions and assuming new roles as screen stars. No longer could they act and maintain creative control over their performances by directing, editing, and the like. Those who were new to the industry were even denied that choice as they were steered toward the screen to fill an industry's hunger for new faces. The stories of both groups of women, the pre-silent pioneers and those who followed, constitute the history of Hollywood in the decades since.

Inventing Hollywood in the 1920s

●

HOLLYWOOD IN THE EARLY 1920s was an exciting place for women. The industry underwent major changes as the nation bounced back from World War I. The formerly strict moral codes loosened as young men returning from war and the women who had waited for them decided to deal with life's uncertainty by enjoying the present. The Jazz Age introduced the flapper, with her short hair, short skirts, and taste for fun, and women in everyday life became more visible and daring. The film industry was forced to change with the times, and many former stars no longer suited the tastes of the new generation of moviegoers. Those who would remain had to adapt.

One of the most visible and innocent reminders of that change was the decision of "America's sweetheart" to cut her hair. Mary Pickford had worn her long sausage curls throughout her teenage years and her twenties. In 1927, at the age of thirty, she ceremoniously and publicly grew up when the curls were cut off. That was the same year that the world discovered "It," in the form of Brooklyn-born Clara Bow, who epitomized the spirit of the Jazz Age as the "It" girl. Part virgin, part

●

vamp, the "It" girl enjoyed life and parties, but her goal was to find a man to love.

Even "The Vamp," Theda Bara, recognized that her days were numbered, as she was forced to make way for actresses such as Pola Negri and Greta Garbo, who exuded a different sort of exotic presence. Where the success of a film in the pre-Hollywood days might be based upon the one star for whom the script had most likely been especially written, studios started to concentrate on first creating good stories and then selecting the right actors and actresses to play the parts. Rather than cast only the lead with care, studios began to take great care in casting even minor roles. The attention to detail created changes in the way scripts were written and films were directed. Instead of writing on the run, or making up the dialogue as filming was in process, screenwriters took on a new importance as the public demanded a more polished product. No longer was the public content simply to see moving images on the screen. More sophisticated tastes meant more sophisticated filming and cutting techniques. In short, the film industry was forced to mature.

The early 1920s offered roles for some of the actresses who had captured the public's adulation in the 1910s, but the numbers were few. Mary Pickford continued to exist within the changing social and moral climate, and she actually thrived in the first half of the 1920s as she remained the "Little Mary" of before. In 1919, she had put her shrewd business sense into a collaboration with Charlie Chaplin, Douglas Fairbanks, and D. W. Griffith, forming United Artists, with the aim of taking creative control of her films. She divorced her first husband, Owen Moore, the next year and married screen idol and business partner Douglas Fairbanks, then had a smash hit in *Pollyana* (1920), in which the twenty-seven-year-old woman played a twelve-year-old girl. Pickford, wanting to shed her "Little Mary" image, played a guitar-strumming Spanish street singer in *Rosita* (1923), and an independent young woman in Elizabethan times in *Dorothy Vernon of Haddon Hall* (1924). Her fans, however, cried out for "Little Mary," and Pickford acquiesced by starring in *Little Annie Rooney* (1925) and *Sparrows*

(1926), both of which did very well at the box office. Part of Pickford's continued success may have been due to the fact that she *was* different from the other screen heroines; she had remained unique. She made her last silent film, *My Best Girl*, in 1927, the same year that she cut off her curls. *Coquette* (1929), Pickford's first sound film and a great success, won her the Academy Award for Best Actress. She made one film with Fairbanks—*The Taming of the Shrew* (1929), which flopped—then had two of her own failures, *Kiki* (1931) and *Secrets* (1933), before retiring from the screen.

Blanche Sweet continued to act throughout the 1920s, appearing in more romantic films than previously. In 1923, she made *Anna Christie* with Thomas Ince, a film that won her great critical acclaim. She ended the major portion of her film career with *The Silver Horde* in 1930, returning to the screen only once in later decades, to play a cameo role in *The Five Pennies*, a 1959 film starring Danny Kaye. Of personal note is Sweet's second marriage in 1936 to actor Raymond Hackett, the brother of Albert Hackett who was married to Frances Goodrich, a noted woman screenwriter from 1933 through 1962.

Despite the limited success of actresses who had established followings in the pre-Hollywood era, audiences no longer wanted the cardboard heroes and heroines of the past, the men with perfectly chiseled features and the sugary, pretty girls. Pretty wasn't as important as that indefinable quality of sex appeal, for both men and women. Realism encroached upon the romantic idealism of most formerly successful films, as audiences began to smirk at the old-fashioned, perennial happy ending. The public demanded that its fighting heroes have dirty faces and torn clothing when the dust cleared, and its heroines could have more than a hint of the vamp even when playing the virgin. And the writers and directors, as well as the actresses, gave the audience what it wanted.

In the 1920s, actresses exaggerated the fantasies of middle-class women viewers. Wearing the most stylish of coiffures and extravagant wardrobes, stars like Gloria Swanson postured and preened, playing the roles of the very rich and pampered in such movies as *Don't Change*

Your Husband (1919) and *Why Don't You Change Your Wife?* (1920). Although women on screen could be flirtatious and sexually playful, the flappers portrayed by Louise Brooks, Colleen Moore, Leatrice Joy, Eleanor Boardman, and Joan Crawford might have bobbed hair and short skirts, but they still watched their reputations. Of course, the change in women's on-screen roles played havoc with the roles of their heroes. One-dimensional villains and heroes were suitable male roles when women were virgins or vamps, but the "new woman" needed a new man.

The ultimate flapper was Colleen Moore, whom writer F. Scott Fitzgerald called "the torch" of the "Flaming Youth" of the Jazz Age. Although she had been acting since the age of fourteen, and had already made thirty-four movies, Moore's role in the 1923 *Flaming Youth* made her a star. Her bobbed hair and shingled bangs started a fashion trend, and the wild parties, frantic dancing, and romance of *Flaming Youth* characterized a generation. The flapper, however, retains her virtue and throws herself off a yacht and into the ocean rather than to submit to sexual advances. In flapper fashion, however, she must be rescued. Once successful, Moore played the role in later movies, such as *Flirting with Love* (1924), *We Moderns* (1925), *Naughty But Nice* (1927), *Her Wild Oat* (1927), *Happiness Ahead* (1928), and *Synthetic Sin* (1928). Throughout all of these movies, Moore acted with a wide-eyed innocence that made her something of a Jazz Age Mary Pickford.

Former Ziegfeld dancer Louise Brooks met the requirements of the flapper in appearance when she was lured to Hollywood by Paramount in 1925. She requires mention more because of her serious political stand against the Hollywood filmmaking machine than for her films. She had a mind of her own, and her career was cut short because her desire for creative control branded her as difficult to work with. Although she made only a few films, most notably *A Girl in Every Port* (1928) and *Beggars of Life* (1928), she refused to conform to the Hollywood pattern and left in 1929 for Germany, where she continued to make movies on her own terms.

Red-haired, pouting Clara Bow, the "It" girl, was the sexy alternative

Louise Brooks (Movie Graphics)

to Colleen Moore and Louise Brooks. In movie after movie, as well as in her personal life, she fulfilled her publicist's claim as being "the hottest jazz baby in films." Born in Brooklyn, she made her first picture. She made fourteen films in the next two years, but her career really caught on with the 1926 film *Mantrap*. The public loved the sexy new heroine who romped through her movie looking like a girl who just wanted to have a good time, no strings attached. Similar to the vamp of a few years before, she pursued and seduced men aggressively, but, unlike the vamp, she posed no danger to her victims. With her, sex seemed to be fun, even though the moral code of the time forced directors to plant more of the sex in the viewer's mind than on the screen.

The public imagination was also fueled by Bow's personal life, which was even more raucous than those of her characters. She was rumored to have had affairs with all of her leading men, as well as with numerous other men along the way. In 1927, Bow starred in *It*, a movie produced by writer Elinor Glyn, who had defined "It" as being sex appeal, a "strange magnetism which attracts both sexes. . . . Physical attraction, but beauty is unnecessary." The movie firmly established Bow as the ultimate silent screen sex symbol. She made more sedate movies as the 1920s wound down, but sound put an end to her popularity as the public could not ignore her heavy Brooklyn accent, which grated on their ears. After a 1931 trial in which her former secretary Daisy DeVoe told tales of drugs, adultery, bribery, and blackmail, Bow's popularity dipped even lower. She made a few nondescript films in the 1930s and retired from the screen.

Where Clara Bow gained a following for her raw sensuality, Gloria Swanson's attraction in the 1920s lay in her overdressed modeling of conspicuous consumption. Like Bow, Swanson lived her screen life in her private life, but her vices were lavish surroundings, vast wardrobes, and men with money. She started acting as an extra and appeared in films made in several pre-Hollywood studios, such as *Teddy at the Throttle*, Mack Sennett's Keystone Studios movie in 1916. The film parodies the romantic adventure movies made by D. W. Griffith at

Gloria Swanson (left) with author Elinor Glyn, the writer who defind "IT" — on the set of The Great Moment *(1921), which Glyn wrote.* (MoMA/Film Stills)

that time and focuses on a love triangle involving a rich society girl, a young man, and the true-blue girl of modest means (played by Swanson) who really loves him. In the film, the young man allows the villain to convince him to leave his true love for the financial comfort of marrying a society girl, as the villain looks forward to profiting from the match. The rich girl is insistent about marrying her suitor as quickly as possible, and his faithful girlfriend doggedly follows them with the aim of saving her young man from disaster. She is thwarted by the villain, who ties her to the railroad tracks to keep her from foiling his plans. As luck would have it, the true-blue girl has a very intelligent dog, Teddy, who arrives to help her and whom she trusts to carry a message to her boyfriend. (Viewers are not expected to question how she manages to write the message while tied to the railroad tracks.) Thanks to Teddy, the boyfriend realizes his true love's danger and comes to her rescue, just as the locomotive is about to crush her. While the couple embrace, Teddy corners the villain and holds him at bay.

After such early work, Swanson really made her impact when Cecil B. De Mille at Paramount decided to cast her in his series of films that flirted with adultery in high society. In *Don't Change Your Husband* in 1919, she plays a wife who divorces her common husband and marries a playboy, then realizes the worth of her first husband and returns to him. She has two fiancés in *For Better, For Worse* (1919), then in *Male and Female* (1919) she plays a society girl who comes to appreciate the common man when she is marooned on a desert island with her butler and others. For part of the latter film, Swanson's character seems to be falling for the butler, but the illusion disappears when they are rescued and she is back in her naturally lavish environment.

In real life, Gloria Swanson personified glamour and glitz with her beach houses, mansions, wealthy admirers, and the like, and moviegoers vicariously enjoyed the lifestyle portrayed in her films and that she also lived. She was among the highest paid actresses in Hollywood by the mid-1920s, and she continued making films with De Mille until 1927, when she decided to produce her own films. She had a huge hit with *Sadie Thompson*, which narrowly slipped by the censor with its story of a prostitute and a hypocritical minister. *Queen Kelly* deserves note because her partner in the deal was Joseph Kennedy, since identified as her lover of the time. The film was made in 1928, but it was so poorly produced and the timing was so bad (a silent film, when sound films were intriguing audiences nationwide) that Swanson abandoned the project in the rough cut. In 1929, Swanson made *The Trespasser*, her first venture into sound. Despite her success in the film, Swanson declined in popularity in the 1930s, because Depression-era audiences who once enjoyed her opulent on-screen presence no longer wanted to be reminded how the rich lived as they struggled to survive. She made her last film of the period *Music in the Air*, in 1934. An attempted comeback film in 1941 failed at the box office. Nine years later, Swanson took the role of Norma Desmond in *Sunset Boulevard* (1950) and left an indelible impression in her portrayal of the aging star who proclaimed, "I'm still big; it's the pictures that got small." Her last screen appearance was in a cameo role in *Airport 1975* (1974).

The silent era in Hollywood produced numerous stars who would go on to fame in later decades, while others simply faded when the sound era entered. Norma Shearer, whom MGM billed as "The First Lady of Screen," started as an extra in *The Flapper* (1920), then appeared in a string of forgettable films until 1924, when she played the first in a long line of sophisticated ladies in *He Who Gets Slapped*. Her popularity grew over the next three years, but her fame skyrocketed after she married movie business "boy wonder" Irving Thalberg in 1927 and he took control of her career. She starred in *The Student Prince* (1927) with the very popular Ramon Novarro, then *The Latest From Paris* (1928). Her success assured, Thalberg maneuvered her into her first sound film, *The Trial of Mary Dugan* (1929). The momentum of this film took her into the 1930s, where she played sophisticated roles in Noël Coward's *Private Lives* (1931) and Eugene O'Neill's *Strange Interlude* (1932), as well as in *The Barretts of Wimpole Street* (1934) and *Romeo and Juliet* (1936). She won the Best Actress nomination for *Marie Antoinette* (1938) and did fairly well in two 1939 films, *The*

Women and *Idiot's Delight*. After turning down the leads in both *Gone With the Wind* (1939) and *Mrs. Miniver* (1942), Shearer made a pair of box-office disasters before retiring from the screen in 1942.

Filmgoers of the 1920s knew Esther Ralston as "The Golden Girl of the Silver Screen" and "The American Venus," and her popularity even spread to England, where a 1929 British poll rated her as more popular than Mary Pickford, Greta Garbo, and Gloria Swanson. She began her career as a bit player and extra in the film *The Deep Purple* (1915) for Peerless-World Studios, then appeared in thirty-six films for a variety of studios until her role as Mrs. Darling in the 1924 Paramount version of *Peter Pan* made her a box-office force. From 1924 through 1929, she starred in twenty-five Paramount movies, most of them silent films, and her box-office value earned her $8,000 per week. Ralston appeared in many of Dorothy Arzner's earliest directing efforts, including the 1927 *Fashions for Women* and *Ten Modern Commandments*, and she also played roles in both drama and light comedy. In 1929, she entered the sound age, appearing in *The Wheel of Life* and *The Mighty*, but her career veered sharply downward as the 1930s began, in part because she refused to play house with MGM head Louis B. Mayer. She told an interviewer in 1983 that Mayer called her into his office on the morning after she had refused his sexual advances and told her that he could have any woman on the lot. Her response was "Any woman but Ralston." MGM refused to renew her option when it expired and rented her out for the remainder of her contract. Although Ralston made twenty-seven more films for different studios, most were low-budget movies until her last two, *Tin Pan Alley* (1940), and *San Francisco Docks* (1941), made for 20th Century–Fox and Universal, respectively.

Although Greta Garbo and Marlene Dietrich would soon follow, Pola Negri became the first European actress in Hollywood when she accepted an offer from Paramount in 1923 to make *Bella Donna*. Born Barbara Apollonia Chalupiec in 1894 in Poland, she attended ballet and acting schools, then performed in Russian cabarets for several years before traveling to Germany and becoming a star in movies in which she consistently played the role of the foreign and exotic seduc-

Actress Esther Ralston with director, Dorothy Arzner (Moma/Film Stills)

tress. With director Ernst Lubitsch, she made a series of movies that were seen in America, prompting offers from numerous Hollywood studios. In Hollywood, Negri again teamed with Lubitsch, appearing in *Carmen* (1918), *Madame DuBarry* (1919), *One Arabian Night* (1920), and *Forbidden Paradise* (1924). The movies were critically acclaimed, but only a few of them were commercially successful. Negri gained brief notoriety when photographs of her grief-stricken face appeared in newspapers worldwide after the death of her lover, Rudolph Valentino, in 1926. Articles implied that the two had planned to marry, and that Negri was devastated by her loss. She continued to make silent movies, but her heavy accent became a liability when the sound era began, and in 1930 she left Hollywood to return to Europe. In 1934, Nazi propaganda minister Joseph Goebbels invited her to return to Germany, where she was strategically deployed in a number of films aimed at desexualizing the German woman and challenging the sexually liberal

Mary Astor with John Barrymore in 1923 (Evans Collection)

view of women presented in the previous Weimar cinema. Among these films were *Mazurek*, directed by Willy Forst in 1935, and *Madame Bovary*, directed by Gerhard Lamprecht in 1937. Negri managed to flee Germany in 1939 and returned to the United States, where she made only two more films, *Hey Diddle Diddle* (1943) and *The Moon-Spinners* (1964).

Other stars who began in the silent screen era but had their greatest successes in the 1930s and 1940s are Greta Garbo, Myrna Loy, Jean Arthur, Mary Astor, Mae West, and Janet Gaynor. The last two deserve mention regarding their successes in the silent era. In 1926, Mae West was jailed for her play *Sex*, but the feisty star went on to score numerous film successes in the 1930s at Paramount Studios, where she wrote and controlled her own work. Janet Gaynor, a top box-office draw throughout the 1930s, has the distinction of being the first performer to win the Academy Award for Best Actress, in 1929.

Although actresses seemed to dominate the 1920s, as the film industry moved from the silent screen to talkies, screenwriters Anita Loos, Frances Marion, and June Mathis also adapted their world view to accommodate the growing Hollywood industry, and Jeanne Macpherson expanded her influence in the film industry as she continued to write many of Cecil B. De Mille's blockbusters at Paramount.

June Mathis stands out among screenwriters of the time because she was a scriptwriter who also served as the head of the scenario department at Metro in 1918—the first production executive in the industry. She is also credited with having developed the writer-director combination of planning the film's action before beginning shooting, a common approach today but one that was radical in the 1920s. Although Mathis wrote hundreds of scripts, her main claim to fame is her insistence while at Metro that it make *The Four Horsemen of the Apocalypse* (1921) and that the film star an unknown bit player named Rudolph Valentino. The film earned $4.5 million for Metro Pictures, making it the top-grossing film of the 1920s. Mathis later starred Valentino in *Blood and Sand* (1922), which contained an underlying sexuality, as did her later film *Ben-Hur* (1926).

Mae West (MoMA/Film Stills)

Mathis was daring for her time in the manner in which she made *Blood and Sand*: she subtly mixed sex with sadism, and a woman in the film is shown to be more callous in love than a man. Dorothy Arzner edited this film, and her skillful blending of footage earned her Mathis's admiration and the assignment to edit the next Metro film, *The Covered Wagon* (1923). Mathis's last film was *Ben-Hur*, considered to be the most effective of all screen versions of the novel and the model for the 1959 extravaganza starring Charlton Heston. She did not complete the film, for she was fired during the final production. Her dialogue and script elements remain in the final cut, which had been revised by Bess Meredyth. Mathis died in 1927 of a stroke at the age of thirty-five.

Frances Marion also wrote screenplays in the 1920s, but her successes and Academy Awards came in the 1930s. Still, her films of the 1920s were notable, as they include *Stella Dallas* (1925), *The Son of the Sheik* (1926), and *The Scarlet Letter* (1927). Her good looks and charisma often led interviewers to question why she chose to remain behind the camera rather than have a screen career. The implication was that beauty and screenwriting were not compatible.

One writer who took that admonishment to heart was Beulah Marie Dix, a Radcliffe graduate who distinguished herself as a playwright before becoming a screenwriter. She was also one of the few women playwrights who had a thorough knowledge of military policies, a knowledge that she exploited in her pacifist plays. In 1926, Dix heeded the advice of her agent, Bibi De Mille, the mother of Cecil B. and William De Mille, and headed for Hollywood to write screenplays for Famous Players–Lasky Studios. Unlike other women in the scenario department who kept their preferences quiet, Dix made known her desire to write for male leads, but she was usually instructed to write for women. Her reason for resisting was that female lead stories usually dealt with lighter subject matter, and she had heavier concerns to explore. She wrote a range of scripts in the 1920s and only five scripts in the sound era, ending her career in 1931.

Adela Rogers St. Johns and Elinor Glyn, neither primarily a screenwriter, earned places of note in the 1920s more through their activities than through their output. St. Johns was a fiction writer who served as a story consultant at MGM and scenarist. She was on the staff of *Photoplay* and wrote profiles of such stars as Gloria Swanson, Tom Mix, and Rudolph Valentino, and she became part of the movie business when three of her magazine serials were optioned for movies. Two of her short stories became the films *Hollywood* (1925) and *Singed* (1927), and she wrote several early westerns for Tom Mix, as well as a 1931 vehicle for Elissa Landi, *Wicked*. Her true historical importance lies in the influence she had on Frances Marion, who credited St. Johns with helping her to gain success in the movie business.

Elinor Glyn was also already an established writer, as well as the reigning queen of the romance novel in England, before she became a Hollywood screenwriter. She also has the distinction of having invented the concept of "It" and of having developed a clear definition of sex appeal, especially in regard to what constitutes "It." She adapted the script *The Romance of the Queen* from her scandalous novel *Three Weeks*, creating a scenario that featured women reclining on fur rugs, as well as a host of other sensuous details that were labeled "pornographic" by critics. Glyn emphasized the need for both male and female characters to possess "It," and in her screenplays, only those who possessed this elusive quality were given the romantic roles. She stayed in Hollywood to write screenplays, including the 1927 hit movie *It*, starring Clara Bow.

Women film editors also came into their own in the 1920s. Margaret Booth, one of the most famous and successful of the industry's film editors in the 1930s, began as an assistant editor for the Louis B. Mayer studios in 1921 and continued to edit through 1979. She remained with the studio when it merged to become Metro-Goldwyn-Mayer in 1924 and became one of its most respected and relied-upon editors during the 1920s and 1930s. Over the years, she edited such films as *The Gay Deceiver* and *Memory Lane*, both in 1926, as well as her first sound film, *A Lady of Chance*, in 1928. She earned an

Novelist / Screenwriter Elinor Glyn (Quigley/Georgetown University)

Academy Award nomination for film editing in 1935 for *Mutiny on the Bounty*.

Sponsored by Universal, Lois Weber had started her own studio, Lois Weber Productions, in 1917 and enjoyed the security of knowing that Universal would finance her films and distribute them, while giving her personal control over their content. Her peak occurred in 1920, when Paramount gave her a five-picture contract at $50,000 per film. As the 1920s moved on, Weber's focus on serious subjects was at odds with the climate of the Jazz Age. She wanted to moralize, but moviegoers wanted to have fun, and her work fell out of favor. Her failed marriage, financial problems, and decreasing popularity drove her to a nervous breakdown after which she directed only a few more films. Cecil B. De Mille hired her to direct the 1927 *Angel on Broadway*, which failed miserably at the box office and met with obstruction because it dealt with prostitution. She made her last film in 1934, *White Heat*, which was never distributed because of its volatile subject matter of race and miscegenation. From then on, she worked sporadically as a freelance script supervisor and died destitute in 1939. In essence, her story reflects the fate of women in the film industry whose careers began with high hopes in the pre-Hollywood era. Once the sound films took on importance, many previously successful female directors and producers were replaced by men, and only one—Dorothy Arzner—managed to succeed in the 1930s.

Arzner, a film editor in the early twenties, used editing as way of getting to know the business. One of her projects was the 1922 *Blood and Sand*, starring Rudolph Valentino. When Paramount offered Arzner an opportunity to direct *Fashions for Women* in 1927, she jumped at the chance. She directed four more films for Paramount in the 1920s: *Ten Modern Commandments* (1927), *Get Your Man* (1928), *Manhattan Cocktail* (1928), and *The Wild Party* (1929). Arzner went on to become the only important female director in 1930s Hollywood, where her real story lies.

During the 1920s, another specialized aspect of the film industry emerged, as the studio wardrobe department became a major consideration in film production, and Natacha Rambova became the first formally identified film costume designer. More elaborate scripts required costume changes, thus forcing a change from the writing of continuity scripts to those that took wardrobe changes into consideration in plotting, so that costumes for each scene would be ready as the scene was to be shot. The earliest films were done mainly in New York, where there were numerous fashion sources to draw on, but most film studios required that actresses arrange for their own clothes and costume rentals. For period films, wardrobes might be quickly created for stars and main characters, while extras and supporting cast would wear a collection of hastily assembled clothes that approximated the needed look. Actresses often wore their own couture gowns in films set in the present, displaying their designer favorite of the moment. Even when wardrobe mistresses were first introduced, little attention was given to individual designs or designers.

The move to Hollywood was also a move away from the large number of fashion sources in the east, and the tendency toward epics, period stories, musicals, and westerns in 1920s and 1930s Hollywood created the need for special costumes that actresses could not be expected to supply from their own wardrobes. As the Hollywood studio system developed, the studio wardrobe departments became more sharply defined, often breaking into five subdivisions: dressmaking, stock materials, finished wardrobe, millinery, and fancy dress. Even if these departments contained hundreds of women (and they were usually women), they labored for the most part without individual recognition. Although the industry began to focus its attention on particular designs and designers in the early 1920s, the Academy Awards did not add a category for Costume Design until 1948.

The first film in which a specific designer is known to have been retained to render a specific vision and to design the costumes is the 1922 *Salome*, starring Alla Nazimova. The flamboyant Nazimova selected young socialite and sometime designer Natacha Rambova, who had been born Winnifred Shaughnessy in Salt Lake City, Utah. Rambova used Aubrey Beardsley's 1894 art *nouveau* illustrations for *Salome* as her guide to dress Nazimova in a range of looks, from bold arabesque patterns to stark white silhouettes. For the Dance of the Seven Veils, Salome was swathed in chiffon veils and her head was covered in a white lacquered wig. Other characters were dressed to suggest deadly night insects, and elaborate headdresses pervaded the film. The original design conceptions shocked audiences and focused attention on Rambova's talents as one of the most inventive designers who would ever work in films as well as a great influence on those designers who followed. Rambova's major flaw was that her magnificent costumes and sets were extremely expensive, and she refused to take budget and money matters into account as she racked up expenditures for her designs. Her work might have been more highly publicized had she not married Rudolph Valentino in 1922. From that point, until their marriage ended in 1925, her visibility was overshadowed by his fame. She had designed to great effect the ultramodern costumes for the 1921 *Camille*, which costarred Nazimova and Valentino. However, in their three years of marriage, Rambova made up and costumed Valentino in *The Young Rajah* (1922), *A Sainted Devil* (1924), and *Cobra* (1925), and her feminization of the star nearly ruined his career.

Claire West became the costume designer for Cecil B. De Mille's productions with the 1919 *Male and Female*, which starred Gloria Swanson. De Mille had long proclaimed that movie magic would be created with the right combination of "sex, sets, and costumes," and West provided him with one major ingredient and in a style that pleased both De Mille and at least one of his stars, Swanson. In *Male and Female*, Paul Iribe was brought in to create the sets and to design costumes for leading lady Gloria Swanson, and Claire West designed mostly for the supporting cast. However, De Mille's insistence on specific artists and designers to work on production design was the first time that a studio acknowledged the importance of creating special costumes for its stars. In 1920, West became costume supervisor for Famous Players–Lasky.

Most of the 1920s served as a period of growth for the film industry, which spent the final years of the silent era creating the image and action that would become evocative of Hollywood. Studios developed, stars arose, and techniques were refined to prepare the way for the glamorous golden years that followed.

The decade saw the creation of the Academy of Motion Picture Arts and Sciences (1926), which gave out awards for 1927–28, 1928–29 and 1929–30. The winner of the Best Actress award in 1927–28 was Janet Gaynor for *Seventh Heaven*. Although a man won the Writing Achievement award in 1928–29, Josephine Lovett was nominated for *Our Dancing Daughters* and Frances Marion was the first woman to win the writing achievement award, for *The Big House* in 1929–30.

Creating Stars in the 1930s

•

A S FILMMAKING INCREASED in respectability and various aspects of the business became formalized, women were replaced by men behind the camera and in the decision-making positions, but screenwriting remained the domain of women. There were more women writing movies during the thirties than during any other period in film history. At the same time, as a star system developed, women were increasingly valued in front of the camera. With this new role came a different set of rewards and new status.

As the movie business grew more sophisticated, so did what appeared on screen. Many screenwriters who had begun their work in film by tentatively plying their trade at the pre-Hollywood studios and in the silent films of the 1920s came into their own once the 1930s were in full swing, and they added memorable films to movie history. Prominent among such writers is Frances Marion, who belongs square-ly in the 1930s. Of the 136 films between 1915 and 1953 in which her name appears in the credits as producer, director, or writer, her biggest successes and years of highest pay in Hollywood belong to this period. She won the Academy Award for Writing in 1930 with *The Big House* and in 1931 for *The Champ*, and every film aficionado is certainly familiar with the very affecting *Anna Christie* (1930), *Min and Bill* (1930), *Dinner at Eight* (1933), and *Camille* (1937), which also bear her name.

Anita Loos, in the film business since her first script sale to D. W. Griffith in 1912, sold more than 200 scripts in the silent era and continued her work in the 1930s, but her role changed. She deserves credit for writing several commercially successful MGM films that starred Jean Harlow, including *Red-Headed Woman* (1932), *Hold Your Man* (1933), as well as the prestigious *San Francisco* (1936) and *The Women* (1939). She also had a hand in writing *Riffraff* (1935), but the script was credited to Frances Marion. Despite the quality and quantity of her work, Loos never received an Academy Award nomination. Nonetheless, she moved away from strictly writing to filling the executive position of script doctor and decision maker in the 1930s. A number of veteran film writers found that their experience from the silent era was a valuable resource to MGM filmmakers in the new age of sound, as Meredyth, Marion, and Loos were frequently called in by MGM as consultants on scripts being shot.

Given the seeming importance of a few women to the film industry in the 1930s, many wonder why more did not assume executive positions in the great studios that seemed to depend upon the largely unacknowledged expertise of their women writers and editors. The answer may lie in the account that Frances Marion gives in her 1971 autobiography, *Off With Their Heads!* It reveals that she was a figure of importance in the MGM of the 1930s and exerted considerable control over projects, but she was spared the frustrations of playing the corporate game of scrambling for and holding on to recognition because she was not officially a member of management. The view is debatable and certainly does not express the feelings of women in latter-day Hollywood who are striving to open more industry management positions to women. In the 1930s, however, the new corporate culture was developing in a frantically growing industry in which production-line techniques were the only way to maintain order. Also, in the first half of the decade, the American economy was struggling to survive a depression. While directors remained contract workers, subject to the whims and dictates of studio heads and of the New York financiers who controlled the bottom line in Hollywood, their jobs were actually less stable than those of writers. Thus, many women remained out of the fight, as long as they were successful and steadily paid as writers or editors. However one might view the writer's position, it's important to keep in mind that producers depended upon the writers, working with them *before* stars and directors were hired on a production. Whatever arguments can be made against such thinking, no one can deny that writers such as Frances Marion enjoyed substantial prestige, as well as the financial rewards that went with it.

Friendship with Greta Garbo gave Salka Viertel her chance to write in Hollywood, and she either wrote or collaborated with other writers on almost every Garbo film made after 1933. Viertel was a Polish actress who had first moved to Germany, where she became a part of the Max Reinhardt company. In the early thirties, she emigrated to Hollywood where, with her director husband, she became a part of Garbo's small circle of intimate friends. When Garbo became dissatisfied with the direction of the *Queen Christina* script in 1933, she asked Viertel to rewrite the material. The result was not only a successful script but also a decade-long collaboration.

In contrast to writers whose work had always been written for the screen, Zoë Akins first established a well-respected writing career in New York before turning to screenplays. Akins started out writing newspaper articles, then published a volume of poetry before she began writing for the stage in 1916, at the age of thirty. Her first stage hit was the 1919 *Declassé*, starring Ethel Barrymore, followed by her next major stage success in 1921, *Daddy's Gone A-Hunting*, which MGM eventually adapted for the screen. With the success of the 1931 *The Greeks Had a Word for It*, filmed in 1932 as *The Greeks Had a Word for Them* to avoid any association with "It," Akins had earned the reputation necessary to gain a favored place as a Hollywood screenwriter. Once in Hollywood, she wrote the screenplays for two movies

Greta Garbo in Queen Christina *(1933)* (Billy Rose Collection/Lincoln Center)

directed by Dorothy Arzner, both featuring Broadway star Ruth Chatterton: the 1930 *Sarah and Son* and *Anybody's Woman*. She again worked with Arzner in writing the 1931 *Working Girls* and the 1933 *Christopher Strong*. The two got along so well together that Akins was willing to take a cut in pay in 1939 in order to work with Arzner on yet another project. Aside from films directed by Arzner, Akins also cowrote the script for the 1937 *Camille*, starring Greta Garbo, and the 1953 *How to Marry a Millionaire*, a reworking of her earlier *The Greeks Had a Word for Them*.

Unlike screenwriters who had never known any other outlet for their writing, Akins was quick to admit that she did screenplays for financial reasons and continued to write for the stage in her free time. In her 1958 obituary in *Time*, she is quoted as having said that "Writing for Hollywood is not difficult. All you have to do is write six pages every day, then grab the money and run for the train." She won the Pulitzer Prize for Drama in 1935 for *The Old Maid*, her adaptation of an Edith Wharton novel that became a 1939 film starring Bette Davis and Miriam Hopkins. For Akins, the death of MGM boy genius Irving Thalberg in 1936 was a devastating blow to her professionally as well as personally. The men who had created the Hollywood film industry had built up their stables of favored writers whom they protected and kept working. With Thalberg dead, Akins felt that she would be left to the mercy of Hollywood politics, so she retreated. She first wrote a novel in 1940, then returned to New York and to her playwriting career, but she kept her California home and Hollywood connections.

Frances Goodrich and her husband and collaborator, Albert Hackett, began a screenwriting partnership in 1930 that lasted through their last film in 1962, *The Five Finger Exercise*. Their first screenplay was *Up Pops the Devil* for Paramount in 1930, which became the 1938 film *Thanks for the Memory*, starring Bob Hope. Their best-known work of the 1930s focused on another couple, Nick and Nora Charles, and the *Thin Man* movies. *The Thin Man* in 1935 and *After the Thin Man* in 1936 were based on the writings of Dashiell Hammett, and their director, W.S. Van Dyke, left the interpretation to the writers, asking only that they give him five scenes containing the Charles couple. Goodrich and Hackett earned Academy Award nominations for their *Thin Man* screenplays in 1934 and 1936.

By 1939, the strain of contract writing bore down on both Goodrich

Frances Goodrich (MoMA/Film Stills)

and Hackett, and they left Hollywood for a year. When they returned, they had made the decision to move freely between the east and west coasts, which they did for the next twenty years. They had a string of hits throughout the 1940s and a few in the 1950s before ending their collaborative screenwriting days in 1962.

Algonquin Round Table wit Dorothy Parker had already established

herself as a member of the New York intelligentsia with her short stories and satiric articles when she moved to Hollywood with her new
and much younger husband, actor Alan Campbell. While Campbell
eagerly turned to writing screenplays, Parker set up the West Coast version of the Round Table with other screenwriters who lived in the
Garden of Allah, former home of silent screen actress Alla Nazimova.
She also immersed herself in political causes, such as organizing the
Screen Writers Guild and founding the Anti-Nazi League; she also
cowrote fifteen screenplays with Campbell in the 1930s. The most
memorable of these scripts was for the 1937 film A *Star Is Born*, for
which she shared an Academy Award nomination for writing with
Campbell and Robert Carson. In 1947, she and Frank Cavett earned
an Academy Award nomination for their original story *Smash Up—The
Story of a Woman*, one of four screenplays she cowrote in the 1940s
before ending her Hollywood career.

Tess Slesinger has the distinction of being the first screenwriter to
bring a case before the Motion Picture Academy. She began her writing
career in New York, where she was first the assistant fashion editor at
the *New York Herald Tribune*, then assistant literary critic at the *New
York Evening Post*. She was also a social activist who was arrested several times for political protests. In 1934, Slesinger published her first
novel, *The Unpossessed*, which related a story about a group of young
intellectuals of the left who work to start a magazine.

She followed the favorable acceptance of her novel with a collection
of short stories, *Time: The Present*, which earned her critical success
and a move to MGM studios in 1935, where she was offered $1,000 a
week to write screenplays. Her first assignment was an adaptation of
Pearl S. Buck's novel *The Good Earth*, later made into a film that was
finally released in 1937. Before its initial release date, Slesinger learned
that her name had been removed from the credits, and she presented
her case to the Motion Picture Academy, which represented her, and
contacted Irving Thalberg. He yielded to pressure from the group, and
Slesinger received the screen credit that she deserved. With her husband, Frank Davis, an assistant producer she met while working on *The

Good Earth, Slesinger wrote *The Bride Wore Red*, directed in 1937 by Dorothy Arzner, and *Dance, Girl, Dance*, a 1940 film directed by Arzner and starring Maureen O'Hara. Slesinger and Davis were nominated for an Academy Award for their 1945 screenplay *A Tree Grows in Brooklyn*.

Sonya Levien was the predominant screenwriter at 20th Century–Fox in the 1930s, and her career stretched into the 1950s. Despite her dedication and prolific pen, she took a circuitous route toward prominence. The daughter of a Russian radical who had escaped exile in Siberia and emigrated to the United States, she spoke four languages and held a law degree from New York University, but, after practicing a short while, she decided that law was not her calling. She began to write, often publishing in *The Women's Journal*, the official publication of the suffrage movement. When Paramount bought several of her stories in 1921, she decided to go to Hollywood, leaving her young son with her husband. She returned east after six months and continued to write. The family moved west in 1926, and Levien resumed screenwriting.

Levien wrote seventy screenplays, thirty-six of them from 1929 through 1939. Among her best-known works of the 1930s are *Daddy Long Legs* (1931), *Rebecca of Sunnybrook Farm* (1932), *Berkeley Square* and *State Fair* (both 1932), *In Old Chicago* (1938), and *The Hunchback of Notre Dame* and *Drums Along the Mohawk* (both 1939). Levien earned an Academy Award nomination (with Paul Green) for *State Fair*. Although all women screenwriters were expected to represent "the woman's point of view" in their work, which is why the blood-and-guts masculine scripts were commissioned from male writers, Levien had a particularly deft touch in creating female characters who were noble, intelligent, and independent. The role of Lana in *Drums Along the Mohawk* is an excellent example: She is an attractive, feminine, and strong pioneer wife who unflinchingly handles frontier hazards. Levien extended her reach into the 1940s, creating strong dramatic roles for Greer Garson in the 1945 *Valley of Decision* and for former sweater girl Lana Turner in the 1947 *Cass Timberlane*. In the 1950s, she also wrote fully dimensional characters for former sex

Sonya Levien (screenwriter) (Quigley Photo Archive/Georgetown University))

objects Ava Gardner (*Bhowani Junction*, 1956) and Kim Novak (*Jeanne Eagels*, 1957). Although only five of her screenplays were filmed in the 1940s, nine appeared in the 1950s, including *The Great Caruso* (1951), *Quo Vadis?* (1951), *The Student Prince* (1952), and *Oklahoma!* (1955).

•

She shared the 1955 Academy Award for story and screenplay with William Ludwig for *Interrupted Melody*.

Film editing took on a new meaning in the 1930s as Hollywood entered its golden age. At MGM, Margaret Booth had built up so solid a reputation that she was entrusted with editing the films of the studio's top money-making stars. She edited Greta Garbo in the 1931 *Susan Lenox: Her Fall and Rise* and the 1937 *Camille*. In 1933, Booth edited Jean Harlow in *Bombshell* and Joan Crawford in *Dancing Lady*. Her triumph of the decade came when the studio assigned her the biggest film of the year to edit, *Mutiny on the Bounty*. She received an Academy Award nomination in 1935 for her work on it. Booth's active editing ended in 1939 when she was appointed supervising film editor at MGM, a position she kept until, in 1968, she returned to active editing.

Former film editor Dorothy Arzner had a major impact on the Hollywood of the 1930s, as she directed a string of films for Paramount, then left that studio to work as a freelance director for RKO, MGM, and Columbia studios. Under contract to Paramount in the 1930s, she directed *Sarah and Son*, *Anybody's Woman*, and *Paramount on Parade* in 1930, *Honor Among Lovers* and *Working Girls* in 1931, and *Merrily We Go to Hell* in 1932. As a freelance director, Arzner did *Christopher Strong* (RKO, 1933), *Nana* (MGM, 1934), *Craig's Wife* (Columbia, 1936), *The Bride Wore Red* (MGM, 1937), *Dance, Girl, Dance* (RKO, 1940), and *First Comes Courage* (Columbia, 1943). Arzner's work on *Dance, Girl, Dance* and *Christopher Strong* has gained a following among feminist film critics in the past two decades. *Dance, Girl, Dance* stars Maureen O'Hara as a dancer who performs for a group of men, and when they become aroused by her dancing, she condemns them for their ogling and voyeurism. In *Christopher Strong*, Katharine Hepburn portrays a pioneering aviator whose exploits exhibit the presence of a strong and competent woman professional.

A new presence—the designer—was felt in Hollywood in the late 1930s, as actresses turned to costumers to create their "look." Designers became actively aware of all aspects of the plot and were responsible for creating a detailed wardrobe plot that showed precisely the sequence of ensembles an actor or actress would wear in the scenes shot. Brief notes were then made in the plot, showing which costumes would be needed for each scene.

Edith Head began to wield her influence when, in 1938, she was made head of the costume department at Paramount Studios and supervised a staff of more than 300. She was the first woman to become a studio design chief, and her costume designs established trends over the following four decades. She became the most famous of Hollywood designers and was nominated for thirty-five Academy Awards, winning eight between 1950 and 1974. Her greatest and most numerous successes occurred in the 1950s.

At Universal Pictures, Vera West was the chief designer in a reign that lasted from 1927 through 1947, with her greatest output taking place in the 1930s. West had owned and operated a clothing salon on Fifth Avenue in New York City before going to Hollywood to design for the movies. Unlike other designers who threw their own tantrums when confronted by temperamental stars, West claimed that she had learned in her salon how to get along with rich, spoiled women who demanded special attention. Thus, her ability to get along made her a popular designer, but not one who was called upon for the really big movies. Her most memorable costumes were designed for Irene Dunne in *Show Boat* (1936), Deanna Durbin in *Mad About Music* (1938), and Marlene Dietrich in *Destry Rides Again* (1939) and *The Spoilers* (1942).

As the studio system strengthened, the 1930s also brought a change in the status of the actress. Winner of the Academy Award for Best Actress for 1929–30, Janet Gaynor entered the decade confident of a successful career in sound movies after moderate success in the twilight years of the silent era. Born Laura Gainor in Philadelphia, she was raised in Chicago and Los Angeles. Her first movie work was as an extra at a number of Hollywood film studios before she was given a screen test by Fox in 1926, which earned her a role in *The Johnstown Flood* (1926). Part of her success was due to good luck and timing. Fox vice president Winfield Sheehan had been looking for a new face to promote to stardom, and the petite and wholesome-looking brunette filled the need. She was paid $100 a week and placed in several movies in which she played sweetheart parts before she landed her role in *Seventh Heaven* (1927), which established her with the public. She was teamed with Charles Farrell in the movie, the first of twelve times in which the two would be paired. *Seventh Heaven* is a sentimental film that tells the story of a poor orphan girl in Paris who is bullied by her sister and forced to make her living on the streets. A sewer cleaner takes pity on her and asks her to move in with him in his seventh-floor walkup. The war temporarily shatters their happiness, but he finally returns blind and in need of her, and they return to their "heaven" on the seventh floor.

Gaynor also had a big hit with her next movie, *Street Angel* (1928), in which she was again teamed with Farrell and played the waif ("street angel" as euphemism for prostitute) who is redeemed by love at the end of the film. They were so popular a team that fans begged them to marry in real life, and Fox's Sheehan capitalized on their bankable chemistry by pairing the two in ten more movies in quick succession. Between *Seventh Heaven* and *Street Angel*, Gaynor was cast as the victim in *Sunrise* (1927), one of the great silent films that, however, did not please her new audience. In the film, she plays a colorless and dowdy farmer's wife whose husband has an affair with a vamplike city woman and plots to kill Gaynor's character. While plotting her "accident," the husband becomes conscience-stricken and decides to abandon his plan, but fate intervenes and she dies, nonetheless, in an accident much like the one he had planned. This trio of films brought industry acclaim and the Oscar to Gaynor. She continued making films for Fox, entering the sound era with *Sunny Side Up* (1930), *Daddy Long Legs* (1931), *Tess of the Storm Country* (1932), *Change of Heart* (1934), *The Farmer Takes a Wife* (1935), *State Fair* (1936), and, as a loanout to MGM, *Small Town Girl* (1936).

Darryl Zanuck took over the financially troubled Fox in 1935 and released the highly paid Gaynor, a millionaire at thirty-one, replacing her with Shirley Temple. She joined the relatively new Selznick

International to make her next film, A *Star Is Born* (1937), an expensively made production that used Technicolor and strengthened Gaynor's star power and earned her another Oscar nomination. The film gathered notoriety as Hollywood and audiences tried to guess the real-life identities of the has-been husband and his rising-star wife. Gaynor made only two more movies in the 1930s, *Three Loves Has Nancy* and *The Young in Heart*, both in 1938, then married costume designer Adrian and retired. She returned to the screen briefly as Pat Boone's mother in *Bernardine* (1957), then made her Broadway debut in 1977 in *Harold and Maude*, but there was no career pinnacle to follow A *Star Is Born*.

Buxom and brazen Mae West moved from Broadway to Hollywood and made sex on the screen fun, with her gyrations, double entendres, risqué songs, and frank sensuality. She was also the only female comic star in the 1930s around whom a movie could be built and who could carry a film on her own. Played for fun, her movies were devoid of plot lines, but they were loaded with her special brand of humor, which pitted West's amoral actions against seemingly respectable and strictly legal obstacles. The most daring of her films, *She Done Him Wrong*, escaped the censorship of later films because it appeared in 1933, the year before the Breen Code went into effect and established moral restrictions. West included several extremely suggestive songs in *She Done Him Wrong*, including her own version of the familiar song "Frankie and Johnny." In the original lyrics, Frankie shoots and kills Johnny because she sees him with another woman, but West's version states that Johnny was doing a little more than just talking with another woman—and they weren't in a public bar in her version. A second song from the movie is suggestively titled "I Like a Guy What Takes His Time," and audiences knew fully that West was talking about sex in her lyrics. The institution of the Breen Code created a greatly subdued Mae West, and the restrictions show in her next film, *Belle of the Nineties*, in which her parody of sex is greatly restrained both in action and in her words. Films such as *Goin' to Town* (1935), *Klondike Annie* (1936), and *My Little Chickadee* (1940), the last mainly a vehicle for

Mae West, 1930s (National Film Archive)

W. C. Fields, seem to have eliminated all trace of West's frank sexuality and fun-loving patter.

Where Mae West made sex fun, Jean Harlow, with her platinum hair, low-cut dresses, and slinky, purring actions, made it dangerous. Although her career lasted only five years, from 1932 until her death in 1937, she became a platinum-blond icon whose physicality inspired sex symbols who followed. The first blond "bad girl" in Hollywood, Harlow, born Harlean Carpenter, brought a new look to the normally dark-haired screen "vamp." After several bit parts in such movies as *Moran of the Marines* (1928) and *The Love Parade* (1929), Harlow caught the attention of producer Howard Hughes, who was then reshooting his epic movie *Hell's Angels*, which had originally been made as a silent. The film combines extensive aerial footage with the slinky and sensual Harlow playing a woman who destroys the friendship of two pilots. Although others have claimed the phrase, Harlow, in *Hell's Angels*, was the first to utter the line "Pardon me while I slip into something more comfortable."

The great success of the movie led to many offers, and Hughes exploited his new possession, whom he had signed to a long-term contract, by loaning her out to other studios. She made *The Public Enemy* with James Cagney for Warner Bros. in 1931 and *Platinum Blonde*, under the direction of Frank Capra, for Columbia the same year. Tired of his new acquisition, Hughes sold her contract to MGM for $60,000, where in *Three Wise Girls* (1932) she played a poor girl whose rich fiancé rejects her when he mistakenly suspects that she has cheated on him. The movie attracted only moderate attention, as did *Red-Headed Woman* the same year, even though Harlow plays a woman who uses her body and her gun to get what she wants in life. Magic erupted on screen that same year when she made *Red Dust* with Clark Gable. The two exuded sexual chemistry on screen, and audiences flocked to watch the movie, which was daring for its time. The pair made four more films in rapid succession.

Although 1932 was a good year professionally for Jean Harlow, she became involved in a public scandal when director Paul Bern, her hus-

Jean Harlow (1930s) (National Film Archive)

band of two months, committed suicide. Rumors abounded, from speculation that Bern was impotent to the finding that his common-law wife of ten years, blond actress Dorothy Millette, had committed suicide only three days after Bern. Whatever the reason, Harlow's pop-

ularity increased with the added aura of sex and scandal, and she continued to crank out films. As the reigning sex goddess, she drew big
audiences for the all-star *Dinner at Eight* and for *Bombshell*, both in
1933, and she had additional hits with *China Seas* and *Reckless*, both
in 1935. The latter film hit too close to home for her comfort, but
MGM knew that fans would eagerly watch a movie about a singer-
dancer whose husband had committed suicide if the lead were played
by none other than Harlow.

After a full schedule of films in 1936, Harlow became engaged to
William Powell, former husband of Carole Lombard. She worked on
Saratoga in 1937, destined to be her last. While filming, she fell ill and
experienced pain as her kidneys stopped functioning. Her mother, a
Christian Scientist, refused to call a doctor, and Harlow died of uremic
poisoning, a sex goddess dead at the age of twenty-six. Once again,
scandalous stories emerged which claimed that her death was due to
alcoholism, a botched abortion, or self-inflicted wounds. Unable to
pass up all of the free publicity, MGM finished *Saratoga* with doubles
who hid behind binoculars and under hats as they attempted to play
Harlow. Two weeks later, the movie was in the theaters and breaking
the box office as the sex queen's last film.

Although she started earlier than Harlow in the film business and
lasted longer, Carole Lombard also died young and tragically. Born Jane
Peters, Lombard had her start when director Allan Dwan spotted her as
a thirteen-year-old and cast her for a part in *A Perfect Crime* (1921).
She played bit parts in numerous movies, and her career nearly ended
in 1926 when an auto accident left her with a badly cut face that
threatened to scar. To help Lombard deal with the aftermath of the
accident, her mother convinced her to join Mack Sennett's comic studio, where she learned the business of being funny and played in a
number of silent comedies and two-reel films. At Paramount, she was
groomed as a sex symbol and cast in romantic parts as the glamorous
sophisticate in such films as *Safety in Numbers* (1930). She rose in the
industry and married successful actor William Powell, of whom she
once said, "The son of a bitch is acting, even when he takes off his

pajamas." After making mainly mediocre movies, she divorced Powell and landed the part that created her fame. In 1934 Howard Hawks cast her in *Twentieth Century*, a comedy about the tensions between a stage director and a former protegée, also starring John Barrymore. Lombard remained wooden and unable to break loose in this screwball comedy, until Hawks told her to simply respond to the taunts of Barrymore's character as she would in real life. Once she had that permission, Lombard displayed her comic abilities in a range of films, of which *My Man Godfrey* (1936), *Nothing Sacred* (1937) and Hitchcock's only comedy *Mr. and Mrs. Smith* (1941), costarring Robert Montgomery, deserve special mention. In 1937, she was the highest-paid actress in Hollywood, making $465,000.

Lombard also took dramatic roles, starring with James Stewart in *Made for Each Other* (1939) and with Charles Laughton in *They Knew What They Wanted* in 1940. In early 1939, she and Clark Gable were listed in a *Photoplay* magazine article entitled "Hollywood's Unmarried Husbands and Wives," and the couple married later that year. In 1942, Lombard made her last film, Ernst Lubitsch's anti-Nazi comedy titled *To Be or Not To Be*. The same year, she joined other Hollywood stars in raising millions of dollars from the sale of war bonds, and she was returning home to Gable, himself soon to leave for military service, when her plane crashed outside of Las Vegas and she died, along with fifteen Army fliers. The nation reacted personally to her death; flags flew at half-mast and many businesses closed. Gable received a telegram of condolence from President Franklin D. Roosevelt, who also awarded Lombard a medal for dying in action. For many, a very special comedic light had been snuffed out.

While Lombard was an open and engaging personality, Greta Garbo became a legend as much for her mysterious private life as for her decision to exit completely from Hollywood after a decade of tantalizing filmmakers with the possibility that she might yet agree to make another film. Her name retains the magic, even though the 1941 *Two-Faced Woman* was her last film; nearly half a century later, she could still draw the attention of the press and the public when she ventured out. As Greta Gustafsson in Stockholm, Sweden, she trained at the Academy of Stockholm's Royal Dramatic Theatre, where director Mauritz Stiller saw her, renamed her, and cast her in his 1924 movie *Gosta Berling's Saga*. When Stiller was hired by MGM, he insisted that Garbo also be hired by the studio. Despite the doubts of both Garbo and MGM, her first American film, *The Torrent* (1926), was a critical and commercial success. Garbo played several different parts in the movie, and she became a star immediately.

While Stiller's career faltered, Garbo began a string of movies that catapulted her to legendary status in the eyes of the public. In 1927, she made *Flesh and the Devil* with John Gilbert, and the two increased the public's interest in their on-screen relationship by conducting an off-screen love affair. Garbo established in this movie a behavior pattern that would reappear in most of her later works, that of the sensuous and irresistible woman who is torn between two men—one her husband and one her illicit love. Her love scenes may have been passionate, but she was also required to pay for her stolen happiness with the ultimate sacrifice. Gilbert appeared with her in several more films, the *Love* (1927) and the *A Woman of Affairs* (1929), as well as *Queen Christina* (1933) one year before his death.

Garbo did not talk on screen until the 1930 *Anna Christie*, which made her first words a matter of major publicity for the film. "Garbo talks!" read the advertisements, and audiences early awaited her first on-screen words, which happened to be "Gimme a vhiskey, ginger ale on the side—and don't be stingy, baby," words made more dramatic by her throaty voice and exotic accent.

As Garbo continued to make films, she remained an enigma to her fans, despite well-publicized affairs with conductor Leopold Stokowski and film director Rouben Mamoulian and constant surveillance by the press. When she made the highly praised *Queen Christina*, she paid John Gilbert back for his support of her early career by insisting that MGM make him her leading man. He had fallen into alcoholic despair in recent years and the studio would not touch him, but Garbo's power as a box-office presence was persuasive. He died a year later. As in most of her films, Garbo loves, suffers, and loses love but, unlike such films as *Flesh and the Devil, Anna Christie, Susan Lenox: Her Fall and Rise* (1931), *Anna Karenina* (1935), and *Camille* (1936), Garbo does not die. Instead, she endures and suffers. Occasionally in her films Garbo has fun among all the grimness of life, especially in *Mata Hari* (1932), in which she played the calculating spy. She breaks taboos as she seduces Ramon Novarro, dances her lascivious dance, and laughs at death. In *Grand Hotel* (1932), she played a high-strung, manic-depressive ballerina, and the movie contains the line most associated with the glamorous recluse: "I vant to be alone."

By 1937, her screen mystique seemed to have worn thin with movie audiences, and *Conquest* did very badly at the box office. Audiences were looking for something light, and Garbo's appearance in the 1939 *Ninotchka* seemed appropriate. She has fun in this movie, playing a coldly doctrinaire Russian who mesmerizes and becomes sexually involved with a capitalist. Garbo laughs out loud in the movie and, unlike in her earlier roles, actually has fun on-screen. Her final film was another comedy, *Two-Faced Woman* (1941), a witless offering that pleased neither its star nor its audiences. Faced with this failure, Garbo decided to leave movies until World War II ended, planning to make a comeback in the late 1940s. Years and projects passed, however, as she half-heartedly considered a range of offerings. She never made another film, but she was honored by the Academy of Motion Picture Arts and Sciences in 1954 with a special award for her legendary performances.

Marlene Dietrich brought another distinctly European presence to Hollywood of the 1930s, creating a worldly and mysteriously sensuous image that continues to influence the film world. Where Garbo sinned and suffered, Dietrich sinned and simply shrugged at a world whose opinion meant nothing to her. She flirted with bisexuality in her cabaret scenes, donned tuxedos in films, and started a fashion trend by wearing slacks. Although her best films were made in the 1930s, Dietrich remained in the public eye through the early 1960s, surfacing sporadically to keep the world from forgetting what constitutes a legend.

Born Maria Magdalena von Losch to a middle-class family in Berlin, Dietrich aspired to a career as a concert violinist, but a serious injury to her wrist put an end to that dream. Instead, she turned to film and studied at the Max Reinhardt Drama School, then appeared in various stage revues, plays, and films. Director Josef von Sternberg noticed her dancing in a revue and signed her to play Lola-Lola, a cabaret singer who ruins the life of a professor obsessed with her, in *The Blue Angel* (1930). Von Sternberg had already selected German actor Emil Jannings for the role of the professor. Dietrich had misgivings about doing the film, fearful that it was "vulgar" and would hinder her career. Instead, Paramount Studios in Hollywood saw the rough cut of the movie and signed her to star with Gary Cooper in *Morocco* (1930).

The Blue Angel was the first of seven movies directed by von Sternberg in which Dietrich ensnares a man in her sexuality, destroys him, and walks away unaffected. She is a cabaret singer in *The Blue Angel*, *Morocco*, and *The Devil Is a Woman* (1935), a housewife who is a former cabaret singer in *Blonde Venus* (1932), a spy in *Dishonored* (1931), a prostitute in *Shanghai Express* (1934), and Catherine the Great of Russia in *The Scarlet Empress* (1934). Playing a woman with a past, Dietrich becomes the world-weary sensualist who has done whatever she must to survive. As she tells costar Clive Brook in *Shanghai Express*, "It took a lot of men to change my name to Shanghai Lily."

As Dietrich's fame in Hollywood increased, Adolf Hitler demanded in 1937 that she leave the United States and return to Germany. Strongly anti-Nazi, Dietrich defied his orders and applied to become a naturalized citizen. She made three disappointing films during this period, all part of Paramount's plan to change the image of her that von Sternberg had created. The three comedies—*Desire* (1936), *The Garden of Allah* (1936), and *Knight Without Armour* (1937)—put mundane lines into the seductress's mouth and placed her at number 126 in a 1937 movie magazine poll of the public's favorite actors and actresses. Paramount bought out her contract, and Dietrich did not make a movie until two years later, when Joe Pasternak at Universal signed her to film *Destry Rides Again* (1939) with James Stewart.

Marlene Dietrich (1930s) (MoMA/Film Stills)

Dietrich plays Frenchy, a saloon girl with a heart of gold who lies, cheats, and fights, then takes a bullet for good guy Stewart at the end. The film was a box-office success, and she quickly appeared in *The Flame of New Orleans* and *Manpower* (both 1941) and three adventure films with John Wayne: *Seven Sinners* (1940), *The Spoilers* (1942), and *Pittsburgh* (1942).

During World War II, Dietrich made three movies, toured military camps, and entertained the American troops, then joined the Allied forces to find her sister when they liberated Belsen concentration camp. When the war ended, Dietrich again made movies, but either the roles or the films were minor. She then played the second lead in *A Foreign Affair* (1948) and had success with *No Highway* (1951) and *Rancho Notorious* (1952). With *Witness for the Prosecution* (1958) and *Judgment at Nuremberg* (1961), she finally had two roles worthy of her talents. Aside from a few cameo roles in the 1960s and Maximillian Schell's fine 1986 documentary about the actress's life and career, Dietrich made no further screen appearances and lived most of her later life in Paris.

Among the most profitable films produced in the 1930s were those of child star Shirley Temple, who reportedly made more than $20 million for Fox before she became a teenager. Her film career began in 1932 with the one-reel series *Baby Burlesk*; her career escalated two years later when Fox signed her to a seven-year contract, for which she was paid $150 weekly. The 1934 musical *Stand Up and Cheer* featured Temple, and the result was a request from Paramount to borrow the young star for its *Little Miss Marker* and *Now and Forever* features, which were released in late 1934. The success of these films resulted in a renegotiation of her contract, raising her salary to $1,000 per week. In 1937 Temple earned $307,000, making her the seventh-highest-paid person in the United States.

Temple made the classic *Heidi* in 1937, then remade Mary Pickford's 1917 hit *Rebecca of Sunnybrook Farm* the following year with even greater success. In the next two years, Temple began to lose popularity at the box office as she approached adolescence. She received her first screen kiss from Dickie Moore in *Miss Annie Rooney* (1942), then appeared in several relatively good movies during the 1940s, including *Since You Went Away* (1944), *The Bachelor and the Bobby-Soxer* (1947), and *Fort Apache* (1948), movies that did not make use of Temple's singing and dancing skills. By 1949, Temple had become a box-office liability, and she stopped making movies. Upon her retirement from the big screen in 1950, Temple married her second husband, Charles Black, and began to take an active role in politics, serving first as a member of the U.S. delegation to the United Nations in the 1960s, as the American ambassador to Ghana in the 1970s and to the former Czechoslovakia in the 1980s.

The latter half of the 1930s welcomed to Universal Studios a talented teenager named Deanna Durbin who starred in her first movie, *Three Smart Girls*, in 1936. Her next picture, *100 Men and a Girl* (1937), established Durbin as a star in the public's eyes, as well as in the studio's coffers. Both films were commercially successful, and her original contract of $150 per week was renegotiated to increase her salary to $1,250 per week with a $10,000 bonus for the completion of each picture. By June 1938, she had become Universal's most important property; the studio once again renegotiated her contract to raise her salary to $1,750 per week with a $50,000 bonus for the completion of each film. The five-year contract also included guaranteed yearly raises of $250 per week for each of the five years. Durbin was well worth the money, because her films were consistently profitable and her success helped to keep an ailing Universal afloat during the late 1930s.

By 1939, Durbin was eighteen years old and had to graduate to playing adult roles. Universal Studios helped her transition by adapting her earlier formula to the young adult: The studio starred her first in *Three Smart Girls Grow Up* (1939), then filmed her first screen kiss in *First Love* (1939). Her later adult roles in the 1940s were commercially successful, and Durbin earned $400,000 for each film. By 1944, Durbin wanted to stop making light comedies and take on more dramatic roles. She convinced Universal to star her with Gene Kelly in

Christmas Holiday (1944), in which she played the opposite of her usual wholesome and peppy character. The clear disapproval of her fans forced Durbin to return to the tried-and-true light comedies and musicals, and they began to lose money at the box office by the late 1940s. In 1948, at the age of twenty-seven, Durbin starred in *For the Love of Mary* and never made another film.

Like many actresses of the 1930s, Myrna Loy began her career in the mid-1920s and went strong through the 1940s, with a sprinkling of films appearing in the 1950s and 1960s. Born Myrna Williams, she danced in the chorus line at Graumann's Chinese Theater in Hollywood, then graduated to very small parts in *What Price Beauty?* (1925) and *Ben-Hur* (1926). Her roles over the next eight years varied from playing leading women to bit parts, as she moved toward the film that would make her name and establish a partnership with William Powell—*The Thin Man* (1934). She had acted with Powell the same year in *Manhattan Melodrama*, a film that may have owed John Dillinger a debt for its unexpected success, for it gained substantial newspaper publicity as the last film the gangster saw before the fatal Chicago shootout that took place in front of the theater where it was playing. From 1934 through 1946, Loy made five more *Thin Man* films, a series based on the Dashiell Hammett novel. Loy also made movies with other leading men, including Clark Gable, with whom she won a 1937 contest held by Ed Sullivan to determine the public's choices as the king and queen of Hollywood. She remained relatively inactive during World War II and made her final *Thin Man* movie in 1947 (her thirteenth teaming with William Powell). She also played the epitome of the American homemaker in *The Best Years of Our Lives* (1946). Loy made two more films in the 1940s, *The Bachelor and the Bobby-Soxer* (1947) and *Mr. Blandings Builds His Dream House* (1948). In the 1950s she acted only rarely. Her greatest triumphs were behind her.

The career of Mary Astor runs the gamut from the silents to the 1960s, but her best work—and greatest fame—was in the 1930s, with the exception of *The Maltese Falcon* in 1941. She began her life as

Lucille Langhanke, the pretty daughter of an ambitious stage father who manipulated his contacts to gain her a bit part in the 1921 *Sentimental Tommy*. Astor next attracted the attention of John Barrymore, who made her his leading lady in *Beau Brummel* (1924) and then his lover. The association helped Astor's career considerably, and she next starred with Barrymore in *Don Juan* (1926) and also appeared in numerous other silent films with such actors as Douglas Fairbanks in *Don Q* and *Son of Zorro* in 1925.

With the advent of sound, Astor left movie acting and appeared on stage to rave reviews. By the mid-1930s, she was offered a range of movie parts from featured player to the leading lady in "B" films. In 1936, her name became known to most Americans when she became involved in a sex scandal and child custody battle. Her estranged physician husband found her intimate diary, which contained entries of her affair with playwright George S. Kaufman, and several portions of the diary, which detailed Kaufman's sexual techniques, were leaked to the press. The news media gave the story front-page treatment, and Astor's career might have been ruined if she had not just appeared in the commercially successful *Dodsworth* (1936). She quickly made *The Prisoner of Zenda* and *The Hurricane*, both successes, in 1937 and emerged from the scandal with her career intact. She made several more movies, then played the role for which she is most remembered—the scheming Bridget O'Shaughnessy in *The Maltese Falcon* (1941). She won the Academy Award for Best Supporting Actress that year for *The Great Lie*, but she believed she should have received it for her role in *The Maltese Falcon* instead. Astor appeared mainly in a variety of matronly roles during the 1940s; then her career began to wind down and she had only a few roles in the 1950s and 1960s.

For Joan Blondell, the 1930s provided the perfect showcase for her talents. Seldom the romantic lead, Blondell made her mark as the wisecracking sidekick or streetwise working girl in the Depression era when many women could relate to her need to work. Her show business career began in vaudeville, where she toured throughout the United States, Europe, and China. She then moved to Broadway in

1927 and appeared in several plays, including *Penny Arcade*, filmed by Warner Bros. in 1930 as *Sinner's Holiday*. She acted with James Cagney throughout most of the 1930s in such films as *Blonde Crazy* (1931), *The Crowd Roars* (1932), *Footlight Parade* (1933), and *He Was Her Man* (1934), then earned the highest critical praise for her role of an established actress being edged out by a newcomer in *Stage Struck* (1936). The successes slowed down as the 1930s ended, and Blondell made fewer movies in the following decades, among these *A Tree Grows in Brooklyn* (1945) and *The Blue Veil* (1951), which earned her the Academy Award nomination for Best Supporting Actress. Blondell played character parts in several movies in the 1950s and 1960s, as well as television in the 1960s, then played small parts in *Grease* (1978) and *The Champ* (1979).

Like Blondell, Loretta Young began in film in the late 1920s, then moved into television as her movie career wound down. Born Gretchen Michaela Young, she was nicknamed "Hollywood's Beautiful Hack" because of her ninety mostly mediocre movies, in which she rarely played leading roles. Young started her film career with bit parts as a child actress. In 1927, she made the silent *Naughty But Nice*, then moved into sound films with *Laugh Clown Laugh* (1928) and *The Squall* (1929). Young played the second lead in John Barrymore's *The Man From Blankleys* (1930), Ronald Colman's *The Devil to Pay* (1930), Jean Harlow's *Platinum Blonde* (1931), and James Cagney's *Taxi* (1932). These roles created an audience for Young at 20th Century–Fox, which starred her in *Ramona* (1936), *Ladies in Love* (1936), and *Three Blind Mice* (1938). Her success in the 1930s did not carry into the first years of the next decade, but Young continued to work in her trade and to earn the respect of her Hollywood colleagues. She appeared with Gary Cooper in *Along Came Jones* (1945), with Orson Welles in *The Stranger* (1946), and with Cary Grant in *The Bishop's Wife* (1947). Young won the 1948 Academy Award for Best Actress for *The Farmer's Daughter* and once again earned an Academy Award nomination in 1949 for *Come to the Stable*. Her last movie was *It Happens Every Thursday* (1953). Afterward, Young concentrated on television, then, with the exception of a couple of TV movies in the late 1980s, retired from show business in 1961.

Musical star Alice Faye also had a strong film career in the 1930s, but her box office appeal lasted only to the midpoint of the following decade. Born Alice Jeane Leppert, she started as a Ziegfeld Follies dancer, then played vaudeville for several years until she was hired to dance in *George White's Scandals* in New York. She had her first film role in 1934 when the dance revue was made into a movie, thus launching her into the public eye. 20th Century–Fox tried to cast her in the image of Jean Harlow by making her a platinum blonde and starring her in such provocatively named movies as *She Learned About Sailors* and *365 Nights in Hollywood*, both in 1934, but audiences soon recognized her talent. She became a box-office success with the 1936 films *Sing, Baby, Sing* and *King of Burlesque. On the Avenue* (1937) featured songs written by Irving Berlin. Faye starred in *In Old Chicago* (1937) and *Alexander's Ragtime Band* (1938), both Academy Award Best Picture nominees, then had big box-office hits with *Rose of Washington Square* (1939), *Lillian Russell* (1940), and *Tin Pan Alley* (1940). She ended the decade of the 1930s as the number-one female star at 20th Century–Fox, but her popularity decreased in the early 1940s, partly because she left for two years to have children but also because the studio began to promote Betty Grable as a challenge to Faye. In 1945, she left the studio after a disagreement over the way in which her role in *Fallen Angel* was edited. She stayed away from the film industry until 1962, when she had a supporting role in *State Fair*. Faye also made a cameo appearance in *Won Ton Ton: The Dog Who Saved Hollywood* (1976) and had a supporting role in *The Magic of Lassie* (1978).

The opportunities were not as great for African-American actresses as they were for Caucasians, yet Hattie McDaniel established a strong film career in Hollywood of the 1930s. Although she may be best known for her role in *Gone With the Wind* (1939), for which she won the Academy Award for Best Supporting Actress and became the first African-American to win an Oscar, McDaniel turned out strong performances in numerous other films in the decade. Her career was one of several firsts. Her early career as a band singer led to her being the first African-American woman to perform on radio. She then began a career in film in 1932, often playing the supporting role of a maid in such films as Marlene Dietrich's *Blonde Venus* (1933) and Mae West's *I'm No Angel* (1933). Most of her movies were set in the South, among them *The Little Colonel* (1935), *Show Boat* (1936), and *Maryland* (1940). McDaniel made *Song of the South* (1946), *Mickey* (1948), and *Family Honeymoon* (1949), then appeared on radio and television until her death in 1952.

No examination of the roles of women in the growing film industry of the 1930s would be complete without mention of Jeanette MacDonald, an actress who specialized in playing rich, spoiled women wooed by rich, equally spoiled men. The women played by MacDonald led with their hearts and eventually fell in love with the poor but sincere heroes who loved them. Although few people might be able to name more than one of the numerous movies she made with several different romantic leads, many people have seen at least one amateur or professional parody of "The Indian Love Call," with which Nelson Eddy serenaded her in *Rose Marie* (1936). Despite her more famous pairing with Eddy, MacDonald first created a strong reputation on Broadway before being lured to Hollywood as sound movies emerged. She actually made her earliest ones with French boulevardier Maurice Chevalier, with whom she starred in *The Love Parade* (1929), *Monte Carlo* (1930), *Love Me Tonight* (1932), and *The Merry Widow* (1934). In 1935, she was paired with Nelson Eddy in the musical *Naughty Marietta*, and audiences enthusiastically cried out for more films starring the new singing screen couple. The pair obliged their audiences and made seven more musicals together, including *Rose Marie* (1936), *The Girl of the Golden West* (1938), *Sweethearts* (1938), and *I Married an Angel* (1942). MacDonald made only one noteworthy nonmusical film, *San Francisco* (1936) with Clark Gable. She was offered only a few minor parts in the 1940s and ended her film career with *The Sun Comes Up* (1949), a Lassie movie.

Claudette Colbert also established a well-respected career on Broadway before becoming a popular Hollywood screen star. She was born Claudette Lily Chauchoin in Paris and moved to New York City when she was six years old. She began a stage career in 1923 at the age of eighteen and worked on stage until 1929. She made a silent film, *For the Love of Mike* (1927), a box-office failure and one of the first movies directed by Frank Capra. Two years later, she made the talkie *The Hole in the Wall*, the first of several undistinguished films, until Cecil B. De Mille cast her in *The Sign of the Cross* (1932), one of his first major biblical epics in the sound era. Colbert followed this with the title role in *Cleopatra* (1934), which brought her fee up to $25,000 per picture, from $10,000 to $15,000 in previous films. That year, Capra again contacted Colbert and asked her to make a picture for the fledgling Columbia Studios, promising that he would pay her twice her usual fee and that it would be completed in four weeks, on her vacation. *It Happened One Night* (1934), made with Clark Gable, established a pattern of clever banter and romantic tension for most of her subsequent films. *It Happened One Night* not only made a fortune for Columbia and established the reputation of the studio, but it earned for Colbert her only Academy Award for Best Actress. She followed this film with both comic and dramatic roles in such films as *Imitation of Life* (1934), *I Met Him in Paris* (1937), *Bluebeard's Eighth Wife* (1938), *Drums Along the Mohawk* (1939), *The Palm Beach Story* (1942), and *The Egg and I* (1947). Her career lost power as she became older, and most of her films of the 1950s are of little interest. After making *Parrish* (1961), Colbert retired from the movies.

The star system was not complete with the end of the 1930s, nor have all of the stars who emerged during this decade yet been identified. Although many actresses, such as Joan Crawford, Bette Davis, Katharine Hepburn, Ginger Rogers, Barbara Stanwyck, Merle Oberon, and Judy Garland, made their first movies in the early 1930s, they went on to thriving careers in later decades and it is in the decades of their greatest triumphs that their stories are told.

Glamour and Growth in the Golden Age: The Late 1930s and the 1940s

•

The years from the late 1930s through the 1940s make up the golden years of Hollywood, characterized by glamorous stars, musical extravaganzas, and substantial growth. The movie industry offered a greater variety of feature films and more diverse stars to lure audiences into the theaters. The musicals and the dramas pulsed with the life infused into characters by directors, writers, and film editors, whose work defined screen personalities and created Hollywood glamour for viewers. Stars became larger than life as they danced across the silver screen in shimmering fabrics in musicals, and as they plotted, planned, and pondered in films that tackled serious, if somewhat melodramatically portrayed, topics related to family and society.

The decade of the 1940s became an era of versatility in the portrayal of women on the screen. The femme fatale and the career woman, each a distinctive type that depended for success upon the combined efforts of the screenwriters, directors, film editors, and actresses, shared marquee space with identifiable types from everyday life, such as the much-loved Mrs. Miniver. Audiences rose to new levels of sophistication in their tastes and demanded diversity in their entertainment and versatility in their stars. Thus, Greer Garson might play the comfortable British matron in *Mrs. Miniver* (1942), then become the alluring woman in *Adventure* (1946), which used as its advertising slogan "Gable's back and Garson's got him."

Women screenwriters were key contributors in the creation of Hollywood's golden age. Writers such as Anita Loos, Frances Goodrich, Sonya Levien, Frances Marion, and Dorothy Parker continued careers that had already peaked in the decades of their greatest successes, while new names appeared on the film credits. Lillian Hellman, Lenore Coffee, Joan Harrison, Alma Reville, Virginia Van Upp, Ruth Gordon, and Sally Benson not only wrote "women's pictures," they also wrote about war and social concerns.

Playwright Lillian Hellman, much like her earlier established colleague Tess Slesinger, exhibited her social concerns in her work, creating serious screenplays that became serious films. Her first effort was *The Dark Angel* (1935), after which she created a screen treatment of her play *The Children's Hour* that was filmed as *These Three* (1936). Her lesbian theme in the latter work was mainly absent from the film because of studio fear that the censors would withhold approval. In 1937, she wrote the powerful screenplay for *Dead End*, a gangster film that, unlike those that had come before, linked crime to poverty. The same year, Hellman also cowrote *The Spanish Earth*, Joris Ivens's great documentary.

Hellman adapted her play *The Little Foxes* for the 1941 movie, which starred Bette Davis, and earned an Academy Award nomination for Best Screenplay that year. With Dashiell Hammett, she adapted her 1941 play *Watch on the Rhine* for the 1943 movie, again starring Bette Davis, and the two writers shared an Academy Award nomination for Best Screenplay. In 1943, Hellman wrote the strongly pacifistic *The North Star* (1943), for which she earned an Academy Award nomination for Best Original Screenplay. The film was edited and retitled in the 1950s as *Armored Attack*, a film she denounced because of the manner in which it manipulated her material. Yet, the screenplay is powerful in its depiction of the 1941 German invasion of Russia and the ensuing tragedy for Russian citizens. The social criticism of her writing attracted attention, and Hellman was called before the House Committee on Un-American Activities during the McCarthy hearings of the 1950s. She was blacklisted after refusing to give the names of well-known Hollywood leftists. As a result, Hellman's film career was halted for more than a decade, and she resurfaced in Hollywood only briefly to write *Toys in the Attic* (1963), and *The Chase* (1966), her last screenplay.

Longtime Hollywood screenwriter Lenore Coffee began her work in silent films in 1919, writing first for such silent screen stars as Clara Kimball Young and for director Cecil B. De Mille. Among these early films were such titles as *Wandering Daughters* and *The Age of Desire*, both in 1923. Her first of many scripts for De Mille was *The Volga Boatman* (1926). Coffee also gained a reputation as a skilled script doctor who, for a $1,000 fee, could transform a poor script into one that could be filmed and aid a studio in recouping some of its investment.

Coffee became known for the "woman's picture," especially in the 1930s, when she wrote starring vehicles for Jean Harlow and Joan Crawford at MGM. Coffee was asked by Irving Thalberg to help the studio transform the twenty-five-year-old Crawford from her flapper roles of the 1920s to a personality that would appeal to audiences of the 1930s. She succeeded with *Possessed* (1931), in which Crawford plays a factory girl who looks for work in New York City and becomes the mistress of a politician. Coffee wrote numerous successful films for both MGM and Paramount in the 1930s and 1940s, including *Suzy* (1936); *The Four Daughters* (1938), for which she earned an Academy Award nomination for Best Screenplay; *The Way of All Flesh* (1940); *Till We Meet Again* (1944); and *Tomorrow Is Forever* (1946). She also wrote the Bette Davis vehicles *The Great Lie* (1942), *Old Acquaintance* (1943), and *Beyond the Forest* (1949). In this last film, Coffee created her version of the 1940s "bad girl," who engages in adultery, murder, and a self-induced miscarriage. At the end of the film, however, the heroine, Rosa, has reconciled with her husband and regrets her earlier behavior. Coffee continued to write screenplays into the 1950s, tailor-

Joan Crawford (1930s) (Billy Rose Theater/Lincoln Center)

ing *Sudden Fear* (1952) for Joan Crawford and ending her long career with *Cash McCall* (1959).

Unlike Coffee, Catherine Turney was new to screenwriting when she started in Hollywood in the 1930s; she had been a playwright in New York and London. *Bitter Harvest*, her play about the relationship between Romantic poet Lord Byron and his half-sister Augusta, drew the attention of Irving Thalberg, who offered Turney a contract with MGM in 1935. While there, she cowrote the rags-to-riches Joan Crawford vehicle *The Bride Wore Red* (1935), a film that all involved preferred to forget. She moved to Warner Bros. where she wrote *Mildred Pierce* (1945), her most famous script and the work that established Turney as a skilled "woman's writer." Murder, betrayal, and incest by proxy (Mildred's despicable daughter commits adultery with Mildred's second husband) were relatively new to women's pictures, which had until then depended for the most part upon sentimentality. The result was that *Mildred Pierce*—and other similar movies that followed—also drew male viewers. Turney used the same approach in writing *The Man I Love* (1947), which starred Ida Lupino, who was only two years away from her directorial debut. The film tells the story of an independent cabaret singer who falls in love with a married jazz pianist. Although the film contains the usual family and romantic scenes, the ending breaks rules as the singer walks away from the man she loves when she learns that she cannot have him. Although some women writers bristled at being associated with the traditional "women's pictures," Turney was practical, acknowledging that writing such scripts with her trademark dark perspective meant an income. She also expressed the feeling that a woman could handle a story about a woman's troubles better than most men could.

Turney eventually wrote for all of the leading actresses at Warner Bros., and became a trusted associate of Bette Davis, who insisted that Turney be allowed on the set during the filming of *A Stolen Life* (1946). That same year, Barbara Stanwyck approached Turney and asked her to develop the studio-owned property *Instruct My Sorrows*, written by Clare Jaynes, into a screenplay; it was released as *My*

Reputation (1946), starring Stanwyck. Turney became known as a skilled adapter of plays, novels, existing films, and other material.

The trend toward darker women's films, however, began before *Mildred Pierce,* and a few throughout the decade sought to portray the psychologically complex reality that existed beneath the neat domestic surfaces of marriage and family. The first to explore this different perspective was *Rebecca* (1940), adapted by Joan Harrison, who had already done *Jamaica Inn* (1939) for Alfred Hitchcock. She shared an Academy Award nomination for Best Screenplay in 1940 for her adaptation of Daphne Du Maurier's novel *Rebecca* and another for Best Original Screenplay that same year for *Foreign Correspondent. Rebecca* was the first of many films that portrayed a woman involved in a dubious relationship that threatens her identity, her sanity, and, eventually, her life. Harrison collaborated with Alma Reville, Hitchcock's wife, on *Suspicion* (1941) as well as on *Saboteur* (1942) before leaving Hitchcock to become an independent film producer.

Harrison produced *Phantom Lady* (1944), *The Strange Affair of Uncle Harry* (1945), *Nocturne* (1946), *They Won't Believe Me* and *Ride the Pink Horse* (both 1947), *Once More My Darling* (1949), and *Eye Witness* and *Circle of Danger,* both in 1950. Most of these films fall into the category of "film noir," a relatively new screen perspective in the 1940s. As successful as Harrison was, she found that her physical attractiveness sometimes made it difficult to be taken seriously by male producers and by the press. The press could not fully be blamed, though, because at least one press release from Universal Pictures described her as "A girl with wavy blonde hair, dimples, and a 24-inch waist [who] could entertain people with something besides crime stories." Despite having proven herself as a feature film producer, Harrison never could escape her association with Hitchcock no matter how great her success. Critics never failed to recall that she had been Hitchcock's writer, and her later successful works as a producer were always reviewed as in the Hitchcock tradition. In the 1950s, she returned to work with Hitchcock on his television series.

Alma Reville cowrote only a few films with Harrison, but her influence was substantial in the making of most Hitchcock films from the 1920s through the 1940s. A skillful writer, film editor, and director, she began as a film editor at the London Film Company in England, working first on *The Prisoner of Zenda* (1915) when she was sixteen. She later met Hitchcock and became his fianceé. She worked as assistant director on the first film he directed, *The Pleasure Garden* (1925), as well as on *The Lodger* (1926). Reville then was a cowriter on *Juno and the Paycock* (1929), *The 39 Steps* (1935), *The Lady Vanishes* (1938), *Jamaica Inn* (1939), *Suspicion* (1941), *Shadow of a Doubt* (1943), and *The Paradine Case* (1948)—all directed by Hitchcock. She also cowrote films for other directors, including *The Passing of the Third Floor Back* (1935) and *It's in the Bag* (1945). Despite Reville's name on the credits of these and other films, historians have allowed Hitchcock's shadow to obscure her work. For the most part, male authors have chosen to relegate Reville's role to that of constructive critic of Hitchcock's impressive oeuvre, pointing out that she worked only on films in trouble after the birth of her daughter.

The curse of being physically attractive that plagued Joan Harrison also cast a pall over the successes of writer-producer Virginia Van Upp. She began as a modestly successful child actress, then later worked as an assistant casting director and assistant agent at Pathé before becoming a secretary to writer Horace Jackson at Paramount Pictures. Van Upp was asked with increasing frequency to finish Jackson's scripts. Her talents were soon recognized, and she was given a contract to write for Paramount, where she created roles for such leads as Carole Lombard and Madeleine Carroll. Van Upp's success brought her to the attention of Harry Cohn, who offered her greater creative control if she would join Columbia Studios; he needed her to create a star-making role for Rita Hayworth. Van Upp not only wrote the script for *Cover Girl* (1944), she also shepherded Hayworth through preparing for the role and dressing for the part. The results pleased Cohn, who now had his star. Hayworth bonded so closely with Van Upp that the star agreed to play the lead in *Gilda* (1946) only if Van Upp would also produce

•

the film. This lead to increased status for Van Upp, who went on to produce other films.

Although Hayworth was the most powerful of the 1940s screen femme fatales, Van Upp was also interested in that other 1940s phenomenon, the career woman. She explored this theme in *Together Again* (1944) and *She Wouldn't Say Yes* (1945), but her career women in both cases marry at the end of the movie and choose the domestic over the professional life. In her own life, Van Upp followed this convention and resigned from Columbia in 1947 to work at her marriage. The move, however, proved to be futile. Two years later, she divorced and returned to writing for Columbia, but her career had lost momentum. Only two of her scripts were produced, but neither *Here Comes the Groom* (1951) nor *An Affair in Trinidad* (1952) was successful. Van Upp then moved to West Berlin and produced propaganda films for the U.S. government before falling ill and retiring from the film business at the age of fifty-two.

Marguerite Roberts went even further in moving away from writing the traditional "women's picture." As early as the 1930s she made her reputation in writing what can only be called "men's films." The women in her screenplays, aside from *Ziegfeld Girl* (1942) and *Undercurrent* (1946), play secondary roles to the male characters. Even movie hero Clark Gable, who appreciated Roberts's style and told her risqué stories, commented that she "writes men with more balls than any other guy on this lot." Professionally, she became one of the boys at MGM because of her love of jazz and horse racing, and she openly stated that she liked working at MGM, where she felt as if she were a member of a club.

Roberts's first screenwriting credit, after working at Fox Movietone City as a secretary for several years, was *Sailor's Luck* (1933), cowritten with Charlotte Miller. Her next credit was *Peck's Bad Boy* (1934), starring Jackie Coogan; she then wrote a melodramatic screenplay about the pitfalls of the film business in *Hollywood Boulevard* (1936). In 1941, she wrote the screenplay for *Honky Tonk*, a rollicking western story about two con artists who attempt to cheat each other; it starred

Clark Gable and Lana Turner. The film pleased Gable, who wanted more from Roberts, and her next work (also for Gable and Turner) was about two war correspondents, entitled *Somewhere I'll Find You* (1942). Roberts also wrote three western films at the behest of studio executives over the course of her long career, including the John Wayne vehicle *True Grit* (1969). In his biography, Wayne gave the movie high praise. Roberts enjoyed the fact that the politically reactionary Wayne was so generous in his praise, particularly given her leftist reputation and her blacklisting during the McCarthy hearings. Among the many writers who were called before the House Un-American Activities Committee during the 1951 hearings, Roberts openly refused to name names, despite the strong urging of MGM, which offered to provide her with a lawyer. When Roberts held her ground, MGM terminated her contract and she received no further screen credits until the 1962 *Diamond Head*. Her career was reactivated, and Roberts wrote six more screenplays in as many years, including *5 Card Stud* (1968).

Before MGM contacted her to write for it, New York writer Sally Benson was a prolific contributor of short stories to *The New Yorker*, as well as a movie critic and newspaper reporter. Benson arrived in Hollywood in 1943 and wrote *Shadow of a Doubt* (1944), followed by *Meet Me in St. Louis*, a musical starring Judy Garland. Next came *Anna and the King of Siam* (1946), for which she shared an Academy Award nomination for Best Screenplay, and *Come to the Stable* three years later. During those years she occasionally returned to the east to write a Broadway script and to continue publishing short stories in *The New Yorker*. Benson adapted Humphrey Slater's political novel *Conspirator* into a 1950 film starring a young Elizabeth Taylor. She wrote other films, including the particularly incongruous (given her background) *Viva Las Vegas* (1964), a vehicle for Elvis Presley and *The Singing Nun* (1968). Benson followed her film career by writing for such television shows as *Dr. Kildare* and *The Chrysler Theater*.

Many other women experienced success as screenwriters in the 1940s. Claudine West shared an Academy Award nomination for Best Screenplay for *Random Harvest* (1942) and won the award that same year for *Mrs. Miniver.* Other women who were nominated during the decade include: Bella Spewack for *My Favorite Wife* (1940), Gladys Lehman for *Two Girls and a Sailor* (1944), Ruth Gordon for *A Double Life* (1947), Frances Flaherty for *The Louisiana Story* (1948), Irmgard Von Cube for *Johnny Belinda* (1948), Shirley W. Smith for *It Happens Every Spring* (1949), Virginia Kellogg for *White Heat* (1949), Helen Levitt and Janice Loeb for *The Quiet One* (1949), and Clare Booth Luce for *Come to the Stable* (1949). In 1946, Muriel Box shared the award for *The Seventh Veil.*

Film editing remained a critical profession for women, although the number recognized for their expertise had decreased from earlier decades. Only two women won the Academy Award for Film Editing during the 1940s: Anne Bauchens for *North West Mounted Police* (1940) and Barbara McLean for *Wilson* (1944). McLean was also nominated for *The Song of Bernadette* (1943), Monica Collingwood for *The Bishop's Wife* (1947).

Costume design became even more important to the film industry, as Edith Head and others built their reputations in Hollywood. Irene (born Irene Lentz) became chief costume designer at MGM in 1941 when the highly successful male costume designer Adrian left the studio after a rift with Louis B. Mayer. Previously a dressmaker who had her own salon-boutique in the prestigious Bullock's store in Los Angeles, Irene created flowing clothes that cling to the body, creating the effect of a living sculpture. Credited as the costume designer for fifty-six films, Irene began her noted designs in 1937 with *Topper.* Her greatest successes, however, occurred in the 1940s, when she designed for Loretta Young in *He Stayed for Breakfast* (1940) and *Bedtime Story* (1941), for Carole Lombard in *Mr. and Mrs. Smith* (1941), and for Claudette Colbert in *The Palm Beach Story* (1942). She earned the Academy Award nomination for the new category of black-and-white costume design for *B.F.'s Daughter* (1948). She designed the costumes for *Key to the City* and *Please Believe Me,* both released in 1950, after she left MGM when her contract expired in 1949. Irene then designed the costumes for *Midnight Lace* (1960), *Lover Come Back* (1961), and

A *Gathering of Eagles* which was released in 1963, the year after she commited suicide. She had always referred to her days at MGM as "a terrible mistake."

It was not until 1948 that the Academy of Motion Picture Arts and Sciences added the category of "Costume Design," thus giving women a new area of recognition. Longtime costume designer Edith Head earned a color category nomination for *The Emperor's Waltz* (1948) and won the award for the black-and-white category for *The Heiress* (1949). Kay Nelson earned a nomination in the color category for *Mother Is a Freshman* (1949). Dorothy Jeakins and Karinska won the color category award for *Joan of Arc* (1948), while Leah Rhodes and Marjorie Best won the color category for *Adventures of Don Juan* (1949).

Women scored one additional Academy Award victory when Mildred Griffiths became the first woman to receive a nomination for Interior Decoration (changed later to Art Direction/Set Decoration) for *National Velvet* (1945).

The star system of the late 1930s produced actresses whose careers continued well into the 1940s and beyond, names that are ingrained in Hollywood lore. Joan Crawford, Katharine Hepburn, Bette Davis, Barbara Stanwyck, Ginger Rogers, and Judy Garland staked their claims in the 1930s, and they held their ground in the decade that followed. Along with newer actresses, they refined roles that had first emerged in the 1930s, and even in the 1920s.

The 1940s femme fatale, like her 1920s predecessor the vamp, exuded a desirable but destructive sexuality that proved fatal to her male victim. The newer, improved version added a driving ambition or self-interest to make her more dangerous, as she lured men into her web and made them powerless to resist her. The deadly femme fatale achieved power at the expense of the men in her life and represented a threat to the normal moral order of life, because such characters usually enjoyed sexual independence and strove for economic independence. Their powerful and dangerous sexuality was represented by long-haired, long-legged actresses who openly and defiantly flouted convention on screen. They were not modest and retiring, nor were they fun-loving airheads. Instead, the femme fatales of the forties strutted boldly, shoulders well padded, and looked the camera and their prey directly in the eyes. Barbara Stanwyck, Rita Hayworth, Joan Bennett, Hedy Lamarr, Veronica Lake, Lana Turner, Lauren Bacall, and Ann Sheridan all played the femme fatale on screen. In *Double Indemnity* (1944), Barbara Stanwyck is the embodiment of the evil and seductive type, a woman who can emotionlessly plot her husband's murder and then lie about it. She seduces the helpless insurance salesman and uses her sexual power over him to convince him to commit the murder. When he has done her bidding and expects to be rewarded, she tries to double-cross him, but he murders her.

Born in Brooklyn and orphaned at an early age, Ruby Stevens might have been expected to develop a tough-girl veneer and to face the world with a chip on her shoulder. As famed actress Barbara Stanwyck, however, she was the consummate professional with both directors and other actors—easy to work with, prompt, and unselfish, although her screen image was that of the tough, cynical female. She entered show business as a chorus girl with the Ziegfeld Follies, then joined the chorus of a Broadway play, *The Noose*, where she quickly moved into the lead and gained attention during her nine months with the show. Stanwyck made her screen debut in *Broadway Nights* (1927), a silent produced by the New York film company First National. It was poorly received by audiences and critics, and Stanwyck decided to return to the stage. However, when her husband, vaudeville comedian Frank Fay, signed a contract with Warner Bros. and left for Hollywood, Stanwyck also signed with the studio. She made two mediocre films, *The Locked Door* (1929) and *Mexicali Rose* (1929), that brought her to the attention of director Frank Capra and Columbia Pictures head Harry Cohn, who signed her to four films: *Ladies of Leisure* (1930), *The Miracle Woman* (1931), *Forbidden* (1932), and *The Bitter Tea of General Yen* (1933).

Stanwyck had made eighty-one movies by the time she was fifty years old and had earned four Academy Award nominations. She was an independent woman who had managed to avoid domination by the Hollywood studio system that ran the lives of many actors and actresses. Her approach was to sign non-exclusive contracts with studios, thus giving her the opportunity to choose her own projects. For the most part, she avoided men's stories and took on a range of female roles that the largely female film audience could empathize and identify with. Rather than men in women's clothing, Stanwyck's characters were fighters who were forced to do combat in a world owned and operated by men. Thus, she had successes in *Night Nurse* (1931), *Annie Oakley* (1935), *A Message to Garcia* (1936), *Stella Dallas* (1937), for which she earned her first Academy Award nomination, and *Union Pacific* (1939). She also worked with Hollywood's best directors, making such classics as Preston Sturges's *The Lady Eve* (1941), Frank Capra's *Meet John Doe* (1941), and Howard Hawks's *Ball of Fire* (1942), for which she received a second Academy Award nomination. These films and others throughout the 1940s cemented her tough-girl image in movies. She starred in *Lady of Burlesque* (1943); *The Strange Love of Martha Ivers* (1946); and *Sorry, Wrong Number* (1948), which earned her another Academy Award nomination. She made her career movie, *Double Indemnity* (1944), in which she conspires to murder her husband, then coolly and without remorse attempts to kill her lover. That performance also won her an Academy Award nomination. In the 1950s, while actresses of her age were no longer being offered starring parts, Stanwyck still made films, beginning with the 1952 *Clash by Night* and continuing through a string of westerns until she yielded to the lure of television. She made several more films in the 1960s, starring as a bordello madam in *Walk on the Wild Side* (1962) and *Roustabout* (1964) with Elvis Presley, then continued to work in television throughout the 1970s and the 1980s.

Rita Hayworth is the mysterious femme fatale in *Gilda* (1946) and *The Lady From Shanghai* (1948). She retains the seductive power over the men in both films, but while she has no overt evil intent to use her power in *Gilda*, in husband Orson Welles's *The Lady from Shanghai*, her short-haired, blond character, Elsa, is a greedy and amoral

Stuart Granger / Rita Hayworth Salome (Moma/Film Stills)

temptress who exhibits no remorse for her powerless male victim. The former Margarita Carmen Cansino, who aspired to dance like her first cousin Ginger Rogers, started as a chorus dancer in 1935. She played mainly seondary roles until *Cover Girl* (1944) with Gene Kelly, followed by *Gilda* (1946). Because she couldn't sing, all of her film songs were dubbed. During the 1950s, she was offered only minor roles, which became fewer in the 1960s and 1970s.

Labeled "The World's Most Beautiful Woman" in 1938, when she arrived in the United States from Austria, Hedy Lamarr had the sensuous looks and the reputation to earn her a place as a 1940s femme fatale. The former Hedwig Eva Maria Kiesler had already scandalized European audiences with her nude swimming scene in the Czechoslovakian film *Ecstasy* (1933). Cast opposite such Hollywood stars as William Powell, Clark Gable, and Spencer Tracy, she exuded an exotic sexuality in *Lady of the Tropics* (1940), *White Cargo* (1942), *Experiment Perilous* (1944), and *Samson and Delilah* (1949), her most successful Hollywood film. Lamarr's career began to decline in the 1950s, and she returned to Europe in 1951; in the late 1950s she made two more unsuccessful movies in the United States.

For sexy Veronica Lake, the hairstyle appears to have made the difference in her career: She rose to stardom quickly in the early 1940s and faded out just as quickly at the end of the decade. More accurately, her change in hairstyle, from provocative to prosaic, coincided with a series of bad management decisions and a waning of public interest in her particular brand of screen allure. Born Constance Ockelman in Brooklyn, New York, in 1922, the former beauty-contest winner adopted her stepfather's name and, as Constance Keane, stormed Hollywood in the late 1930s with her long blond hair that covered her brow and cheek provocatively and invited sexuality. She appeared in five films in 1939 and 1940 before changing her name to Veronica Lake. Her early minor roles soon earned her the lead in *I Wanted Wings* (1941), followed by *Sullivan's Travels* (1941) with Joel McCrea. With Alan Ladd she filmed the highly successful *This Gun for Hire* (1942) and *The Glass Key* (1942) as well as the less successful *The Blue Dahlia*

(1946) and *Saigon* (1948), movies in which she played the tough and sensual yet vulnerable blonde. Throughout the 1940s, she appeared in thirteen other films, among them *I Married a Witch* (1942), *Bring on the girls* (1945), *Hold That Blonde* (1945), and *Variety Girl* (1946), which exhibited her feline sex appeal fully.

As the film offers disappeared, Lake began to drink heavily and she became even less bankable. Despite her reluctance to leave the glamour of Hollywood, where she had been a star, she turned to television. From 1950 through 1952, Lake appeared as a guest star on such shows as *The Lux Video Theatre*, *The Bert Parks Show*, Sid Caesar's *Your Show of Shows*, and Milton Berle's *Texaco Star Theatre*, just to meet her financial obligations.

Hollywood studios no longer made offers, but Lake eagerly accepted one from Lippert Pictures for a low-budget Mexican film, *Stronghold* (1952). The B-grade movie, which took less than two months to film, did nothing to resurrect her career. Lake appeared sporadically in theater-in-the-round productions and touring productions in the Midwest, the South, and New England throughout the 1950s, but her drinking eventually made her performances unreliable. In 1962, a reporter for the *New York Post* discovered her working as a barmaid at the Martha Washington Hotel on East 29th Street in New York. The resulting attention brought Lake many offers for Las Vegas engagements, off-Broadway parts, and chances to do television. Unwilling to accept what she perceived as charity, Lake chose to become the hostess for a Saturday night film program in Baltimore. Several stage roles and two grade-Z movies, *Footsteps in the Snow* (1966) and *Flesh Feasts* (1973), followed, but drinking dominated her life and bloated her face. In 1973, Lake was admitted to a hospital in Vermont, where she died on July 7 of acute hepatitis.

Lana Turner arrived in Los Angeles with her mother at the age of nine. The star, whose well-developed figure would earn her the nickname of "The Sweater Girl" in pinup photographs, attended Hollywood High and was discovered at the age of fifteen by a writer for *The Hollywood Reporter*. Warner Bros. gave her a chance and filmed her in *They Won't Forget* (1938), but the results were disappointing and the studio released her. Turner moved to MGM, which groomed her for stardom; the studio first gave her featured roles in films that were part of established successful series—*Love Finds Andy Hardy* (1938) and *Calling Dr. Kildare* (1939). Then it began the pinup campaign. Sexy melodramas followed in the early 1940s, which strengthened her image. She made her most popular films, though, after World War II, among them *The Postman Always Rings Twice* (1946), *Green Dolphin Street* (1947), *Cass Timberlane* (1947), and *The Three Musketeers* (1948). Her popularity decreased substantially in the 1950s, and only the scandal that followed her daughter's killing of Turner's gangster boyfriend revived her career, leading to successes in *Peyton Place* (1957), which brought her an Academy Award nomination as Best Actress, and *Imitation of Life* (1959). She made several films in the 1960s, but only *Madame X* stands out. She died in 1995.

A tough blonde with sex appeal, the former Betty Joan Perske, renamed Lauren Bacall, had a seductive voice and a come-hither manner that made her an interesting choice as the love interest for Humphrey Bogart. Working as a model in New York, she was discovered when the wife of director Howard Hawks saw her picture on the cover of *Harper's Bazaar* and suggested to Hawks that Bacall would be perfect for his latest project. The nineteen-year-old girl with the smoky voice and the Veronica Lake hairdo was paired with Humphrey Bogart in *To Have and Have Not* (1944), and the two married the following year. They costarred in *The Big Sleep* (1946), *Dark Passage* (1947), and *Key Largo* (1948), with Bacall playing her sensuous but tough role in all three. She appeared alone in several films in the 1950s, among them *Young Man With a Horn* (1950), *How to Marry a Millionaire* (1953), and *Written on the Wind* (1957), but her image underwent a change as her box-office appeal lessened. She appeared more on Broadway in the 1960s and had supporting roles in *Harper* (1966), *Murder on the Orient Express* (1974), and *The Shootist* (1976).

Ann Sheridan often played the feminine, sexy, and resilient woman in movies during the 1940s, but her on-screen glamour failed to keep her career momentum going beyond that decade. The former Clara Lou Sheridan made her debut in a Paramount film, having won the role as the prize in a 1933 "Search for Beauty" contest. After playing bit parts in several films, she changed her name and moved to Warner Bros., which publicized her as "The Oomph Girl" and gave her tough-blonde roles in such films as *Angels With Dirty Faces* (1938), *They Made Me a Criminal* (1939), *They Drive by Night* (1940), and *City for Conquest* (1940). Her star performance in *Kings Row* (1942) made her a strong box-office draw, and she continued her success in a range of films through the last half of the 1940s, ending with *I Was a Male War Bride* (1949) with Cary Grant. The scripts offered to Sheridan in the 1950s were poorly written, and she quit making movies to enter television, where she became one of the first Hollywood stars to appear in a daytime soap opera.

Another stereotype that became fully developed in films of the 1940s was the "career woman," a female character who deviated from the wife-and-mother norm of the period and who usually faced a knotty conflict between her career and her traditional role. Career-woman movies first appeared in the 1930s, and such roles were often played by Rosalind Russell, Bette Davis, Joan Crawford, Katharine Hepburn, and Barbara Stanwyck. As early as *Christopher Strong*, directed by Dorothy Arzner and starring Hepburn, the pattern and the lesson to be learned were made clear. Highly intelligent women, single-minded in their pursuit of a career, sacrifice love for their ambition, only to learn by the end of the film how wrong they have been. Examples of this appear in *Woman of the Year* (1942), with a variation of the same type of woman whose inherent warmth and compassion vie with her drive for a career, as shown in *Pat and Mike* (1952) and *Mildred Pierce* (1945). Some actresses—Rosalind Russell among them—played career women as confident and fun-loving, smart and sexy, while others took the route of Joan Crawford, whose brittle career women were a blend of success and pain.

Joan Crawford was one of the rare actresses who could play both the femme fatale and the "career woman." She entered show business by winning a Charleston contest in her home state of Texas, then became a chorus girl on Broadway under her real name of Lucille Fay Le Sueur. In 1925, Harry Rapf discovered her and took her to MGM, where she appeared in *Pretty Ladies* (1925), using the stage name of Billie Cassin. After placing her in several movies, MGM decided to give her the star treatment. The studio ran a fan magazine contest to rename her, but the winning name, "Joan Arden," already belonged to another actress, so the runner-up name became hers. As Joan Crawford, she appeared in numerous films, none successful, until her lead role as a wild flapper in the silent film *Our Dancing Daughters* (1928) brought her to the filmgoer's attention. She reprised this role in the silent *Our Modern Maidens* (1929), also a great success, then made her sound debut in *Hollywood Revue of 1929*.

In 1931, MGM strove to change Crawford's flapper image into something more durable, and she was cast in *Possessed* (1931) as a poor working girl who goes to New York to find a job and becomes the mistress of a politician. This was the first of many roles in which she played poor but honest girls with ambition who succeed in making their way in this world, yet endanger all that they have accomplished for love. From 1931 through 1937, Crawford made numerous films for MGM, most box-office hits, among them *Letty Lynton* and *Grand Hotel* (both 1932). Although the cult of the career woman had not yet begun, Crawford wore the broad-shouldered look in *Letty Lynton*. In 1938 and 1939, she had a string of box-office failures, then had a hit with *The Women* (1939), in which she played the villainous Crystal Allen. She had only two more hits in the next five years, and MGM dropped her contract. She moved to Warner Bros., where she waited two years until the right script came along. That script was *Mildred Pierce* (1945), which gave new life to Crawford's dying career and created her new persona, that of a tough, ambitious woman who is in control. She won the Academy Award for Best Actress for *Mildred Pierce*. Her later films for Warner Bros. cast her in essentially the same role: *Humoresque* (1946), *Possessed* (1947), *Daisy Kenyon* (1947), and *Flamingo Road* (1949).

The tough-talking Crawford persona, complete with aggressively masculine qualities, carried into her films of the 1950s, most of which had only moderate success. Good roles for aging actresses were nearly nonexistent, and Crawford took what there was, mostly playing the older woman who falls in love with a much younger man who deceives or murders her. Her increasingly exaggerated physical appearance had a campy look, with the heavy eyebrows, red set lips, and sculpted cheekbones. The look was appropriate for Robert Aldrich's *What Ever Happened to Baby Jane?* (1962), her hit horror film with Bette Davis that gained a substantial following. Crawford followed this with a string of horror movies, including *Straitjacket* (1964), *Berserk* (1967), and *Trog* (1970), her final film.

Katharine Hepburn also portrayed strong women on screen, but her roles combined the qualities of a patrician beauty and cultured intelligence with a defiant independence. Her roles have ranged from light comedy to tragedy, and over her long career she has won four Academy Awards for Best Actress. Starting out in summer stock in 1928, Hepburn later starred in the hit Broadway play *The Warrior Husband* in 1932 and drew offers from Fox, Paramount, and RKO. She agreed to make one film for RKO, *A Bill of Divorcement* (1932), and expected to return to the stage afterward, but the picture was so great a success that she made thirteen more for RKO and won the Academy Award for Best Actress for *Morning Glory* (1932). Her upper-class diction, her habit of wearing men's clothes, and her film failures made her box-office "poison" by the late 1930s. She had made $175,000 for *Bringing Up Baby* (1938), a comic masterpiece, and when she was offered only $10,000 in 1939 for a film role, Hepburn decided to return to the stage, where she hired Phillip Barry to write a play for her. The play was *The Philadelphia Story*, a smash hit on Broadway to which Hepburn owned the film rights. When Hollywood sought these rights, Hepburn held the upper hand, and studios were forced to give her the lead role if they wanted to make a movie of the play. MGM made the film, using Cary Grant and James Stewart in the male leads to bolster Hepburn's

•

Katherine Hepburn in Stage Door *(1937)* (National Film Archive)

shaky box-office position. The result was a major success and the reju-
venation of Hepburn's film career.

The 1940s marked the beginning of a string of film successes, beginning with the first pairing of Hepburn with Spencer Tracy in *Woman of the Year* (1942). Their nine films were very successful at the box office, in large part because of their on-screen chemistry but also because of their long-standing affair. In 1951, Hepburn starred in *The African Queen* as a psalm-singing spinster to Humphrey Bogart's unshaven riverboat captain. She played a similar role, as the spinster in *The Rainmaker* (1956), and won two Academy Awards for Best Actress during the 1960s: for *Guess Who's Coming to Dinner?* (1967), her last film with Tracy, who died soon after, and *The Lion in Winter* (1968). She starred with John Wayne in *Rooster Cogburn* (1975), then earned her final Oscar for *On Golden Pond* (1981). Hepburn's most recent role was a cameo appearance in *Love Affair* (1994), which starred Warren Beatty and Annette Bening.

Blessed, like Hepburn, with a long and successful career, Bette Davis began making films in 1931 and made her last one in 1987. Also like Hepburn, she began her career on stage, starting in New England theater companies. She starred in the successful Broadway play *Broken Dishes* (1928), which brought her to the attention of Universal Studios. Her first screen role was that of the good sister in *Bad Sister* (1931). She then made a series of unimportant films until she moved to Warner Bros. Movie audiences were riveted by her performance as the young tramp in *Cabin in the Cotton* (1932), and she was even more successful in *20,000 Years in Sing Sing* (1933), which costarred Spencer Tracy. In 1934, RKO wanted to borrow Davis for the lead in *Of Human Bondage*, but Warner Bros. refused until Davis eventually wore Jack Warner down; the movie made her a star. She followed with *Dangerous* (1935), winning the Academy Award for Best Actress that year, but she then made the mistake of agreeing to appear in a series of mediocre movies for Warner Bros. Davis finally rebelled when handed the script for *God's Country and the Woman* and refused to make any more second-rate pictures. She was suspended and fined $5,000 per week. Violating her contract, she went to England to make several films. Warner finally capitulated. When the company offered not only to pay her court damages but also to give her the lead in *Marked Woman*

Betty Davis in 1939 (National Film Archive)

(1937) with Humphrey Bogart, she returned to the United States. Two years later she wanted the part of Scarlett O'Hara in *Gone With the Wind* and David Selznick wanted Davis to play the part, but Warner Bros. would agree to lend Davis only if Selznick would use Errol Flynn in the Rhett Butler part. When Selznick refused, Warner refused to release Davis for the picture. Instead, Warner created *Jezebel* (1938), a variation on *Gone With the Wind*, as a starring vehicle for Davis. It brought her her second Academy Award for Best Actress.

From 1939 through the early 1940s, Davis starred in a series of box-office hits, from *Dark Victory* and *The Private Lives of Elizabeth and Essex*, both in 1939, through *All This and Heaven Too* (1940), *The Letter* (1940), *The Little Foxes* (1941), *Now Voyager* (1942), *Watch on the Rhine* (1943), and *Mr. Skeffington* (1944). After World War II ended, Davis's career faltered and nearly ended as her films became increasingly less successful. In *Beyond the Forest* (1949), Davis played what the advertisements described as "a midnight girl in a nine o'clock town" who has an abortion, commits adultery and murder, and then dies after a long and boring scene in which she crawls over railroad tracks for what seems to be miles. The high point of the movie is Davis's often-quoted camp line regarding her home—"What a dump!" Disgusted with the script, Davis threatened to walk off the set unless Warner Bros. released her from her contract when the movie was complete. The studio agreed, and Davis moved to 20th Century–Fox where she turned in a powerful performance in *All About Eve* (1950).

Few roles came her way in the 1950s, and in 1961 Davis took the initiative. She paid for a full-page advertisement in the trade papers announcing her availability for work. She was offered one of the two lead roles, with Joan Crawford, in *What Ever Happened to Baby Jane?*, a psychological thriller for which she earned an Academy Award nomination for Best Actress. She later made three more horror films, *Hush . . . Hush . . . Sweet Charlotte* (1965), *The Nanny* (1965), and *The Anniversary* (1967). Davis had roles in *Burnt Offerings* (1976) and *Death on the Nile* (1978), then starred with Lillian Gish in *The Whales of August* (1987). In 1977, she was the first woman to earn the Life Achievement Award of the American Film Institute.

Among the most underrated of the actresses who enlivened the movie screens of the late 1930s and the 1940s, Ginger Rogers has become better known for the ten musicals she made with Fred Astaire than for her other sixty films. Pushed into a show business career at the age of fourteen by her strong-willed mother, a retired Marine Corps sergeant, the former Virginia Katherine McMath started as a substitute dancer in a vaudeville act, then won a Charleston contest in 1926. She danced on the vaudeville circuit throughout the late 1920s before landing a central role in the Broadway musical *Top Speed* (1929). The next year, she had another strong stage role in *Girl Crazy*, which caught the attention of Paramount, who starred her in several low-budget films at their Astoria, New York, studio. She then moved to Hollywood, where she made several forgettable films for Warner Bros. before the studio recognized her musical gift and cast her in *42nd Street* (1933) and *Gold Diggers of 1933* (1933). She next worked for RKO, which cast her as the dance partner to second lead Fred Astaire in *Flying Down to Rio* (1933). The pairing was fateful. Audiences were so enthusiastic that RKO rushed the two through filming of *The Gay Divorcée* (1934), another wildly successful film. Rogers made seven more films with Astaire in the last half of the 1930s: *Roberta* (1935), *Top Hat* (1935), *Swingtime* (1936), *Follow the Fleet* (1936), *Shall We Dance* (1937), *Carefree* (1938), and *The Story of Vernon and Irene Castle* (1939).

During the 1940s, Rogers played serious dramatic roles and comedy, beginning with *Kitty Foyle* (1940), for which she won the Academy Award for Best Actress. She also starred in such comedies as *Tom, Dick, and Harry* (1941) and *The Major and the Minor* (1942), ending the decade with a musical and her final film with Astaire, *The Barkleys of Broadway* (1949). She appeared sporadically in films during the 1950s and 1960s and returned to the stage to star in *Hello, Dolly!* on Broadway and *Mame* in London. In the 1970s and 1980s, Rogers limited her activity to a few rare television appearances.

Although she had her first screen role at the age of fourteen, Judy Garland, born Frances Gumm in Grand Rapids, Michigan, was already a show business veteran. She had been performing from the age of three as one of "The Gumm Sisters," a vaudeville act with her two older sisters. She made a one-reel film for MGM in 1936, *Every*

Sunday, which also starred the fifteen-year-old Deanna Durbin. MGM used the singing and dancing Garland—the little girl with the big voice—in several minor musicals during the late 1930s, then paired her with Mickey Rooney in *Thoroughbreds Don't Cry* and *Love Finds Andy Hardy* (both 1938), the first of many Andy Hardy movies they made together. One of her best-known roles, Dorothy in *The Wizard of Oz* (1939), she nearly lost to Shirley Temple, whom MGM executives wanted. "Over the Rainbow" became her theme song. Ironically, it had almost been edited out of the film in the final cut.

After *The Wizard of Oz* and two more Andy Hardy films, Garland was cast with Gene Kelly in *For Me and My Gal* (1942). She then filmed *Meet Me in St. Louis* (1944) with director Vincente Minnelli, whom she soon married. Garland departed from musicals to film the dramatic World War II movie *The Clock* (1945), then returned to musical roles in *The Harvey Girls* (1946), *The Pirate* (1948), and *Easter Parade* (1948). MGM had planned to star Garland with Fred Astaire in *The Barkleys of Broadway* (1949), but she backed out of the project because of ill health. Ginger Rogers, eleven years her senior, took her place with old partner Astaire.

By the 1950s, Garland was becoming increasingly unreliable on the set. After she was replaced by Betty Hutton in *Annie Get Your Gun* (1950) she committed herself to star in *Royal Wedding* (1950) and *Showboat* (1951), then failed to appear on the set and was fired by MGM. After three years of concert appearances, Garland made *A Star Is Born* (1954) for Warner Bros. and regained her film audience when the film drew both popular support and critical raves, as well as an Oscar nomination for her as Best Actress. Despite the success of the film, she appeared in no others until her dramatic role in *Judgment at Nuremberg* (1961), for which she earned an Academy Award nomination for Best Supporting Actress. Garland made two more films, *A Child Is Waiting* and *I Could Go On Singing* (both 1963). For the remaining six years of her life, until her death from an accidental drug overdose in 1969, Garland gave concert and cabaret performances.

The late 1930s and the 1940s in Hollywood were a time of glamour and growth in the film industry, and many young actresses appeared on the scene like shooting stars, then rapidly disappeared, leaving behind little trace that they had ever existed. Those who found an "image" played the image until the roles ran out, while the smart actresses developed acting style and skill, ignoring image in favor of substance.

Ingrid Bergman was an actress who did not play to type but instead took roles that intrigued and challenged her. Born in Sweden and orphaned at an early age, she studied at the Royal Dramatic Theater in Stockholm, then played a small role as a maid in *Munkbrogreven* (1934) before making twelve films over a five-year period. Her performance in *Intermezzo* (1936) caught the attention of Elsa Neuberger, David Selznick's talent scout. Selznick bought the rights to the film and brought Bergman to Hollywood to remake the film. In *Intermezzo: A Love Story* (1939), Bergman played the "other woman" in the life of a married violinist and, as required of the period, she expresses shame in the movie, telling her married lover "I'm ashamed. . . . And I hate being ashamed."

Bergman followed the guilt-ridden adulteress by playing a debauched bar maid in *Dr. Jekyll and Mr. Hyde* (1941), then played the heroine, Ilsa Lund, in *Casablanca* (1942). The script had started out as a play entitled *Everybody Goes to Rick's*, and Warner had originally planned to star Ronald Reagan as Rick, Ann Sheridan as Ilsa, and Dennis Morgan as the anti-Nazi freedom fighter. A change of director resulted in a change of cast, and Bergman won the romantic role of the decade as the woman torn between her noble husband and her passionate former love.

Bergman also played a heroine in *For Whom the Bell Tolls* (1943), then the victimized wife in *Gaslight* (1944), for which she won an Academy Award for Best Actress. She had not been the first choice for these two films, or for *Saratoga Trunk* (1945), which all became box-offices hits for her. The role of Maria in *For Whom the Bell Tolls* was first played by Vera Zorina, who left the production and opened the way for Bergman. The role of the wife nearly driven mad by her husband in *Gaslight* was first offered to Irene Dunne and then Hedy

Ingrid Bergman, 1930s (Evans Collection)

Lamarr. Vivien Leigh turned down the role in *Saratoga Trunk* before Bergman was chosen. Bergman then made *Spellbound* (1945) and *Notorious* (1946) with Alfred Hitchcock. When Selznick tried to sign her to another seven-year contract, she turned him down. Freed from the studio contract system, Bergman made several poorly received pictures, then put her career on hold when, still married to her first husband, she went to Italy and began an affair with director Roberto Rossellini and had his child. Even though she soon married Rossellini, Hollywood denounced her, and she was referred to as "America's apostle of degradation" on the floor of the U.S. Senate. She made six movies with her new husband and, in addition to the first child, produced a set of twins before the marriage collapsed. Bergman began the steep climb back to success when 20th Century–Fox starred her in *Anastasia* (1956), for which she won the Academy Award for Best Actress. She made relatively few movies from the late 1950s through the 1970s; among them *Indiscreet* (1957), *The Inn of the Sixth Happiness* (1958), and *Murder on the Orient Express* (1974), for which she won the Academy Award for Best Supporting Actress, stand out. Her last film, *Autumn Sonata* (1978), in which she played a dying concert pianist, brought Bergman an Academy Award Nomination.

There were so many others who contributed to the glamour of Hollywood's golden years. Pinup queen Betty Grable blended sexy with wholesome to become one of the most popular and highly paid singing and dancing actresses of the era. "The Blonde Blitz," Betty Hutton, appeared in a string of musicals and lent her exuberance and flair for comedy to numerous films. Dorothy Lamour's exotic beauty and playful sexiness made her a favorite actress in jungle films and took her "on the road" with Bob Hope and Bing Crosby in seven movies. Claire Trevor made an art of playing the morally loose woman and earned three Academy Award nominations and one Oscar for Best Supporting Actress for *Key Largo* (1947). Merle Oberon, Maureen O'Hara, and Joan Fontaine dazzled audiences in numerous dramatic roles, and Gene Tierney's *Laura* (1944) has become a film classic. British-born Vivien Leigh and Olivia de Havilland appeared in *Gone With the Wind* (1939), for which Leigh won the Academy Award for Best Actress, and both won Oscars for their fine dramatic performances in other films over the years. Irene Dunne proved equally adept in musical comedy and drama, garnering five Academy Award nominations over the years. Film studios began to groom new solo comedy stars in the late 1940s,

Vivien Leigh, 1939 (Movie Graphics)

but women did not fare too well in this area. Only Lucille Ball, whose first roles were in drama, managed to star in a number of comic film roles before she began her phenomenal success in television.

The end of the 1940s closed the door on an era in Hollywood. Many former screen luminaries were dying out as tastes in movies—and lifestyles generally—changed after World War II. Women screenwriters, film editors, and others behind the camera lost ground when the studio system began to break up, and even fewer women than before would be found in decision-making positions as movies entered the second half of the twentieth century.

A Decade of Transition: The 1950s

•

THE DECADE OF THE 1950s was a time of contrasts in Hollywood, as well as throughout the nation. It was a time of economic growth and of deep conservation, of a professed belief in two old values mixed with a sense of unease that maybe the old values no longer held all the answers. American men who had helped to fight oppression overseas in World War II and the women who had kept America's factories humming while the men were at war now settled into their comfortable tract houses. Senator Joseph McCarthy waged war against communism on the home front and bullied many Hollywood figures into naming names or else suffer the consequences of blacklisting. The nation rejected the popular 1940s screen image of the competent career woman in favor of the "dumb blonde" sex goddess at one end of the spectrum and the sweet heroine at the other. Racial discrimination was rampant, yet Dorothy Dandridge became the first actress of African-American descent to earn an Academy Award nomination for Best Actress, for her performance in *Carmen Jones* (1954).

Women's pictures decreased in popularity during the 1950s, and

both the female stars of these movies and those who wrote the screenplays were less in demand as the decade began. Most of the big names
of the 1940s were now out of favor with a new generation of filmgoers.
The hard-edged glamour queens of the previous decade were no longer
welcome on the silver screen, nor did the public want to see the plucky,
virginal heroines of musicals simply dance their way to happiness. Ann
Miller might high step her way through *Small Town Girl* (1953), but
audiences were more likely to warm to Gwen Verdon as the seductive
Lola in *Damn Yankees* (1958), or to Mitzi Gaynor in *South Pacific*
(1958).

Sexual allure and virginal pluckiness were still desirable characteris-
tics, but alone they were not enough; characters had to be more accessible and believable to the public, and more substance and story were
required as well. Thus, Marilyn Monroe might be the sex goddess on
screen, dressed glamorously and fawned over by numerous suitors, but
she had to seem approachable to the bored husband in *The Seven-Year
Itch* (1955) or to the cowboy in *Bus Stop* (1956). In like manner, the
seemingly sweet and innocent heroines, such as those played by Doris
Day or Debbie Reynolds, and in a less cloying manner by Audrey
Hepburn, might start out as inaccessible, but they became attainable
by the film's end. The cool blonde complicated the mix, as her sensuality was intensified by her aloof appearance and apparent lack of sexual interest, yet she could also be reached. Grace Kelly was the epitome
of this type.

Despite the relatively small number of women screenwriters in the
1950s, several of the most memorable films of the decade were written
or cowritten by women. Nine screenplays by Frances Goodrich, with
husband and collaborator Albert Hackett, were filmed, including
Father of the Bride (1950), *Father's Little Dividend* (1951), *Seven Brides
for Seven Brothers* (1954), *A Certain Smile* (1958), and *The Diary of
Anne Frank* (1959). Lillian Hellman was first offered the opportunity
to adapt the memoir *The Diary of Anne Frank* for the stage, but she
sent it to Goodrich and Hackett, who won a Pulitzer Prize for Drama

and a Tony Award. Their screenplay also earned them a third Academy Award nomination for writing.

Isobel Lennart was one screenwriter who managed to maintain a healthy output as she moved from the 1940s into the 1950s. She began writing for MGM in the early 1940s, after working her way up from the typing pool to script girl. Lennart wrote numerous scripts for MGM, mostly light comedies and musicals such as *Anchors Aweigh* (1944) and *Meet Me in Las Vegas* (1956). She also wrote several screenplays for 20th Century–Fox. Beginning with *The Affairs of Martha* (1942) through *Funny Girl* (1968), twenty-six of Lennart's screenplays were filmed, including *The Inn of the Sixth Happiness* (1958), an enormously popular vehicle for Ingrid Bergman. She received two Academy Award nominations, for *Love Me or Leave Me* (1955) and for *The Sundowners* (1960).

Dorothy Kingsley has the distinction of being the only woman screenwriter in Hollywood of the 1940s and 1950s who went to Hollywood after establishing a career as a radio comedy gag writer. Fortunately for Kingsley, the reluctance of studio executives to take a chance on her skills was overcome with the help of actress Constance Bennett, who introduced her to the right people to market her talent. Her early claim to fame lay in an unusual specialty: She wrote seven films for Esther Williams, the swimming star, including *Bathing Beauty* (1944), *Neptune's Daughters* (1949), *Dangerous When Wet* (1953), and *Jupiter's Darling* (1955). She also cowrote *Kiss Me Kate* (1953); *Seven Brides for Seven Brothers* (1954), for which she shared an Academy Award nomination; *Pal Joey* (1957); *Green Mansions* (1959); and *Can-Can* (1960). The Disney remake in 1994 of *Angels in the Outfield* owes its story to Kingsley, who wrote the original script with George Wells in 1951, the year the film was first made. Advertisements for the Disney version appropriately mentioned the Kingsley-Wells script. Kingsley's final screenplay was for *The Valley of the Dolls* (1967), an adaptation of the Jacqueline Susann novel of the same name.

One of the most noted women in screenwriting partnerships of the 1950s was Ruth Gordon, who also made a name for herself as a

Broadway and Hollywood actress. Gordon collaborated with her husband, Garson Kanin, on four films: *A Double Life* (1947), *Adam's Rib* (1950), *Marrying Kind* (1951), and *Pat and Mike* (1952), and earned Academy Award nominations for all but *Marrying Kind*. Gordon also wrote an autobiographical play entitled *Years Ago*, which she turned into a screenplay for *The Actress* (1953), starring Spencer Tracy, Teresa Wright, and Jean Simmons. Her combination of successful screenplays and a long and memorable acting career is unique in Hollywood history. Gordon began as a bit player in silent films and later became a character actress in the 1940s, appearing in such roles as Mary Todd Lincoln in *Abe Lincoln in Illinois* (1940) and *Dr. Ehrlich's Magic Bullet* (1940). From the late 1940s through the mid-1950s, she wrote for the screen and then left Hollywood for a decade to appear on Broadway. When Gordon returned to Hollywood, she resumed her acting career, appearing first in *Inside Daisy Clover* (1965), *Lord Love a Duck* (1966), *Rosemary's Baby* (1968), for which she won the Academy Award for Best Supporting Actress and the cult film *Harold and Maude* (1970). As Gordon entered her seventies, she became highly in demand, playing a series of eccentric old women throughout the late 1970s and early 1980s.

Betty Comden and partner Adolph Green were nightclub performers before they began to write Hollywood screenplays in the mid-1940s. The team introduced a new concept to the Hollywood musical—actors and actresses singing and dancing in the streets and in other everyday settings rather than performing on a stage within the movie. Their first writing effort was *Good News* (1947), followed by *The Barkleys of Broadway* and *On the Town* (both in 1949), *Singin' in the Rain* (1952), *The Band Wagon* (1953), *It's Always Fair Weather* (1955), *Auntie Mame* (1958), *Bells Are Ringing* (1960), and *What a Way to Go!* (1964).

Only Dorothy Arzner had achieved any success as a director during the 1930s and the 1940s, and unfortunately the paucity of female directors continued into the 1950s. One of the best among this select group was Ida Lupino. Despite the fact that her output of seven films as a director may not equal that of most male directors of the time, her

Betty Comden — Screenwriter 1950s (MoMA/Film Stills)

efforts as a screenwriter, producer, and director in the 1950s are note-worthy.

Lupino acted in more than fifty Hollywood films in the 1930s and the 1940s, playing sexy, sultry roles, before she left acting for directing. She made her first six movies in her native England and came to

Hollywood in 1934 at the age of fifteen, a platinum blonde cast in a series of ingenue parts. Her first Hollywood movie was *Search for Beauty*. None of her roles in the 1930s made a lasting impression, but she matured into a popular screen figure in the 1940s. Her first success was in *They Drive By Night* (1940) with Humphrey Bogart. This role led to another pairing with Bogart in *High Sierra* (1941), a movie that earned them both box-office recognition. That same year, she also appeared in *The Sea Wolf* and *Out of the Fog*, then made *The Hard Way* (1943), for which she won the New York Film Critics Award for Best Actress. When Warner Bros. continued to offer the best roles to its main star, Bette Davis, throughout the 1940s, Lupino realized that her future at the studio was limited; she decided to leave acting to form Emerald Productions, later renamed Filmakers, Inc., with her then-husband, Collier Young. She wrote *Not Wanted* (1949) with Paul Jarrico and produced the film and later assumed directing duties when the director became ill three days after shooting began.

As with all of her films in the 1950s, *Not Wanted* was a "problem" film that cost less than $160,000 to make and cast relatively unknown actors and actresses in all roles. This first film dealt with the difficulties experienced by an unmarried mother who gives up her baby, then faces kidnapping charges when she longingly cradles another couple's baby. *Outrage* (1950) focused on the difficult subject of rape and the extensive effects on the victim, while *Never Fear* (1950) dealt with the struggles of a dancer who contracts polio and then must come to terms with her future. Lupino followed these films with *Hard, Fast and Beautiful* (1951), *The Bigamist* (1953), and *The Hitchhiker* (1953), all dealing with the alienation and displacement in postwar America of people who are trapped by class issues and social structures. *Hard, Fast and Beautiful* focuses on a mother's sacrificial love and obsessive ambition for her daughter, whom she aims to make a star on the competitive tennis circuit. In *The Bigamist*, Lupino looked at male and female victims in her story of a traveling salesman who creates two distinct lives and two families. Male characters were the focus of *The Hitchhiker*, in which two fishing friends offer a stranger a ride, only to

Ida Lupino (Evans Collection)

learn that he is a mass murderer. Lupino switched roles in *Private Hell 36* (1954), producing and cowriting the film while hiring someone else to direct it. As in *The Hitchhiker*, this film's principal focus is on male characters, this time examining police corruption.

Lupino's production company disbanded when her marriage to Young ended. She then turned to television, where she directed episodes of action and dramatic series, including *The Twilight Zone*, *The Fugitive*, *The Untouchables*, and *Have Gun, Will Travel*. In 1966, Lupino directed *The Trouble With Angels* for Columbia Pictures. This was her last big-screen directorial effort, although she continued to work in television.

Women film editors in the 1950s remained a largely anonymous entity, as they had for four decades, but several received Academy Award nominations. Anne Bauchens, first nominated in 1934 for *Cleopatra* and the winner in 1940 for *North West Mounted Police*, earned two nominations—for *The Greatest Show on Earth* (1952) and for *The Ten Commandments* (1956). In 1951, Adrienne Fazan earned an Academy Award nomination for editing *An American in Paris*, then won the film editing award for *Gigi* (1958); she was the only woman to win during the 1950s and only the third woman to win since the award was first given in 1934. Other Academy Award nominees for editing were Barbara McLean for *All About Eve* (1950), Dorothy Spencer for *Decision Before Dawn* (1951), Alma Macrorie for *The Bridges at Toko-Ri* (1955), and Viola Lawrence for *Pal Joey* (1957).

In contrast to other behind-the-scenes areas, the decade of the 1950s was a fruitful period for female costume designers, who outnumbered their male counterparts not only in physical numbers but also in the number of Academy Award nominations they earned. Edith Head continued to design costumes at Paramount. She received her greatest number of Oscar nominations during the 1950s and won the Academy Award for Costume Design five times in the decade. Head designed costumes for all of the Paramount *Road . . .* films of the 1940s, and created a fashion trend with the simple, shoulder-tied, boat-necked linen dresses designed for Audrey Hepburn in *Sabrina* (1954). She also created costumes for Mae West over the years, from the first designs for *She Done Him Wrong* (1933), through the all-white clothes that West wore in *Myra Breckenridge* (1970) and the clothes in West's comeback film *Sextette* (1979). West claimed to like Head's designs because they were " 'alluring without being vulgar' " because she (West) liked " 'gowns that have a little *insinuendo* [*sic*] about them.' " In a career that has spanned so many years, Head has garnered thirty-five Academy Award nominations for Best Costume Design. She earned Oscars for eight films: *The Heiress* (1949), *All About Eve* (1950), *Samson and Delilah* (1950), *A Place in the Sun* (1951), *Roman Holiday* (1953), *Sabrina* (1954), *The Facts of Life* (1960), and *The Sting* (1973). Head also has the distinction of being the only costume designer to appear as herself in two films, *Lucy Gallant* (1955) and *The Oscar* (1966).

Helen Rose also became a known force at MGM. She is largely responsible for contributing to the look of good taste coupled with understated allure that characterized the movie costumes of stars in this decade. Rose began her design by creating costumes for chorus girls and "shimmy" dancers who strutted their assets in low-priced nightclubs then graduated to the Ice Follies before becoming a staff designer at MGM in 1943. Although she created designs for more than 200 films during her 23 years at MGM, the costumes that she designed for most of the major stars of the 1950s stand out. When she created the wardrobe for Elizabeth Taylor in *Father of the Bride* (1950), her wedding gown design caused a flurry of interest among New York manufacturers who immediately copied the design for an eager public. Rose received her first Academy Award nomination for Best Costume Design in a Color Film for *The Great Caruso* in 1951. The next year, she created the movie clothes for Lana Turner for her two great screen successes, *The Merry Widow*, for which Rose received the 1952 Academy Award nomination for Best Costume Design in a Color Film, and *The Bad and the Beautiful*, for which Rose won the Academy Award for Best Costume Design in a Black-and-White Film. She was nominated for the same award each year for the next four years, for *Dream Wife* (1953), *Executive Suite* (1954), *I'll Cry Tomorrow* (1955), and *The Power and the Prize* (1956), and she won the award for *I'll Cry Tomorrow*. Rose also received a nomination for Best Costume Design in a Color Film for *Interrupted Melody* (1955). The designer was responsible for Grace Kelly's sophisticated and simple look in *The Swan* (1956) and created three memorable costumes for Elizabeth Taylor for her role as "Maggie the cat" in the 1958 *Cat on a Hot Tin Roof*—a slip, a simple blouse and skirt, and a white chiffon gown. The overwhelming popularity of the gown led Rose to create her own wholesale garment business.

The big-budget musical became the domain of Irene Sharaff, whose first success was the design of costumes for the ballet scene in *An American in Paris* (1951), for which she shared (with Walter Plunkett) the Academy Award for Costume Design in a Color Film. Her skill lay not only in costuming (her dance garments brought to mind the paintings of such French painters as Lautrec and Degas) but in creating a series of eclectic backgrounds that suggested the streets of Paris. Sharaff had a strong understanding of the ballet and of the need for costumes that could adapt to the movements of the dancers; she paid close attention to fabric, shape, and construction. She also knew how to project visual excitement in her choice of color and pattern. She created costumes for other popular musicals in the 1950s, including *Call Me Madam* (1953), *Brigadoon* (1954), *Guys and Dolls* (1955), *The King and I* (1956), and *Porgy and Bess* (1959). She received Academy Award nominations for Best Costume Design and won for *The King and I*. Although the majority of productions for which Sharaff designed costumes were released in the 1950s, she continued to work in the 1960s and garnered Academy Award nominations for her work on *Flower Drum Song* (1961) and *Cleopatra* (1963), and she won the Academy Award for Best Costume Design in 1961 for *West Side Story*.

Hollywood's women of the 1950s may have been sexy, sweet, or cool, but they were also accessible, which made them safe to men and approachable. The diversity of the roles they played, and of the actresses themselves, made the 1950s a decade of transition in Hollywood.

Ava Gardner, Jane Russell, and Susan Hayward entered the decade

with film experience, but their best films were made in the 1950s. Ava
Gardner was a versatile actress who projected a sultry sensuality, and
she could play any number of nationalities and variety of woman on
screen. Born the daughter of a tenant farmer in Grabtown, North
Carolina, the former Ava Lavinia Gardner had dreamed of being a New
York secretary, but instead she became one of the last of the studio-
made glamour girls. Marriages to Mickey Rooney, Artie Shaw, and
Frank Sinatra made her an object of gossip, and her darkly sensual version of the femme fatale captured the public imagination. She played
the femme fatale in *Whistle Stop* (1945), *The Killers* (1946), and *The
Hucksters* (1947), and she was the goddess of love in *One Touch of
Venus* (1948). In the 1950s, Gardner experimented with slightly different roles. She played a redemptive woman who dies to be with a ghost-
ly sea captain in *Pandora and the Flying Dutchman* (1951) and a jazz-
age loser in *The Snows of Kilimanjaro* (1952). She took her major risk
in *Show Boat* (1951), playing Julie Laverne, a girl of mixed race. It was
a role Judy Garland was originally set to play but that many thought
would have been better played by Lena Horne. Nonetheless, Gardner
was believable in the role. Several of her other films of the 1950s were
equally well received, especially *Mogambo* (1953), a remake of the
Clark Gable–Jean Harlow vehicle *Red Dust* (1932). Gardner also had
successes with *The Barefoot Contessa* (1954) and *Bhowani Junction*
(1956), but her later films were less successful. Two exceptions were
The Sun Also Rises (1957) which was a huge hit, and her role as a hotel
proprietor in Mexico in *The Night of the Iguana* (1964), which showed
her to her best advantage and drew praise for her performance.

Despite an output of only twenty-five films during her Hollywood
career, Jane Russell helped to establish the role of the sex symbol that
dominated the 1950s movie screen. *The Outlaw*, filmed in 1941 but
not released for the first time until 1943, brought Russell recognition,
but movie censors protested the long and lingering shots of Russell's
bosom. Howard Hughes, the disgruntled and obsessive producer of the
film, shelved it until 1946, when he released it again, but in a modified
form. Hughes owned Russell's contract, and he kept her out of films

Ava Gardner (Evans Collection)

during this waiting period to prevent any box-office failures that might harm *The Outlaw* upon its eventual release. He allowed her to film only *Young Widow* (1946). After the second release of *The Outlaw*, Russell made two movies with Bob Hope, *The Paleface* (1948) and *Son of Paleface* (1952), and *Double Dynamite* (1951) before the film that brought her the most positive recognition of her career—*Gentlemen Prefer Blondes* (1953), with Marilyn Monroe. She starred in what amounted to a sequel in 1955, *Gentlemen Marry Brunettes*, a film that joins *The Tall Men* (1955) and *The Revolt of Mamie Stover* (1956) as being among her best work. The rest of Russell's films of the 1950s were poorly received by audiences, and she retired from movies for a nightclub career. After seven years, she returned to films in several supporting roles before leaving movies for good. She appeared on television in the 1970s as the spokeswoman in commercials for a brassiere manufacturer, touting undergarments for full-figured women.

Unlike Gardner and Russell, Susan Hayward was more the actress and less the sex symbol, and her female audiences could relate to her portrayals of women who overcame great obstacles and survived. The former Edythe Marrener made her film debut at nineteen in *Hollywood Hotel* (1937), a beginning that led to four Academy Award nominations for Best Actress and one Best Actress Oscar in the years to follow. Hayward's roles in the 1930s and 1940s, aside from her role of an alcoholic in *Smash-Up: The Story of a Woman* (1947), which earned an Academy Award nomination, were solidly acted but largely mundane. In the 1950s, she starred in biblical epics and in a series of films that dealt with the problems of contemporary women. *David and Bathsheba* (1951) and *Demetrius and the Gladiators* (1954) did respectably well at the box office, and Hayward earned Academy Award nominations for *My Foolish Heart* (1950), *With a Song in My Heart* (1952), *I'll Cry Tomorrow* (1956), and *I Want to Live* (1958), for which she won the award for Best Actress. Hayward appeared in several badly made films in the 1960s and early 1970s, then left the movies in 1972, three years before she died of a brain tumor.

Blond comedian Judy Holliday also appeared in films during the

Susan Hayward — 1958 Oscar for I Want to Live (Billy Rose / Lincoln Center)

1940s and managed to become a film comedy star in the 1950s, a feat that Lucille Ball did not manage. Similar to Holliday, Ball played both straight drama and then comedy in movies of the 1940s, but she failed to ignite the public interest. She went on to revolutionize the new medium of television, and with comedy partner and husband Desi

Judy Holliday and Broderick Crawford in Born Yesterday *(1950)* (MoMA/Film Stills)

Arnaz she set the standard for situation comedies. Holliday, on the other hand, flourished on the big screen. With her Academy Award–winning performance as the shrewd "dumb blonde" Billie Dawn in *Born Yesterday* (1950), as well as her roles in *It Should Happen to You* (1954), *Phffft* (1954), *The Solid Gold Cadillac* (1956), *Full of Life* (1957), and *Bells Are Ringing* (1960), she made comedy sexy and fun. Unlike her platinum-blonde predecessors of the 1930s, Holliday went for the laughs in an innocent manner, outsmarting those around her with her "dumb" act. This was not the approach of Mae West or

Carole Lombard, but it worked well in the 1950s, especially so for Holliday. She also played a dramatic role in *The Marrying Kind* (1952), but audiences preferred her comedic roles.

The early 1950s also welcomed other actresses whose careers had flourished in past decades. Jane Wyman, June Allyson, Cyd Charisse, and Ann Miller carried active careers into the 1950s but could claim only modest success in this period of transition. For the most part, the public no longer accepted the syrupy-sweet behavior of a June Allyson role. Viewers were also losing interest in Jane Wyman, who could not compete with the new breed of film actress, despite her success in *Johnny Belinda* (1948), *The Glass Menagerie* (1950), and *Magnificent Obsession* (1954), for which she earned an Academy Award nomination. Both actresses recognized that their time was past and turned to television, which welcomed them. Cyd Charisse and Ann Miller continued to dance, but even Charisse's success in *The Band Wagon* (1953) and *Brigadoon* (1954) and Miller's in *Small Town Girl* (1953) were not enough to sustain movie careers. The old Hollywood musical was passé, and so were dancers who simply danced on an artificial stage. Audiences demanded more story with their songs, and they found what they wanted in musicals such as *Guys and Dolls* (1955), *Damn Yankees* (1958), and *South Pacific* (1958), all of which starred actresses who sometimes danced rather than dancers who sometimes acted.

Although primarily a sex symbol, Marilyn Monroe was one of the new breed of actresses who also danced in films. Monroe's film career spanned less than fifteen years and included only eleven starring roles, but she, along with Elizabeth Taylor and Judy Garland, became a popular icon. Born Norma Jean Mortenson to a mentally unstable mother who was frequently institutionalized, she spent her early life in a series of foster homes. After marriage at sixteen, she found a job packing parachutes at a defense plant, where a photographer for the magazine *Yank* took her picture with other women workers and used it to illustrate an article. A modeling agency saw Monroe's picture and signed her, then changed the brown-haired girl into a blonde.

Marilyn Monroe, 1950s (Movie Graphics)

As Monroe modeled, she also auditioned for movie roles and signed a contract with 20th Century–Fox, where she had bit parts in *Scudda Hoo! Scudda Hay!* and *The Dangerous Years* (both 1948). Unimpressed with her screen presence, Fox dropped her contract, and she prevailed upon her latest companion, Joseph Schenck, a sixty-nine-year-old producer at Fox, to use his widespread contacts to help her. Within days, Harry Cohn of Columbia Pictures offered Monroe a contract and cast her in *Ladies of the Chorus* (1949). Columbia also dropped her contract, and Monroe set out to gain parts on her own, landing a small role in *Love Happy* (1949), the last Marx Brothers movie. Her role caught the attention of Johnny Hyde, a William Morris agent, who took over her career and became her lover. He found her roles in *The Asphalt Jungle* and *All About Eve* (both 1950), in which her elegant date, played by George Sanders, introduces her as "a graduate of the Copacabana School of Dramatic Art." Hyde died soon after arranging for Monroe a seven-year contract with 20th Century–Fox. In two years she appeared in six films that capitalized on her sexual attraction rather than on her acting ability. After playing the dumb blonde in *As Young as You Feel* (1951) and appearing in *Love Nest* (1951), *Let's Make It Legal* (1951), *Clash by Night* (1951), *We're Not Married* (1952), and *Monkey Business* (1952), Monroe was cast in *Niagara* (1953), which allowed her to act and focused attention on her as Joseph Cotten's scheming wife. In her next film, *Gentlemen Prefer Blondes* (1953), she blossomed as Lorelei Lee and showed off her talents as a comedienne while exhibiting her ability as a dancer and singer with her rendition of "Diamonds Are a Girl's Best Friend." *How to Marry a Millionaire* (1953) followed, but despite Monroe's show of versatility, the studio once again cast her as a dumb blond in *There's No Business Like Show Business* (1954) and *The Seven-Year Itch* (1955). Even her dramatic role in *River of No Return* (1954) allowed her no depth of characterization.

By this time, tired of being typecast, Monroe left for New York to study with Lee Strasberg at Actors Studio. When she returned to Hollywood, Fox agreed to rewrite her contract, allowing her to have approval over both her scripts and her directors. *Bus Stop* (1956) showed that she could act, but her progress suffered a setback with *The Prince and the Showgirl* (1957), made with Laurence Olivier. Monroe had begun to grow difficult. She was constantly late, blew her lines, ignored the director, and generally alienated others on the set.

During the filming of *Some Like It Hot* (1959), Monroe seemed to have conquered some of her demons and was dazzling as the comedic Sugar Kane, out to snag a wealthy husband. As a ukulele-playing singer, she acted in the role her public expected, that of the dumb blonde and inefficient gold digger whose dreams do not quite come true. *Let's Make Love* (1960) with Yves Montand was a box-office failure, but United Artists tried to bolster Monroe's sagging popularity by pairing her with the aging Clark Gable in *The Misfits* (1961). By this time, Monroe was completely dependent upon sleeping pills and other substances. Although the filming was drastically slowed down by her emotional problems and difficulty in remembering lines, the film was eventually finished. She began work on *Something's Got to Give* (1962) but was fired because her continual lateness, tantrums on the set, and generally unprofessional behavior placed the film way behind schedule. Monroe died that year of a drug overdose, and the mysterious circumstances have left unanswered the question of whether she died a suicide or a victim of murder.

Marilyn Monroe set the standard for sex symbols in the 1950s, combining the vulnerability of a little girl with the savvy of the blonde, buxom woman. If imitation is the sincerest form of flattery, then the later emergence of Jayne Mansfield, Diana Dors, Kim Novak, and Carroll Baker, among many others, should have thrilled her. Dissatisfied as Monroe may have become with her roles, the public wanted more, and every studio seemed to create its own Marilyn Monroe clone. Some were more successful than others.

Jayne Mansfield was a publicity hound who created an exaggerated image of the sex goddess, complete with pink Hollywood mansion, pink Jaguars, tight clothing, and a reputation for being a woman who could not help herself where men were concerned. Her films were forgettable, but the image she projected in the late 1950s and into the

Jayne Mansfield (1950s) (Evans Collection)

early 1960s was hard to ignore because of her gifts as a self-promoter. Her biographer claims that her sex goddess appeal was so widespread that John Lennon asked to meet her when the Beatles came to the United States on their first American tour. She graciously met the group at Whiskey a Go-Go, a thriving discotheque frequented by celebrities.

Born Vera Jane Palmer in Bryn Mawr, Pennsylvania, in 1933, Mansfield dreamed of being a movie star and held on to that dream as her family moved to Texas, where she became pregnant and then married as a teenager. She kept her first husband's name through three later marriages but never forgot the difficult early years when her family refused to accept her dream of stardom.

Mansfield's first movie was *The Female Jungle* (1955), a low-budget independent film; she played a nymphomaniac and earned less than $200. Her perseverance in calling at the studios paid off with a screen test at Warner Bros.; she was signed to a contract at $75 per week. Already twenty-two years old and desperate to break into the movies, Mansfield risked a publicity stunt at a press affair being given for Jane Russell's new film *Underwater* (1955). Urged on by a photographer friend who had managed to get her an invitation, she appeared in a red bikini and postured as other photographers took pictures of her and ignored the "nice girls working at RKO"—Debbie Reynolds, Mala Powers, and Lori Nelson, who were part of the publicity. Then, on cue from her friend, Mansfield dove into the water, ostensibly to swim underwater. Her bikini top strap broke as planned and she hurried out of the water and toward the bath house with her hands modestly covering her breasts as photographers frantically snapped pictures. This was the first of numerous staged events for the press that Mansfield orchestrated over her decade in Hollywood. The pictures that flooded the newspapers brought her to the attention of producers who borrowed her from Warner Bros. to film *The Burglar* (1956) with Dan Duryea. From there, Mansfield took on a role in the Broadway play *Will Success Spoil Rock Hunter?*

The play, a sendup of Hollywood, made Mansfield the darling of

Broadway and the special darling of newspaper columnist Walter Winchell, who danced the mambo with her at El Morocco in New York. It also brought her to the attention of 20th Century–Fox, which offered her the lead in *The Girl Can't Help It* (1956) and a seven-year contract. Mansfield felt that she had really arrived and bought a mansion on Sunset Boulevard that she turned into a pink movie star palace, complete with a pink heart-shaped bathtub and a pink-tiled, heart-shaped swimming pool. For effect, she walked her pet leopard, tied with pink satin ribbon, down Hollywood Boulevard. She also fell in love with Mickey Hargitay, a one-time member of Mae West's onstage entourage and a professional body builder, and married him against her studio's wishes. *The Wayward Bus* and the film of *Will Success Spoil Rock Hunter?* were released in 1957, and Mansfield began a Las Vegas act with Hargitay in 1958. The *Las Vegas Sun* reported that she "wiggles and waggles and warbles and does some acrobatic maneuvers with Mickey Hargitay." Backed by a male chorus, she squealed and postured in a number of sheet costumes covered with strategically placed spangles.

By 1960, her relentless self-promotion had made her the most-written-about actress of the year. She continued to perform in nightclubs, then went to Rome to make *Panic Button* (1964) with Maurice Chevalier. By now, Mansfield had tired of the sex goddess image, despite being awarded the title of the "World's No. 1 Sex Symbol" by the world press in 1964. After she divorced Hargitay, she hoped to change her image and become a dramatic actress, but she had four children to support and was forced to take the roles offered. Despite her new goals, she and fellow sexpot Mamie Van Doren made *Las Vegas Hillbillies* (1966), a film that was created to capitalize on her body and not on her acting skills.

Marriage to director Matt Cimber promised a change in career direction when they filmed *Single Room Furnished*, but Mansfield and her lawyer/lover were killed in an automobile crash in 1967, a grisly accident in which Mansfield was first reported to have been decapitated. Although the rumor persists, later newspaper accounts revealed that her blonde wig, thrown from the car in the crash, was mistaken for her head. Contrary to her grand desires to remain forever in Hollywood, she was buried, at her mother's insistence, in Argyle, Pennsylvania, not in Hollywood's Forest Lawn Cemetery.

Carroll Baker was another pretender to the throne of sex goddess Marilyn Monroe. She tried to make her mark in mid-1950s Hollywood after a small part in the Esther Williams film *Easy to Love* (1953) and roles in several television commercials and a Broadway play, but her first real opportunity was a small role in *Giant* (1956). She followed this with her role as the sexy child bride suffering from arrested development in *Baby Doll* (1956), for which she earned an Academy Award nomination, something her idol Monroe had never received. Baker then appeared in *The Big Country* (1958), followed by *The Carpetbaggers* (1964) and the lead in *Harlow* (1965), a role that had been offered to Monroe years before and that she had refused. The box-office failures of these two films killed Baker's Hollywood aspirations and she went to Europe, where she made exploitation films through the late 1960s and early 1970s. Her attempted Hollywood comeback in 1977 was a resounding failure.

In contrast, British sex symbol Diana Dors and studio-created sex goddess Kim Novak, both marketed as challengers to the sex queen's throne, did not allow themselves to be victimized by the system. Dors was hailed as Britain's answer to Marilyn Monroe, but she refused to succumb to the vulnerable sex kitten image. Of the sixty-three films she made between 1946 and 1984, her best ones appeared in the 1950s. Although she projected the needed sexual allure and her physical endowments were impressive, Dors chose her roles with care to avoid being typecast. Her most memorable role in this decade was in *Yield to the Night* (1956), called *Blonde Sinner* in the U.S., in which she played a fictional character based on Ruth Ellis, the last woman hanged for murder in Britain. Dors offset her sex goddess image by appearing for most of the film without makeup and wearing a baggy white nightgown, a trick she used in several other movies to remind

•

audiences that she was more than a sexy blonde with a well-endowed body.

Kim Novak rivaled Marilyn Monroe in popularity as a leading blond sex symbol in the 1950s, and she actually owed her fast start to Monroe. Several years before Columbia Pictures signed Novak, studio head Harry Cohn had cast Monroe in one film and then had ended the association, only to watch her become a major box office success. In 1954, Cohn was looking for a blonde sex goddess, and Kim Novak was the starlet he chose to develop as the next Monroe. The studio changed her hair color from light brown to blond, gave her acting lessons, and launched a publicity campaign to hail her as the new sex goddess. Novak earned back Columbia's investment in such films as *Pushover* (1954), *Phffft* (1954), *Five Against the House* (1955), and *The Man With the Golden Arm* (1955). In 1956, she surpassed Monroe as the top box-office earner after starring in *Picnic*, but bad casting in *Jeanne Eagels* and *Pal Joey*, both in 1957, lowered her popularity. Novak climbed back on top with the two films she made with James Stewart in 1958, *Vertigo* and *Bell, Book and Candle*, both box-office successes. She made several successful films in the early 1960s, including *The Adventures of Moll Flanders* (1965), then, after making *The Legend of Lylah Clare* (1968), she left Hollywood. Since then, she has appeared only in a few carefully chosen movies or television series.

Tight skirts and plunging necklines might have created heat waves among many 1950s screen spectators, but others defined sexy as being synonymous with Grace Kelly, Deborah Kerr, and Audrey Hepburn. While other blonde sex symbols smoldered, Grace Kelly was cool and aloof—the ice princess with the passion carefully restrained beneath the surface. Monroe might swivel her hips and coo breathlessly and Mansfield might spill out of her neckline, but Kelly merely had to look, and her every move afterward had meaning. She appeared in only eleven films during her five years in Hollywood, yet Grace Kelly became one of the screen's important leading ladies. The daughter of a wealthy businessman and a model, Kelly aspired to modeling before appearing on Broadway in August Strindberg's *The Father* in 1949. This

Grace Kelly (1955) (National Film Archives)

led to a walk-on role in *Fourteen Hours* (1951). Stanley Kramer saw her and decided to cast the unknown as the passive young Quaker wife of threatened town sheriff Gary Cooper in *High Noon* (1952). The film made her a hot box-office property, and she next starred in *Mogambo* (1953), a remake of the Clark Gable–Jean Harlow film *Red Dust* (1932). Kelly played a prim and proper wife whose marriage is threatened by the sultry Ava Gardner. Once again, screen audiences made the film a hit, and Kelly earned an Academy Award nomination for Best Supporting Actress.

Kelly made four well-received films in 1954—the routine adventure film *Green Fire*, the two Hitchcock thrillers *Dial M for Murder* and *Rear Window*, and *The Country Girl* for which she won the Academy Award for Best Actress. Unlike her earlier roles, Kelly played a bitter wife who must cope with an alcoholic husband determined to resurrect his singing career. She appeared in only four more films before marrying Prince Rainier III of Monaco. They met while she was on location in the south of France shooting *To Catch a Thief* in 1955, the same year that she made *The Bridges at Toko-Ri*, a Korean War action thriller. Her final two movies appeared to reflect the story of her life. *The Swan* (1956) tells the story of a noble girl in 1910 Hungary who is groomed to marry a crown prince, while *High Society* (1956) was a remake of *The Philadelphia Story*, which relates the dilemma of a society girl who must choose between suitors. Kelly, who married her prince and retired from the movies, died a tragic death in 1982 when her car swerved off a road and plunged down a mountainside.

Deborah Kerr was another, like Kelly, whose sexual allure was subtle but promising beneath an exterior reserve. Unlike Kelly, Kerr had a long Hollywood career; she made forty-four films and earned six Academy Award nominations for Best Actress. She began making films in 1941, with her debut in *Major Barbara*, but her major successes appeared in the 1950s. Kerr made *King Solomon's Mines* in 1950, followed by *Quo Vadis* (1951), *The Prisoner of Zenda* (1952), and *Julius Caesar* (1953). Her cool exterior was shed in *From Here to Eternity* (1953). She played an officer's wife who passionately makes love to army sergeant Burt Lancaster in the Hawaiian surf, a role for which she earned an Academy Award nomination. From 1956 through 1960, Kerr received Academy Award nominations for her roles in *The King and I* (1956) with Yul Brynner, *Heaven Knows, Mr. Allison* (1957) with Robert Mitchum, *Separate Tables* (1958) with Burt Lancaster and David Niven, and *The Sundowners* (1960) with Robert Mitchum. She also exercised her subtle allure in *Tea and Sympathy* (1956), *An Affair* to *Remember* (1957), and *Bonjour Tristesse* (1958). She was brilliant as the spinster daughter of a minister in *The Night of the Iguana* (1964), but the decade demanded a more effusive personality than Kerr's. After making *The Arrangement* (1969), she retired from making movies.

Actress-singer Doris Day became one of the biggest stars of the late 1950s, despite her virginal image in a decade of buxom, platinum-blonde sex symbols. The former Doris Von Kappelhoff began as a big-band singer, who had the good fortune to be under consideration by Warner Bros. when Betty Hutton, the star of their musical *Romance on the High Seas* (1948), became pregnant and had to leave the film. Day was tested and signed to a contract, then assigned the role. The film was well received at the box office, and the ingenue became an overnight success. She was cast in several mediocre films before taking the lead in the highly successful *Calamity Jane* (1953), which made Day a major Hollywood star. She appeared in other hit movies of the 1950s, including *Young at Heart* (1954), *The Pajama Game* (1957), and *Teacher's Pet* (1958), as well as the dramatic films *Love Me or Leave Me* (1955) and Hitchcock's *The Man Who Knew Too Much* (1956).

Day's sweet and sunny on-screen personality suited audiences of the late 1950s and early 1960s, as did the series of sex comedies she made, starting with *Pillow Talk* (1959). She followed this with six more: *Lover Come Back* (1961), *That Touch of Mink* (1962), *The Thrill of It All* (1963), *Move Over Darling* (1963), *Send Me No Flowers* (1964), and *Do Not Disturb* (1965). Day also filmed *Please Don't Eat the Daisies* (1960) and the musical *Billy Rose's Jumbo* (1962), but her films of the late 1960s failed to draw the same audiences. As social mores and sexual attitudes changed, Day's formerly sophisticated sex comedies became outmoded, and audiences had difficulty accepting that her career women would exercise such elaborate restraint in relationships. Day retired from the movies after making *With Six You Get Eggroll* (1968).

Debbie Reynolds is another actress of the 1950s whose sweet and wholesome image appealed to audiences for a time, but whose popu-

Doris Day — *1950s/60s* (Evans Collection)

larity decreased as changing mores made that image archaic. The former Miss Burbank of 1948 was signed by Warner Bros. and appeared in *June Bride* (1948). Reynolds moved to MGM in 1950, where she was cast as the lead in *Singin' in the Rain* (1952). She appeared in several mediocre films, including *I Love Melvin* (1953), *The Affairs of Dobie*

Gillis (1953), *Susan Slept Here* (1954), and *The Tender Trap* (1955). In 1957, Reynolds starred in *Tammy and the Bachelor*, which became one of her most successful films; it also produced her hit recording of "Tammy." Her career became secondary to the notoriety of her personal life when her husband, singer Eddie Fisher, left her for actress Elizabeth Taylor in 1959 in a much-publicized breakup. The sweetly wholesome Reynolds was viewed as the victim by audiences who sympathized with the "good girl" wronged by the "bad girl." Both *The Unsinkable Molly Brown* (1964) and *The Singing Nun* (1966) were box-office successes, but they were the last of their type to do so well as changing audiences were no longer attracted by the sentimental romances in which Reynolds specialized. Aside from roles in *That's Entertainment* (1974) and *Aloha, Paradise* (1981), a short-lived TV series she made no further screen appearances until Oliver Stone's *Heaven and Earth* in 1994, playing Tommy Lee Jones's mother.

Not all of the sex symbols of this decade were blond, as the popularity of Dorothy Dandridge and Elizabeth Taylor could attest. A glamorous African-American singer and actress, Dandridge attracted as much publicity in the 1950s as did Marilyn Monroe and Elizabeth Taylor, but her professional and personal lives were substantially more difficult. The beautiful, fair-skinned actress was often cast as a sensuous temptress, and her most memorable roles were as the sultry leading lady in *Carmen Jones* (1954), for which she earned an Academy Award nomination for Best Actress, and the sexy but evil Bess in *Porgy and Bess* (1959). Dandridge could also point proudly to other accomplishments. Not only was she the first African-American star to earn an Academy Award nomination for Best Actress, but she was also the first to appear on the cover of *Life*. In addition, Dandridge was the first leading African-American actress to engage in an interracial relationship on screen, in the movie *Island in the Sun* (1957). Despite the notoriety that she won for her sultry, seductive roles, Dandridge would have preferred to build a reputation based on her dramatic abilities, which she exhibited in *Bright Road* (1953) in her role of the dedicated young teacher who is devoted to her students.

Elizabeth Taylor (Evans Collection)

Glamour, excess, and illness have characterized the film career and life of Elizabeth Taylor, who has won two Academy Awards for Best Actress and earned three nominations during a career that encompasses fifty films. Taylor was a child actress, making her first film at the age of ten when she appeared in *There's One Born Every Minute* (1942). Universal dropped her contract after the film, convinced that she had no box-office appeal. She then made *Jane Eyre* (1944) for 20th Century–Fox, *National Velvet* (1945) for MGM, and *Life With Father* (1947) for Warner Bros. In 1949, only seventeen years old, she married Hilton Hotel chain heir Nicky Hilton, whom she divorced only months later. It was the first of her eight marriages.

Although *Cleopatra* (1963) was her most famous movie, both for its great cost and for her highly visible affair and subsequent marriage to the already married Richard Burton, Taylor made her best films in the 1950s. She appeared in *Conspirator* (1950), *The Big Hangover* (1950), and *Father of the Bride* (1950), which became her most successful film of the decade. Good scripts came her way, and she starred in A *Place in the Sun* (1951), *The Last Time I Saw Paris* (1954), and *Giant* (1956). Later in the decade, she earned an Academy Award nomination for Best Actress for roles in *Raintree County* (1957), *Cat on a Hot Tin Roof* (1958), and *Suddenly, Last Summer* (1959). Taylor's roles in the 1950s exhibited her versatility, and she played the loving wife or daughter as easily as the hard-edged temptress.

In real life, she was labeled a homewrecker. In 1958 she became romantically involved with Eddie Fisher, who was still married to Debbie Reynolds, after a second divorce and the death of her third husband, Mike Todd. Reynolds had made a career of playing the wholesome heroine, and the public sympathized with her as the wronged wife when Fisher asked for a divorce and married Taylor in 1959. Even though Taylor won the Academy Award for Best Actress for her role in *Butterfield 8* (1960), her popularity rating was low and did not rise until she suffered the first of her many major illnesses, a bout with a rare pneumonia virus, which attracted public sympathy.

The extravagance of *Cleopatra* (1963), as well as her $2 million salary and her steamy affair with Burton, made Taylor extremely popular with the press as newspapers and magazines followed the action both on and off the set. She and Burton would later marry, then divorce and remarry, and they appeared together in several forgettable films during the 1970s and 1980s. Of these movies, only *Who's Afraid of Virginia Woolf?* (1966), which won Taylor her second Academy Award for Best Actress, and *The Taming of the Shrew* (1967) are commendable. Taylor's films in the 1970s were box-office failures, and her only one after the 1960s to garner positive reviews was *The Mirror Crack'd* (1981). She married politician John Warner in 1976 and divorced him in 1981; her eighth marriage took place in 1991 to Larry Fortensky, a man more than twenty years her junior whom she met in a drug and alcohol treatment clinic. Tha marriage went on the rocks in 1995.

As the 1950s ended, well-known faces competed with starlets and ingenues on the silver screen as Hollywood prepared, along with the rest of the country, to embark upon a social and sexual revolution. Starlets like Angie Dickinson, whom producer Howard Hawks claimed to have discovered, would find that the climate of the 1950s, which fostered their rise, changed dramatically in the following decade. And ingenues like Sandra Dee, Carol Lynley, Tuesday Weld, and Yvette Mimieux, already on the horizon in the late 1950s, would excite interest in a decade that would make stars of Jane Fonda, Natalie Wood, Ann-Margret, and Joanne Woodward.

Sex and Tumult:
The 1960s

•

T HE HOLLYWOOD FILM INDUSTRY became increasingly heterogeneous in its offerings during the 1960s, reflecting the social revolution in the America of that decade. The screen attempted the socially relevant, with such movies as *To Kill a Mockingbird* (1962), *Lilies of the Field* (1963), and *Guess Who's Coming to Dinner* (1967); these films won for their stars Best Actor or Best Actress Oscars, but many of the Best Picture awards during the decade still went to musicals or to lighthearted fare. Blond teen queens vied with dark, troubled outsiders to capture the youth market, and gamines shared the screen with sex goddess carryovers from the 1950s. The public welcomed with equal enthusiasm the dark pessimism of *West Side Story* (1961) and *In the Heat of the Night* (1967) and the rambunctious fantasy of *Tom Jones* (1963), *My Fair Lady* (1964), *The Sound of Music* (1965), and *Oliver!* (1968), all winners of the Academy Award for Best Picture. Overall, although the diversity of women's roles on screen increased, their influence was less pervasive than it had been in the early years of the industry.

•

The 1960s, for example, produced significantly fewer films based on scripts written by women. As existing screenwriters—many of whom had been writing for decades—gradually left the scene, fewer new women scenarists were invited to take their places. During the decade, only six Academy Award nominations for Best Screenplay went to women, and no woman won the award. Despite the decreasing numbers, though, women managed to influence the making of some of the best-known films of the decade. Isobel Lennart, most productive in the 1950s, earned an Academy Award nomination for *The Sundowners* (1960), and Marguerite Duras was nominated that same year for *Hiroshima, Mon Amour*. In 1962, Eleanor Perry was nominated for *David and Lisa*. Harriet Frank Jr. shared the nomination with her husband for *Hud* in 1963, as did Phoebe Ephron that same year for *Captain Newman, M.D.* The final nomination of the decade went to Bridget Boland for *Anne of a Thousand Days* in 1969.

Eleanor Perry became a screenwriter in her forties, after a career of writing educational plays, mystery novels, and a Broadway play. She had trained as a psychiatric case worker, and this interest emerged in her first screenplay, *David and Lisa* (1962), which dealt with two mentally disturbed adolescents. Her success with the script and Academy Award nomination led to numerous offers from Hollywood for film adaptations of novels concerned with mentally ill adolescents or other topics dealing with shattered families, broken lives, and social problems. She refused these, preferring to explore the effect of the nuclear threat on children in *Ladybug, Ladybug* (1963) and to examine the American dream in her adaptation of John Cheever's short story *The Swimmer* (1968). Several of her other scripts were also produced, including *Trilogy* (1969), based on three stories by Truman Capote, with whom she shared credits, and *Last Summer* (1969).

Perry's already considerable influence in Hollywood increased when four of her screenplays appeared on film in the early 1970s: *Diary of a Mad Housewife* (1970), *The Lady in the Car With Glasses and a Gun* (1970), *The Deadly Trap* (1972), and *The Man Who Loved Cat Dancing* (1973). *Diary of a Mad Housewife*, starring Carrie Snodgress, had a feminist angle rare for its time. Still, Perry claimed that she did not go far enough in setting Tina, the "mad" housewife, free. In retrospect, Perry felt that she should have liberated Tina by having her get a job or go to school, rather than liberate herself through a man. Perry also placed a feminist twist on *The Man Who Loved Cat Dancing*, which led to problems with MGM and the assignment of several male writers to the film. She left screenwriting but continued to campaign to encourage more young women to write and to direct films.

Harriet Frank Jr. cowrote numerous films with her husband, Irving Ravetch, from the late 1950s through the early 1970s, beginning with *The Long Hot Summer* (1957), starring Paul Newman and Joanne Woodward. They adapted William Faulkner's novel for the 1959 film *The Sound and the Fury*, starring Yul Brynner. Most of the films made from their screenplays appeared in the 1960s, and their adaptation of Larry McMurtry's novel *Horseman, Pass By* into *Hud* (1963), also starring Paul Newman, earned them Academy Award nominations. Among other films in the 1960s based on Frank's screenplays are *The Dark at the Top of the Stairs* and *Home From the Hill* (both 1960) and *Hombre* (1967). In later decades, Frank also shared screenwriting credits for *Conrack* (1974), *Norma Rae* (1979), *Murphy's Romance* (1985), and *Stanley and Iris* (1990).

Women film editors earned nominations in six of the ten Academy Award years of the decade, but their numbers were fewer than in previous years. Viola Lawrence earned the nomination for *Pepe* in 1960. Anne Coates was nominated in 1962 and 1964 for her work on *Lawrence of Arabia* and *Becket*; Dorothy Spencer was nominated in 1963 for *Cleopatra*, Majorie Fowler was nominated for *Doctor Doolittle* in 1967, and Eve Newman shared the nomination with Fred Feithsham in 1968 for *Wild in the Streets*.

The number of women working with set direction increased in this decade. In 1960, Julia Heron shared the Academy Award with three male set designers for color set direction for the spectacle *Spartacus*. Grace Gregory and three male designers received a nomination in 1963 for black-and-white set design for *Love With a Proper Stranger*, and

Jocelyn Herbert and Josie MacAvin shared a nomination with two male set designers that same year for color set design for the movie *Tom Jones*. In 1965, Josie MacAvin earned the nomination for her sole black-and-white design of the set for *The Spy Who Came in From the Cold*.

The greatest increase in influence for women behind the scenes occurred in costume design, once also a male domain. Every year of the decade saw several women nominated in this category. Edith Head received Academy Award nominations for costume design every year except 1967 and 1968, for the movies *Pepe* (1960), *A Pocketful of Miracles* (1961), *The Man Who Shot Liberty Valance* (1962), *Love With a Proper Stranger* (1963), *Wives and Lovers* (1963), *A New Kind of Love* (1963), *A House Is Not a Home* (1964), *What a Way to Go* (1964), *The Slender Thread* (1965), *Inside Daisy Clover* (1965), *The Oscar* (1966), *Sweet Charity* (1969), and *Airport* (1970). She won the award for black-and-white costume design in 1960 for *The Facts of Life*.

The success of Irene Sharaff in the 1960s extended her influence beyond her already strong recognition in the industry. She won the Academy Award for costume design in 1961 for *West Side Story* and again in 1966 for *Who's Afraid of Virginia Woolf?* Her unique approach to design made her a popular costume designer in this decade, and one who was frequently called upon by producers with big-budget films. She received five more nominations during the decade: for *Can-Can* (1960), *Flower Drum Song* (1961), *Cleopatra* (1963), *The Taming of the Shrew* (1967), and *Hello, Dolly!* (1969).

Although less frequently nominated, seven other women gained prominence in this area for their costume designs in high-profile, big box-office pictures. Mary Wills won the 1962 award for *The Wonderful World of the Brothers Grimm*, and Dorothy Jeakins won in 1964 for *The Night of the Iguana* and was also nominated for *The Sound of Music* (1965) and *Hawaii* (1966). Julie Harris (not the actress) and Phyllis Dalton both won Academy Awards in 1965, Harris for black-and-white costume design in *Darling* and Dalton for color design in *Doctor Zhivago*. In 1966, Elizabeth Haffenden and Joan Bridge shared the award for A *Man for All Seasons*, and Margaret Furse won in 1969 for *Anne of a Thousand Days*.

On-screen, women widened their sphere of influence only slightly as they portrayed more varied roles, but several actresses do merit recognition for having, however briefly, stood out among the masses. The sex symbol of the 1960s evolved from the image of the blatant sex goddess of the previous decade to take on a variety of guises, each appealing to different segments of the movie audience. One of many young woman to court the youth market, teen queen Sandra Dee bore the blond hair of a Monroe or a Mansfield, but her sex appeal was more that of the innocent ingenue than of the seductress. Teen movie magazines chronicled her love life and revealed her "innermost thoughts," as well as her makeup tips, and she became a hot commodity in Hollywood; industry power brokers saw the adoration of a generation of young female moviegoers translate into ticket sales.

Ann-Margret exerted a different influence, because her audience extended beyond the teen market. She wore tight tops and toreador pants, but she could also dance and sing competently, as well as play the innocent when necessary. She even exhibited dramatic ability in her later work. Physically attractive and dramatically proficient Joanne Woodward and Natalie Wood started out in relatively well-received roles in the 1950s, but both actresses exhibited their acting range and reached career heights during the 1960s, when box office translated into influence. Sophia Loren, while pleasing to view, proved that dramatic ability also counted for something, although her physical endowment was the real on-screen money maker and the basis of her early influence. Added to this mix of actresses, whose influence in the 1960s depended on box office revenues rather than the off-screen business sense of their later contemporaries, were Julie Andrews with her musical talents, the elegant and fragile Audrey Hepburn, and the musically and dramatically adept Shirley MacLaine.

The late 1950s fostered a number of movies aimed at the teenage market, and young stars like Sandra Dee, Carol Lynley, and Tuesday Weld emerged in films like *The Reluctant Debutante* (1958), *Gidget*

Audrey Hepburn (Evans Collection)

(1959), and *Tammy Tell Me True* (1961). The most popular of these teen queens was Sandra Dee, who made films into the early 1970s. Born Alexandria Zuck in 1942 in Bayonne, New Jersey, she began modeling at the age of eight when her mother and stepfather moved to Manhattan. She exerted no influence as a Hollywood power broker but she functioned as a representative of what made box office in early 1960s. When her stepfather died, the twelve-year-old Dee became her mother's sole financial and emotional support. Shortly after, movie producer Ross Hunter flew Dee and her mother to Hollywood for the young girl's screen test; her mother lied and said that Sandra was fifteen years old, instead of thirteen.

The screen test went well, and Hunter loaned Dee out to MGM to make *Until They Sail* (1957) with Paul Newman. She then made *The Restless Years* and *Teach Me How to Cry*, both in 1957. Her popularity soared after the teen beach movie *Gidget* (1959) and her first romantic screen role, in *A Summer Place* (also 1959) with Troy Donahue. Several of Dee's movies made social statements: *A Summer Place* confronted the problem of an unwanted teen pregnancy, and her next picture that same year, *Imitation of Life* with Lana Turner, dealt with the problem of racism. The success of these pictures led to her being cast in *Portrait in Black* (1960), a thriller with Lana Turner and Anthony Quinn. In 1960, she also filmed the light comedy *Come September* with Rock Hudson and Gina Lollobrigida, a movie that featured young singer-composer Bobby Darin, whom she would marry. In 1961, Dee made one further movie, *Tammy Tell Me True*, before giving birth to her only child, Dodd. The next year Dee starred with Darin in *If a Man Answers* (1962), a film about two lovers trying to outdo each other in stirring up jealousy. These films made Dee a box-office success, and she continued to make movies, finishing *Tammy and the Doctor* in 1963, then *A Man Could Get Killed* (1965), and *Doctor, You've Got to Be Kidding*, a light comedy with George Hamilton and Bill Bixby, in 1966.

Her influence in Hollywood increased as the box-office profits on her films increased, but Sandra Dee the person entertained no illusions of control or of individual influence, a common plight of women in the decade. Profit was power, and income was influence. As the last of the contract players and one who had begun in films at the age of fourteen, Dee had a limited shelf life as a hot Hollywood commodity. She grew up, left her teens, and found herself with a sticky-sweet image she couldn't shake and an image that was at odds with her real-life existence as a wife and mother in her twenties. She made her last movie for Universal in 1968, *Rosie!*, a light comedy starring Rosalind Russell. In 1969, Sandra Dee appeared in her final film, a commercial bomb titled *The Dunwich Horrors*. At twenty-five, the former teen queen found her career over. In merely a decade, Dee and other ingenues had gone from star power to obscurity.

Ann-Margret offered the public a different image—the sex kitten—an image that could age gracefully if handled correctly. Her career began when, as Ann-Margret Olsson, she won a Chicago talent show at age thirteen, only seven years after emigrating from Valsjobyn, Sweden. She became a singer with a group formed by friends and had the good fortune to audition with George Burns for his Las Vegas holiday show. He recommended that she use her audition costume of tight top, toreador pants, and high heels as her stage costume, which she did until Burns's wife and fellow entertainer, Gracie Allen, warned that patrons and others were getting the wrong idea about the nineteen-year-old sensation. That "wrong idea" was actually the right idea in terms of career-building potential.

Even as she sang in Las Vegas, Ann-Margret had her eye on Hollywood and auditioned whenever possible. She received her break in 1960 and made thirty-eight movies in the next fifteen years. Ann-Margret made her debut in *Pocketful of Miracles* (1961), with Bette Davis, and then appeared in *State Fair* (1962), in which she gave Pat Boone his first on-screen kiss. In 1962, she starred as the wholesome, innocent sweetheart in *Bye, Bye, Birdie*, a musical satire of the induction into the army of rock-and-roll king Elvis Presley. She starred with him in *Viva Las Vegas* (1964), playing the role of "Rusty," a swimming teacher to Elvis Presley's "Lucky," a race car driver.

In 1964, Ann-Margret made the film noir *Kitten With a Whip*, her first dramatic role, in which she played a character she described as a "renegade, schizophrenic, reform school escapee." The film was a box-office success, but her early fans rejected the new "bad girl" image. This was followed by *Bus Riley's Back in Town* and *The Pleasure Seekers* (both 1964). Film offers continued, and her roles in a string of movies throughout the second half of the decade took her from a sensuous wife in *The Cincinnati Kid* (1965) to light romantic adventure as a clothing buyer in *Made in Paris* (1966) to the hooker with a heart of gold in the remake of *Stagecoach* (1966).

Decreased profits at the box-office resulted in mediocre roles as Ann-Margret lost her appeal and her audience in the late 1960s. With the loss of box-office clout came the corresponding loss of decision-making power in her choice of roles. She regained some of her status after several years, when she made her comeback in *Carnal Knowledge* (1971), directed by Mike Nichols, a film that brutally dissected contemporary sexual attitudes and relationships. Audiences loved her as Bobbie Templeton, the sexpot who is betrayed both by her men and by her own sexuality. The film was banned in some cities, but it made Ann-Margret hot again and earned her an Academy Award nomination for Best Supporting Actress. Offers once again came in, and she was able to choose her roles, rather than settle for them but the choices she made were unwise. She continued to make films in the 1970s and the 1980s, winning the Golden Globe for Best Actress in 1976. Her most recent films were *Grumpy Old Men* (1994), with Jack Lemmon and Walter Matthau, and its sequel. She currently concentrates more on stage shows than the movies.

Although the 1960s may have been a dry period for some actresses, Joanne Woodward and Natalie Wood gave some of their finest dramatic performances and wielded considerable clout in the choice of roles because of their high visibility and strong box office receipts. Woodward has long been associated with husband Paul Newman, whom she married in 1958 and who directed a couple of the films in which she starred, but her solo efforts as a character actress established her as a very talented and highly acclaimed performer. Winner of the

Academy Award for Best Actress for *The Three Faces of Eve* (1957), she also gave fine dramatic performances in *The Long, Hot Summer* (1958), and *The Sound and the Fury* (1959). She then moved into the 1960s and starred with Newman in *From the Terrace* (1960) and *Paris Blues* (1961) and made several other forgettable films, but her solo performances in *The Stripper* (1963), *A Big Hand for the Little Lady* (1966), *A Fine Madness* (1966), and *Rachel, Rachel* (1968) earned critical praise. In the 1960s, she could choose her own roles, but her influence waned as she made fewer and less commercially successful films in the 1970s. Nonetheless, the association with Newman has been helpful in keeping Woodward among those to whom Hollywood still defers, despite her relative lack of on-screen influence in recent years. She continued making feature films throughout the 1970s and more rarely into the 1980s, including *The Effect of Gamma Rays on Man-in-the-Moon Marigolds* (1972), *Harry and Son* (1984), and *The Glass Menagerie* (1987) but has appeared largely in television movies in recent years.

Former child actor Natalie Wood, most notable as the pretty and sincere little girl in *Miracle on 34th Street* (1947), earned three Academy Award nominations in her twenty-five years as an adult performer, and it was in the 1960s that she became established as a film industry presence. Her first adult role was in *Rebel Without a Cause* (1955), for which she earned the Academy Award for Best Supporting Actress, but she was eclipsed by costar James Dean's powerful performance. Her other films of the 1950s were generally mediocre, but that changed in the next decade. She began the 1960s strongly in *Splendor in the Grass* (1961) and earned an Academy Award nomination for Best Actress. The hit movie *West Side Story* (1961) followed; she became a major box-office draw and remained so throughout the decade. In 1963, Wood starred with Steve McQueen in *Love With the Proper Stranger* and earned her third Academy Award nomination. She then starred with some of Hollywood's leading men in such successful films as *Sex and the Single Girl* (1964) with Tony Curtis, *Inside Daisy Clover* (1966) with Robert Redford, *This Property Is Condemned* (1966) with Redford, and *Bob & Carol & Ted & Alice* (1969) with Elliott Gould and Robert Culp. Wood went on a hiatus from filmmaking for much of the 1970s, making only a few movies, then returned in 1981 to star in a major feature film titled *Brainstorm*. Wood had nearly completed shooting the movie when she drowned under mysterious circumstances in a late-night boating accident.

British-born Julie Andrews has used both box-office power and her marriage to producer-director Blake Edwards as the means of establishing influence in Hollywood. She has also had to deal with the bittersweet curse of being forever associated with the prim and proper characters of Mary Poppins and Maria Von Trapp, however much she has tried to change this image. Mainly a musical stage actress in both England and the United States, she gained early fame as Eliza Doolittle in the Broadway version of *My Fair Lady* but she lost that role in the movie version to Audrey Hepburn. Better luck came her way, however, when she took the title role in the Walt Disney film *Mary Poppins* (1964) and walked off with the Academy Award for Best Actress. She then landed the choice musical role of Maria Von Trapp in *The Sound of Music* (1965), a film that appealed to a nation on the brink of major social upheaval; it earned her a second Academy Award nomination for Best Actress, as well as substantial box-office power. These two films, with their broad audience appeal, made her a widely recognized performer in the first half of the 1960s. Her marketability increased when the Theatre Owners of America voted her Star of the Year in both 1966 and 1967, but the quality of her films in the second half of the 1960s was relatively poor, with *Thoroughly Modern Millie* (1967) the most successful among them.

Andrews's few films in the 1970s received moderately good reviews, and she decided that an image change was needed to improve her choice in films. She decided to transform herself from the primly proper Mary Poppins and Maria Von Trapp into an actress with an added sexual dimension. In the 1981 film *S.O.B.*, directed by Edwards, Andrews briefly appeared topless. This stirred up discussion, but it did little to increase the number of positive film reviews or ticket sales.

Aside from *Victor/Victoria* (1982), which earned her a third Academy Award nomination for Best Actress, Andrews's films in the 1980s were box-office disappointments.

The gaminelike Audrey Hepburn, with her natural poise and aristocratic appearance, chose to avoid any conscious efforts at exerting influence in the film industry. Whatever power she might have acquired in Hollywood deal-making resulted from her ability to generate box-office revenue, and such incidental power appeared to suit her. Like Julie Andrews, she might have suffered a fate of being typecast, but she managed to captivate audiences with her fragile beauty and stylish poise in diverse film roles that brought her five Academy Award nominations for Best Actress and one Oscar.

Hepburn began as a high-fashion model in London and appeared in several English films before coming to Hollywood. She made sixteen films in the United States, beginning with *Roman Holiday* (1953), for which she won the Academy Award for Best Actress. From this initial success, Hepburn was cast with Hollywood's most successful leading men in a series of well-received films. She won an Academy Award nomination for *Sabrina* (1954), in which she starred with Humphrey Bogart, then made *War and Peace* (1956) with husband Mel Ferrer, *Funny Face* (1957) with Fred Astaire, *Love in the Afternoon* (1957) with Gary Cooper, *Charade* (1963) with Cary Grant, and *My Fair Lady* (1964) with Rex Harrison.

For Hepburn, success on screen translated into deal-making power. Her most successful box-office hits began with *The Nun's Story* (1959), for which she earned her third Academy Award nomination, followed by *The Unforgiven* (1960) and *Breakfast at Tiffany's* (1961), which brought her her fourth. Hepburn played in several more romantic comedies, including *Paris When It Sizzles* (1964) and *How to Steal a Million* (1966), then changed course and appeared in the serious marital drama *Two for the Road* (1967). The following year, she played a blind woman trapped in her home by a killer in *Wait Until Dark* (1968) and earned her fifth Academy Award nomination. Hepburn left the film business at the height of her popularity and influence in 1969 to marry a physician and live in Rome. When she came out of retirement to make *Robin & Marian* (1976) with Sean Connery, she was still revered, but her influence in Hollywood was just a memory, and her rare film appearances of the 1980s were badly chosen.

Shirley MacLaine is most unusual among the diverse actresses of the 1960s whose names had the power to open doors. The story of her start in the movie business has a fairy-tale quality to it, and her New Age insights have extended her reach beyond the silver screen. Overall, her years of greatest influence in the film industry were concentrated in the 1960s, except for two later successes, one in each of the decades following. MacLaine started in show business as a chorus dancer on Broadway, then became the understudy to Carol Haney, the star of *The Pajama Game*. Haney broke her ankle and MacLaine went on after only four days of rehearsal. The rest of the story is pure Hollywood. MacLaine was a hit on stage, and movie producer Hal Wallis saw her perform sometime later and signed her to a five-year movie contract.

MacLaine's first films were Alfred Hitchcock's *The Trouble With Harry* and the Martin and Lewis comedy *Artists and Models* (both 1955), followed by *Around the World in Eighty Days* (1956). After she earned an Academy Award nomination for her role as the love-starved young woman in *Some Came Running* (1958), which also starred Frank Sinatra, she was offered choice roles as she moved into the 1960s, her best decade. She danced and sang her way through *Can-Can* (1960) and then earned her second Academy Award nomination for *The Apartment*. She followed with the hit movie *Irma La Douce* (1963). It earned her a third Academy Award nomination and proved to be her last success for several years. In 1969, *Sweet Charity* did poorly at the box office, but MacLaine's performance was lauded, and for a short time she retained her veto power regarding film roles. She gave a good performance in the 1970 *Two Mules for Sister Sara*, made with Clint Eastwood, then won a fourth Academy Award nomination for her role as the regret-filled mother in *The Turning Point* (1977) who gave up a dancing career for domesticity. MacLaine's performance in *Terms of Endearment* (1983) exploited her dramatic potential in her portrayal of a mother who must help her dying adult daughter cope; this part won her the Academy Award for Best Actress. MacLaine has starred in nine films between 1983 and 1995, and also retains a highly visible image through her writing and her production of documentary films.

These actresses were not the only influences in Hollywood during the 1960s, but they best exhibit the diversity among influential actresses that characterized the period. Geraldine Page, winner in 1961 of the Academy Award for Best Actress for her role in *Summer and Smoke*, made several highly acclaimed movies during this decade, but her successes, while modest, are also spread out evenly over the two decades following. She earned eight Academy Award nominations for the twenty-five films she made during her film career. In the 1960s, however, her performances in *Sweet Bird of Youth* (1962) and *You're a Big Boy Now* (1967), both of which earned her Academy Award nominations, as well as in *Toys in the Attic* (1963), Disney's *The Happiest Millionaire* (1967), and *Whatever Happened to Aunt Alice?* (1969), made her a women of note in the film industry. She retained her modest yet firm stature in the business until her death in 1987.

Jane Fonda also scored several big successes in this decade, with *Cat Ballou* (1965), *Any Wednesday* (1966), and *Barefoot in the Park* (1967). She also gained notoriety for her starring role in her then-husband Roger Vadim's science fiction sex fantasy *Barbarella* (1968). Despite earning an Academy Award nomination for Best Actress in 1969 for *They Shoot Horses, Don't They?* and winning the Oscar for Best Actress for *Klute* (1971), she wielded little influence in the industry until she returned to films after her antiwar activities. Her biggest box-office clout came in the 1970s.

Faye Dunaway was a Hollywood golden girl for a time when she earned the Academy Award nomination for Best Actress as Bonnie Parker in *Bonnie and Clyde* (1967) and starred in the 1968 hit movie *The Thomas Crown Affair*. Nonetheless, she did not really become a leading lady who could make others listen until the 1970s, when she had taken control of her talent and of her professional life.

Goldie Hawn and Barbra Streisand also appeared in successful films during the 1960s, but few people would claim that either exerted any influence of note in this period. Hawn first appeared in a bit part in Disney's *The One and Only Genuine Original Family Band* (1968). The following year, she skyrocketed to the top of her profession in *Cactus Flower* (1969), for which she won the Academy Award for Best Supporting Actress. She would become one of the most powerful women in Hollywood in the 1980s and 1990s, but Hawn had no idea in 1969 of how to exploit her new status. She even admitted as much in an interview with Rex Reed when she told him, "My greatest regret is that I won an Oscar before I learned how to act." It was not until later that Hawn and Streisand learned how to use their success to develop their own properties and to control their professional lives.

Barbra Streisand appeared in the commercially successful *Funny Girl* (1968), after stage appearances in *I Can Get It For You Wholesale* (1962) and the 1964 Broadway production of *Funny Girl*. Streisand also won the Academy Award for Best Actress for *Funny Girl* (1968), an honor that she shared in a tie with Katharine Hepburn who was honored for *The Lion in Winter* (1968). Her rapid success translated into numerous film roles throughout the 1970s, but she wielded little influence in the business until she became more involved in the production of her films and assumed control in various ways in the following decades.

For these actresses and many others, early box-office success meant high visibility, but they took years to develop an influence—and Hollywood also needed time to become open, once again, to that influence. For women in Hollywood, the 1960s were the preface to a long battle toward regaining elements of control in the American film industry.

The Slow Climb Back: The 1970s

•

THE DECADE OF THE 1970s was one of slow but steady growth in the number of women entering or reentering facets of the film industry that had been closed to them for decades. The number of women screenwriters acknowledged by the Academy of Motion Picture Arts and Sciences increased, as did the number of women film editors. A few women directors also emerged in the last years of the decade, but their influence would not be felt for several more years.

What made this decade remarkable is that women, for the first time in Academy Award history, earned nominations as producers for Best Picture. And in 1973, Julia Phillips became the first woman to win an Academy Award for Best Picture, for *The Sting*, an honor she shared with husband Michael Phillips and Tony Bill. Julia Phillips was once again nominated for the award in 1976 for *Taxi Driver*. In 1979, Tamara Asseyev shared the nomination for Best Picture with Alex Rose for *Norma Rae*. These numbers may appear unremarkable until one considers that no woman had ever been nominated in the Best Picture category—and in the decade and a half since, only three women have been given this acknowledgment.

In the 1970s, women reentered the management areas of the film industry, moving higher in the studio executive hierarchy. Three women became vice presidents of production at two prominent studios: Nessa Hyams and Rosilyn Heller at Columbia and Marcia Nasatir at United Artists. The last woman to reach so high a level as a production executive was Virginia Van Upp in the 1940s. The influence of these three women vice presidents extended far beyond their decision-making roles within their individual studios. Production executives wield considerable power in determining what appears on screen, and thus every facet of the filmmaking process feels the impact of decisions made at this level. Actresses, set designers, directors, writers, and everyone else connected with a film owes his or her job—or lack of one—to a production executive's decision to make one type of film over another, to choose one project to back over another. The ramifications of these three appointments were great.

In this same decade, a curious phenomenon also emerged, as actresses made efforts to emulate their predecessors of five decades earlier by turning to writing, directing, and producing as a means of assuming greater creative control over the final film. Jane Fonda started her own production company to produce *Coming Home* (1978), a film in which she also starred. Anne Bancroft was one of the first actress-writer-directors with her 1979 film *Fatso*. Bancroft also created a first in the industry when she hired Brianne Murphy to shoot the film, making her the first woman director of photography.

Even on-screen roles began to exhibit a new direction. Heroines of some films took on a new power and became the protagonists, examining and dealing with problems in their lives, however unsuccessfully, and thus moving the narrative forward. Ellen Burstyn's role in *Alice Doesn't Live Here Anymore* (1974) is only one example of this.

Women writers produced the screenplays for many of the most widely known films of the decade. Among the most influential in this period was Jay Presson Allen, who would later turn to producing, with *Prince of the City* (1981) and five other films. She wrote the screenplays for *Cabaret* (1972), *Travels With My Aunt* (1972), and *Funny*

Lady (1975). Carole Eastman, first an actress, wrote *Five Easy Pieces* (1970) at the specific request of a former colleague, Jack Nicholson, then wrote *The Fortune* (1975). Nancy Dowd effectively changed the image of the woman screenwriter with her screenplay for *Slap Shot* (1977), which many men in the industry considered so vulgar and realistically violent a portrayal of hockey that they refused to believe a woman could have written it. The reaction had a positive effect for women screenwriters, because it forced many male decision makers to rethink their perceptions of the types of films that women could and should write. *Slap Shot* opened, if only a little, the door to greater writing opportunities for women.

None of these films earned Academy Award nominations, but others written by women in this decade did. In 1970, Renee Taylor shared an Academy Award nomination with Joseph Bologna and David Goodman for *Lovers and Other Strangers*. Penelope Gilliat earned a nomination for *Sunday, Bloody Sunday* (1971), and Suzanne de Passe shared nomination honors with Terence McCloy and Chris Clark for *Lady Sings the Blues* (1972). Gloria Katz was one of the screenwriters nominated for *American Graffiti* (1973), and Gladys Hill shared a nomination for *The Man Who Would Be King* (1975). In 1978, Nancy Dowd earned a nomination for writing the original story for *Coming Home*, an interesting follow-up to her violent and bloody *Slap Shot*. Valerie Curtin was nominated for best screenplay for her work on *...And Justice for All* (1979), and Harriet Frank Jr. was similarly acknowledged for *Norma Rae* (1979). The range of topics in screenplays by women nominated for the Academy Award for Screenwriting in the 1970s shows an extension of their influence in the industry.

Women film editors took on a renewed prominence as nine women earned Oscar nominations for editing during the 1970s and two won Academy Awards for their skill. Thelma Schoonmaker, who would go on to edit a large number of films in the 1980s and 1990s, earned a nomination for editing *Woodstock* (1970). In 1975, Lynzee Klingman shared a nomination for editing *One Flew Over the Cuckoo's Nest*, and Eve Newman was nominated in 1976 for her work on *Two-Minute*

Warning. In 1977, Marcia Lucas, with Paul Hirsch and Richard Chew, won the Academy Award for film editing for her work on *Star Wars,* and Lisa Fruchman shared a nomination for *Apocalypse Now* (1979). In 1979, Susan E. Morse moved to a position of prominence when she became the editor of Woody Allen's *Manhattan.* Her professional collaboration with Allen has continued.

The best known and most influential film editor of the decade was Dede Allen. She had built a strong reputation throughout the 1950s and edited *The Hustler* (1961), *America, America* (1963), *Bonnie and Clyde* (1967), and *Alice's Restaurant* (1969). She was also one of the first editors to demand and to receive a cut of film profits. In the 1970s, Allen chose her projects carefully. She edited two of Sidney Lumet's most critically acclaimed films, *Serpico* (1973) and *Dog Day Afternoon* (1975), earning an Academy Award nomination for the latter. Allen also edited *Little Big Man* (1970), *Slaughterhouse Five* (1972), *Night Moves* (1975), and *Slap Shot* (1977). Actor-directors Paul Newman and Warren Beatty have called upon Allen when making their own films, and she edited *Harry and Son* (1984) for Newman and Beatty's *Reds* (1981).

In 1973, Verna Fields shared a nomination with Marcia Lucas for *American Graffiti,* and two years later Fields won the Academy Award for film editing for her work on *Jaws* (1975). More important to the role of women in the industry, however, was Fields's appointment as vice president of feature production at Universal Studios in 1976.

The 1970s also welcomed the return of film editor Margaret Booth, who had ended thirty years as a supervising film editor for MGM in 1968 and returned to active film editing in a free-lance capacity. In 1972, she edited John Huston's *Fat City,* followed by a string of other, better-known films. Booth edited *The Way We Were* in 1973, followed by four Neil Simon comedies: *The Sunshine Boys* in 1975, *Murder by Death* in 1976, *California Suite* in 1978, and *Chapter Two* in 1979. She was recognized in 1977 by the Academy of Motion Picture Arts and Sciences with a Special Award for her years of fine work.

The scarcity of women directors in the industry of the 1970s made the press portray Elaine May as an anomaly in 1971 when she first wrote the screenplay and then directed the film of *A New Leaf*. A Mike Nichols comedy partner before becoming an actress, May was lauded as a pioneer in the writer-director role for women, although she had actually just rediscovered the role. (Jeanne MacPherson had been a writer-director with Cecil B. De Mille in the infancy of the film industry.) Before *A New Leaf*, May had used the pseudonym Esther Dale when she adapted Lois Gould's novel *Such Good Friends* for the screen. Her next success was another comedy, *The Heartbreak Kid* in 1972, which she directed, followed by *Mike and Nicky* (1976), which she wrote and directed. In 1978, May cowrote with Warren Beatty the screenplay for *Heaven Can Wait*, for which she received an Academy Award nomination for Best Screenplay; she then served as an uncredited cowriter on *Tootsie* (1982). She also cowrote and codirected with Beatty the colossal 1987 failure *Ishtar*. Her period of greatest influence was the 1970s, but she joins others in observing that her major failure with *Ishtar* in the 1980s struck a blow for women in the industry, because it was the first time that a woman director had been entrusted with so large a budget, as well as the correspondingly large expectations for success.

Other women directors followed in the decade. In 1975, Lina Wertmuller became the first woman to be nominated for the Academy Award for Best Director, for her work on *Seven Beauties*. Joan Micklin Silver directed the acclaimed *Hester Street* (1975), followed by *Between the Lines* (1977), a comedy about the demise of a counterculture newspaper. In 1979, Silver directed *Chilly Scenes of Winter* (1979), an adaptation of an Ann Beattie novel. She continued into the 1980s with the commercially successful *Crossing Delancey* (1988) and *Lover Boy* (1989). To a great extent, Silver has addressed the issue of Jewish women and the patriarchal world that confined them. The 1970s afforded her influence in an industry bereft of women directors, although her major directorial success did not emerge until the late 1980s with *Crossing Delancey*.

Several long-established women costume designers exerted strong influence in the 1970s, led by Edith Head, who earned Academy Award nominations for *Airport* (1970), *The Man Who Would Be King* (1975), and *Airport '77* (1977). She also won her eighth Academy Award for costume design for *The Sting* (1973), making her the most frequently honored Oscar winner, man or women. Margaret Furse earned nominations for *Scrooge* (1970) and *Mary, Queen of Scots* (1971), and Dorothy Jeakins earned a nomination for *The Way We Were* (1973). Fourteen other women designers earned Academy Award nominations for costume design during the decade, and four newcomers won the award: Yvonne Blake for *Nicholas and Alexandra* (1971), Theoni V. Aldredge for *The Great Gatsby* (1974), and Ulla-Britt Soderlund and Milena Canonero for *Barry Lyndon* (1975).

The decade also saw the emergence of costume designer Ann Roth, who, although she did not earn Academy Award nominations in the 1970s, began to establish a strong presence in the industry and to gain the respect and support of directors and producers. She was prolific in in the 1970s and designed the costumes for eighteen films, including *The Owl and the Pussycat* (1970), *Klute* (1971), *The Goodbye Girl* (1977), and *Coming Home* (1978). Her name and her work became well known among the era's decision makers, and her influence has continued on through the 1980s and into the 1990s.

The area of set design has slowly opened to women in the film industry, but the number of women recognized in this field remains small. Production designer Patrizia Von Brandenstein earned respect for her work in such films as *The Candidate* (1972), *Girlfriends* (1978), and *Breaking Away* (1979), and the number of productions for which her services were retained as well as her influence increased in the 1980s. Ruby Leavitt twice shared an Academy Award nomination for set design during the 1970s—for *The Andromeda Strain* (1971) and for *Chinatown* (1973)—while Pamela Cornell shared the nomination for *Scrooge* (1970). In 1979, Linda Descenna shared a nomination for her work on *Star Trek: The Motion Picture*. Because of the relative scarcity of women in what remains a male-dominated area, those women who

•

have been recognized for set design have also gained some influence in the film industry.

Few actresses exerted any true influence in Hollywood in the 1970s simply as actresses. In some cases, women who had acted in the previous decade gained influence by turning their talents to the additional areas of directing or producing films on their own. Of those actresses who wielded influence solely in the 1970s, many have faded from the ranks of Hollywood power brokers, because the period was one of fads. Raquel Welch is an example of an actress in this period with both high name recognition and physical endowments whose influence was limited. She was a 1960s starlet whom 20th Century–Fox turned into a sex symbol. Despite making numerous films, all of which depended upon her sex appeal, Welch enjoyed only a brief period of influence. In the 1960s, her physical presence drew viewers to *Fantastic Voyage* (1966), *One Million Years B.C.* (1967), *Bedazzled* (1967), and *One Hundred Rifles* (1969); clearly no one came to see her act. In the 1970s, she could still draw an audience and backers for such films as the sex satire *Myra Breckinridge* (1970) and *The Wild Party* (1975), but her era of even minor influence was over.

Liza Minnelli, like Welch, enjoyed some limited influence in the film industry of the 1970s and then faded. The daughter of actress Judy Garland and director Vincente Minnelli, she has been famous since birth. However, while Liza does not need a last name to be recognized, her films are largely forgettable. Her screen debut in *Charlie Bubbles* (1967) has become a cult classic, but the reviews were poor. One critic referred to Minnelli as "the supreme deadweight" in the movie. *Lucky Lady* (1975) was a commercial flop, and *A Matter of Time* (1976), directed by her father, miscast Liza in a part that drew much criticism from reviewers. Liza's problem was that her song-and-dance talents should have been showcased, as they were in *Cabaret* (1972) and *New York, New York* (1977). Her success in *Cabaret* led to speculation that Liza would become the new musical star who could lead audiences back to screen musicals, but poor film choices followed and made her a hard sell in Hollywood. With her Oscar-winning turn as Sally Bowles, she made the screen version of Bob Fosse's *Cabaret* a classic. Then her stock plummeted with several failures. *New York, New York* and *Arthur* (1981) briefly resuscitated her image.

Prominent in the 1970s, Sissy Spacek remains a good actress, but she no longer wields the influence that her successful films in the decade gave her. Her Texas twang has, to some extent, limited her to playing southern or southwestern roles, but she nevertheless has played a wide range of characters throughout her career. Spacek's films of the early 1970s, including her debut film, *Prime Cut* (1972), *Badlands* (1973), and *Carrie* (1976), made her familiar to movie audiences, and also did very well financially. Armed with such successes, Spacek had her pick of roles but chose poorly. Most of her later 1970s films were disappointing, and with each successive film she lost more of her influence in the industry. She earned the Academy Award for Best Actress for her portrayal of Loretta Lynn in *Coal Miner's Daughter* (1980), but by then no longer had the power to pick out the choicest roles. Even so, Spacek earned relatively good reviews for *Raggedy Man* (1981), had a hit with *Missing* (1982), and earned an Academy Award nomination for *Crimes of the Heart* (1986). She remains respected as an actress, but she never regained the influence she enjoyed in the 1970s.

The early success of Faye Dunaway in *Bonnie and Clyde* (1967) and *The Thomas Crown Affair* (1968) was only a prelude to her mid-1970s emergence as a strong leading lady in *Chinatown* (1974) and *Network* (1976). She was too inexperienced in the 1960s to capitalize fully on the Best Actress nomination she earned for her role as Bonnie Parker. By the mid-1970s, she should have exploited the influence that her Academy Award nomination for *Chinatown* and her Oscar for Best Actress in *Network* had brought her. By the end of the decade, however, bad choices had canceled out the success of her earlier roles, although she continued to act in films throughout the 1980s and even attracted critical acclaim for her role in *Barfly* (1987).

Diane Keaton, on the other hand, gained prominence in Hollywood as an adaptable actress who could be counted upon to give a good performance in comedy and drama. Keaton made her film debut in *Lovers*

Diane Keaton in the 1970's (Evans Collection)

and Other Strangers (1970). She worked well in comedic films produced by Woody Allen, such as *Play It Again, Sam* (1972), *Sleeper*
(1973), *Love and Death* (1975), *Annie Hall* (1977), for which she won
the Academy Award for Best Actress, and *Manhattan* (1979). At the

same time, she was also a solid dramatic talent who could play the wife of a future Mafia don in *The Godfather* (1972) and *The Godfather II* (1974), as well as a sexually promiscuous teacher in *Looking for Mr. Goodbar* (1977). She then entered the 1980s and won wide acclaim for her role as political radical Louise Bryant in Warren Beatty's *Reds* (1981) and in the small but well-received *Shoot the Moon* (1982). In the last half of the 1980s, Keaton appeared in such well-received films as *Crimes of the Heart* (1986), *Baby Boom* (1987), and *The Good Mother* (1988). In the 1990s, Keaton has extended her influence to directing, in addition to her strong screen roles in *Father of the Bride* (1992) and *Father of the Bride II* (1995). Her first efforts were rock videos, including Belinda Carlisle's *Heaven Is a Place on Earth*, then episodes of *China Beach* and *Twin Peaks*. Keaton's first major directorial project, the quirky documentary *Heaven* (1987), was a critical disaster, but her latest, *Unstrung Heroes* (1995), brought thundering applause when screened at the Cannes Film Festival in May 1995.

Jane Fonda emerged as an independent force in the late 1970s, after a series of successful roles in the 1960s marked her as a sex symbol actress, most notoriously for her role in the erotic science fiction space adventure *Barbarella* (1968). She earned an Academy Award nomination for her role as a Depression-era marathon dancer in *They Shoot Horses, Don't They?* (1969) and won the Academy Award for Best Actress for her role as a prostitute in *Klute* (1971). A year later, her radical antiwar pronouncements made her an outsider in Hollywood and led to her ostracism by the film industry for several years. It was not the first time that Fonda had drawn negative attention to herself. In the early 1960s, she had provoked controversy by making such overtly sexual movies as *Walk on the Wild Side* (1962) and *The Chapman Report* (1962), and the huge billboard advertisements for *Circle of Love* (1965) had pictured her nude on a bed. She may have shocked people culturally then, but she committed a more egregious sin against society when, in the early 1970s, she openly spoke out against U.S. government policy in Vietnam, sympathized with the Viet Cong (earning

•

Jane Fonda (Movie Graphics)

the nickname "Hanoi Jane"), and joined leftists in trying to convert American soldiers into revolutionaries.

By 1976, all was forgotten, if not forgiven, in Hollywood and she appeared to have made peace with the system. Her late-1970s films contained familiar themes to appeal to middle-class audiences. In *Fun with Dick and Jane* (1976), George Segal and Fonda made a big-budget attack on corporate crime, while *Julia* (1977) was a big-screen, anti-fascism melodrama. In *Coming Home* (1978), a film made by Fonda's newly formed production company, IPC, Fonda played the wife of a Vietnam veteran who returns home physically whole but mentally shattered, and she, in turn, falls in love with a hospitalized veteran who is mentally whole but physically shattered. The modern western *Comes a Horseman* (1978) and the Neil Simon comedy *California Suite* (1978) were well received by audiences, as was *The China Syndrome* (1979) with its nuclear plant disaster theme. In 1981, she had a hit with Lily Tomlin and Dolly Parton in *Nine to Five*, a film that pushed her further up the Hollywood scale of influence. All was forgiven as Fonda became a moneymaker and, thus, a driving force in the industry. In 1981, she appeared in *On Golden Pond* with her father, Henry Fonda, who won the Academy Award for Best Actor shortly before he died. The actress turned to making exercise videos in the 1980s, venturing into only three movies before *The Morning After* (1986), for which she earned an Academy Award nomination for Best Actress. She also produced and starred in *Old Gringo* (1989) through her own company but has had little to do with Hollywood in recent years. Although Fonda's marriage to Ted Turner in the early 1990s could only add to her clout in the film industry, she has chosen not to exercise her potential muscle.

Barbra Streisand, influential in Hollywood throughout the 1980s and 1990s, first became highly involved in her own films in the 1970s. After winning the Academy Award for Best Actress for *Funny Girl* (1968), then failing to do well at the box office or with the critics with her next two films, *Hello, Dolly!* (1969) and *On a Clear Day You Can See Forever* (1970), she made a string of films of mixed quality in the early 1970s. *The Owl and the Pussycat* (1970) and *What's Up, Doc?* (1972) were box-office successes, but *Up the Sandbox* (1972) received a lukewarm reception. In 1973, Streisand had an overwhelming success in *The Way We Were*, a love story with Robert Redford as her romantic lead. Despite skeptics who asserted that she had neither the looks nor the sound to make a credible object of romance for the type of male character portrayed by Redford in the movie, both audiences and critics acclaimed her performance, and the film and Streisand's recording of the theme song did extremely well.

Streisand did not match this success with any of her films of the later 1970s, and she became increasingly dissatisfied with the quality of these productions. As Streisand's reputation for being "difficult" on the set increased, so did her determination to take greater control of the films in which she appeared. The comedy *For Pete's Sake* (1974) and *Funny Lady* (1975), the sequel to *Funny Girl*, did poorly at the box office. Streisand became the first woman in modern film history to found a production company when, in 1969, she joined Paul Newman and Sidney Poitier in forming the First Artists Production Company. Each pledged to produce three movies for the company, which later included Dustin Hoffman and Steve McQueen. *Up the Sandbox* (1972) was the first of her three pictures for the new company, followed by *A Star is Born* (1976), and *The Main Event* (1979), all three partially financed by her New York company Barwood Productions.

Her remake of *A Star is Born* earned commercial if not critical success, and it marked an important evolution in Streisand's career. She insisted on composing the theme song, "Evergreen," with Paul Williams, and the song won the Academy Award for Best Song that year. She increased her involvement with her next film, *The Main Event* (1979), by becoming co–executive producer on the project. Four years later, Streisand used her growing influence to produce, direct, cowrite, and star in *Yentl* (1983). The resounding box-office success of the movie confirmed Streisand's power in the film industry and established the foundation for a strong presence in the 1980s and 1990s.

The 1970s also saw a number of stars who began to build reputations in the film industry, but their periods of greatest influence actually occurred later. Jessica Lange's well-received films of the 1970s actually laid the foundation for her numerous successful films during the 1980s. Her film debut in the remake of *King Kong* (1976) was

Meryl Streep (Evans Collection)

inauspicious, at best, but she managed to turn the criticism around when she played a prominent role in Bob Fosse's *All That Jazz* (1979). Her successful performance led to a strong repertoire of films in the

1980s, which gave her the credibility to demand increasingly good material.

Jodie Foster, who became a powerhouse in the late 1980s and early 1990s, had already developed a level of influence in the 1970s film industry, that enabled her to be more selective in her choice of roles. She made her film debut in *Napoleon and Samantha* (1972), then had a bit part in *Alice Doesn't Live Here Anymore* (1973). Three years later, she played a teenage prostitute in *Taxi Driver* (1976), a film that starred Robert De Niro and brought her instant recognition. She made several more films throughout the decade, but then her career appeared to wind down while she took time off to attend Yale University. By the late 1980s, she had rejuvenated her film career with *The Accused* (1988), which won for her the Academy Award for Best Actress. From that point, Foster seized control and emerged in the 1990s as a figure of prominence.

Meryl Streep gained respect in Hollywood in the 1970s with such films as *The Deer Hunter* (1978), for which she earned an Academy Award nomination for Best Actress, *Manhattan* (1979), *The Seduction of Joe Tynan* (1979), and *Kramer vs. Kramer* (1979), for which she won the Academy Award for Best Supporting Actress, but the extent of her influence in the decade was limited. Streep's performances in the 1980s varied in quality, but she made some wise role decisions toward the end of the decade that have increased her influence in the 1990s.

Many women had their brief hours of recognition, but others simply faded with the end of the decade. Those few who learned from their experiences, however, have become moving forces in a rapidly changing industry.

Women at the Top:
The 1980s

•

WOMEN FORCED HOLLYWOOD to reopen its doors to them in the 1980s; positions from the boardroom to both sides of the camera could finally be called women's work. They took over some of the most powerful jobs in town. Even on-screen roles were affected as more secure actresses rebelled against the meager "bimbo or bitch" choices offered them, and chose to write their own scripts, deepening the roles for women characters. The truly motivated also obtained their own backing and formed their own production companies. This revolution extended to women behind the camera, many of whom were rewarded during the decade with Academy Awards and other industry recognition for their efforts. In short, the 1980s signaled women's return to the business aspect of the film industry for the first time since its infancy.

In 1980, Sherry Lansing became the first woman to head an already-established studio, as president of 20th Century–Fox, (Pickford, Swanson, and Streisand headed studios that they themselves had created) a position she held for three years before leaving to become an

•

Sherry Lansing (© Paramount Pictures)

independent film producer. Despite years of work in the business, three years at MGM, and two and a half years at Columbia, Lansing was still described by newspapers and poorly informed magazines—who seemed to dismiss her years of professional growth—as the "former model" who had become the head of a major film studio. Her frustrations were understandable, because Lansing became a studio head at the age of thirty-five, and her modeling days had ended when she was twenty-two. While at Columbia, she developed *The China*

Syndrome (1979) and *Kramer vs. Kramer* (1979). At Fox, however, she was denied the power to give the go-ahead to projects and left after three years. She lost no time in forming her own production company and, with *Kramer v. Kramer* producer Stanley Jaffe, produced *Fatal Attraction* in 1987. She conceived of the movie as having a strong feminist slant, yet audiences and critics accused her of having produced an anti-feminist film. Despite criticism to the contrary, Lansing asserted that the character played by Glenn Close brought a new dimension to the concept of one-night stands and created a strong female threat that fights back and refuses to be a victim. Even given the poor press, the film, which had been made on a budget of $14 million, became a runaway hit and in 1995 recorded total gross earnings of $156.6 million. Lansing also coproduced *Black Rain* (1988) and *The Accused* (1988) through the independent production company.

Other women assumed once male-only roles in industry positions that gave them decision-making power. In 1981, Paula Weinstein was named president of the motion picture division at United Artists. She came to the position after working for years as an agent with the William Morris Agency, where she represented, among others, Jane Fonda and Donald Sutherland. Weinstein grew up in the film industry: her mother was producer Hannah Weinstein, a close friend of Lillian Hellman's. Paula Weinstein left United Artists late in the decade and, with her husband, Mark Rosenberg, formed an independent production company, Spring Creek Productions. In 1989 she produced *A Dry White Season*.

Dawn Steel began as director of merchandising at Paramount Pictures and became the president of production in 1984. While at Paramount, she brought *Footloose* (1984), *Top Gun* (1986), and *The Untouchables* (1987) to the screen. Rumors of friction with the president of the studio's motion picture division were rife when she left in 1987. Only months later, she was named president of Columbia Pictures, where she became the first woman in the industry to oversee both the production and the marketing operations of a studio. At Columbia, in 1989 she brought to the screen *Ghostbusters II*, *Casualties of War*, *When Harry Met Sally . . .* , and *Look Who's Talking*, along with numerous others. She left the job in 1990, claiming exhaustion and disillusionment with the business.

In 1984, Kathleen Kennedy became the president of Amblin Entertainment, the company founded by Steven Spielberg. Kennedy began in the business as a production assistant on Spielberg's *1941* (1979), then took on additional producing responsibility while working on *Raiders of the Lost Ark* (1981). She made her producing debut on the extremely successful *E.T. The Extraterrestrial* (1982) and shared with Spielberg an Academy Award nomination for Best Picture. As president of Amblin, Kennedy produced the three *Back to the Future* films, *The Color Purple* (1985), and *Who Framed Roger Rabbit* (1988).

More women began to produce feature films than in any previous decade, and women were responsible for many of the most successful films. Producer Lauren Shuler-Donner established a reputation for getting her pictures in on time and within budget. Her debut as a solo producer was with *Mr. Mom* (1982), starring Michael Keaton. She followed this effort with two "Brat Pack" movies: *St. Elmo's Fire* (1985), which did well among teenagers and featured Rob Lowe, Emilio Estevez, Judd Nelson, Demi Moore, Andrew McCarthy, and Ally Sheedy, and *Pretty in Pink* (1986), a "Cinderella" story, featuring Molly Ringwald, Jon Cryer, Andrew McCarthy, and Annie Potts. In 1989, Shuler-Donner produced *Three Fugitives*, a comedy that starred Nick Nolte and Martin Short. In 1992, she and husband Richard Donner merged production companies and continued to produce films that brought in strong revenues at the box office.

Other women built their reputations as producers during this decade. Lucy Fisher, who began as a reader at United Artists, later headed worldwide productions at American Zoetrope, Francis Ford Coppola's studio. She moved to Warner Bros. in the early 1980s as executive vice president and handled the production of *Gremlins* (1984), *Greystoke: The Legend of Tarzan, Lord of the Apes* (1984), and *The Witches of Eastwick* (1987). Mildred Lewis earned an Academy Award nomination for Best Picture for coproducing *Missing* (1982). In

1984, Arlene Hart earned an Academy Award nomination for Best Picture for her production of *Places in the Heart*. And in 1987, Linda Gottlieb produced *Dirty Dancing*, which became a major box-office success and seemed to signal a solid future for its producer.

Barbra Streisand made her presence felt in this decade, beginning with her first film, *Yentl* (1983). Streisand took on all of the creative roles—cowriting, directing, producing, and starring in the film. She also defied convention by putting her own twist on the conventional boy-meets-girl musical motion picture, for her main character rejects marriage at the end in favor of growth and independence. Streisand addressed the position of Jewish women in a patriarchal world, and she created a female character who defies the male mandate that only men can have access to knowledge. She also produced the drama *Nuts* (1987) and took her momentum into the 1990s, where she co-produced and directed *The Prince of Tides* (1991). Beyond her work in film, Streisand assumed a powerful role in Hollywood as a longtime proponent of women helping women in the business. She continues to use her visibility to draw attention to political issues in which she deeply believes. As she said in her 1992 address to members of Women in Film, "Speaking for myself, I have a deep commitment to making films about positive transformation and the unlimited potential for human growth."

The business of screenwriting and producing took an interesting turn in 1984 when Gale Ann Hurd cowrote and produced *The Terminator*. Hurd admits to a taste for action dramas, and she indulged her taste throughout the decade by also producing such films as *Aliens* (1979), which starred Sigourney Weaver, *Alien Nation* (1988), and *The Abyss* (1989). She began her film career working at New World Pictures, which was headed by the king of the B-pictures, Roger Corman. Gaining the confidence of studios was at first difficult, but the success of *The Terminator* coupled with *Aliens'* gross of $82 million in the United States gave Hurd credibility. She was one of the few women to be given a free hand in producing big-budget, big-set films.

Directing took on a different appearance in the 1980s. Actresses turned to directing in an effort to make films that the studios ignored. In 1986, Sondra Locke directed and starred in *Ratboy*. Other actresses, including Dyan Cannon, Diane Keaton, and Lee Grant, directed experimental, documentary, and mainstream films. Perhaps more important to the position of women in the industry, new female directors appeared on the scene who had not emerged from the acting ranks, and they quickly acquired credibility.

Susan Seidelman became one of the best known of the new women directors. She broke into commercial film with the art house success *Smithereens* (1983). It earned her the necessary visibility and the financial backing to write and direct the medium-budget film *Desperately Seeking Susan* (1985). The story of a bored suburban housewife who seeks to escape to a more glamorous life starred popular American recording star Madonna, on the ascendance at that time as an international star. This casting helped to draw audiences, but the film's unprecedented success is also due to its playful handling of a timely feminist theme. Seidelman made three more feature films during the 1980s: *Making Mr. Right* (1987), *Cookie* (1989), and *She-Devil* in 1989, thus establishing herself as a leading woman director.

Martha Coolidge made her feature film directorial debut with the independently produced *Valley Girl* (1983), which starred Nicolas Cage. The low-budget film was planned to attract the teenage market, but its huge commercial success surprised Coolidge and became her means of breaking into the established film industry. Paramount commissioned her to direct *Joy of Sex* (1984), starring Christopher Lloyd, another film aimed at the teenage market. Nonetheless, Coolidge attempted to distance herself from the film because of its blatant exploitation. Her big-budget opportunity came with *Real Genius* (1985), starring Val Kilmer, a science fiction comedy aimed once again at the teen market. By the middle of the decade, Coolidge became frustrated with the compromises necessary to remain successful in mainstream Hollywood and left.

Australian director Gillian Armstrong enjoyed a brief burst of popularity in the early 1980s after Hollywood discovered her film *My*

Brilliant Career (1979), based on the novel by Australian woman novelist Miles Franklin. Her film marked an important stage in Australian filmmaking because she was the first woman in forty-six years to direct a narrative feature. She then made *Starstruck* (1982), *Mrs. Soffel* (1994), and *High Tide* (1987). Only *Mrs. Soffel* did reasonably well at the box office, and the credit for that was the drawing power of its stars, Mel Gibson and Diane Keaton.

Other women directors emerged in this decade, some of whom would exert only brief influence, while others would influence the film industry into the 1990s. Amy Heckerling, who would later write the screenplays for *Look Who's Talking* (1989) and *Look Who's Talking Too* (1990), made her directing debut with *Fast Times at Ridgemont High* (1982), then directed *National Lampoon's European Vacation* (1985) and *Look Who's Talking*. Randa Haines attracted favorable attention with her direction of *Children of a Lesser God* (1986), which starred Marlee Matlin; Donna Deitch directed *Desert Hearts* (1985); and Catlin Adams wrote, directed, and coproduced *Sticky Fingers* in 1988. Former television actress Penny Marshall directed her first big-screen feature film, *Jumpin' Jack Flash* (1986), followed by *Big* in 1988, then went on to major successes in the 1990s.

The decade offered new opportunities to women writers. Hilary Henkin was one of the few women given the opportunity to write for the action genre. Hers was the original script for the police action thriller *Fatal Beauty* (1987), which starred Whoopi Goldberg. In 1989, Hers was the original script about a boy wrongly committed to a mental institution in *Lost Angels*, starring Donald Sutherland, but lost the right to screen credit in arbitration. Her final script of the decade was for *Roadhouse* (1989), a thriller starring Patrick Swayze as a kickboxer with a doctorate in philosophy. Henkin continued to write into the 1990s, and she both wrote and produced *Romeo Is Bleeding* (1994), a classic hard-boiled thriller that featured a tough, larger-than-life heroine.

Journalist Nora Ephron gained prominence in the 1980s as a screenwriter with *Silkwood* (1983), directed by Mike Nichols and starring

Meryl Streep and Cher. She claimed that she used her experience as a journalist to formulate in a screenplay the true story of activist Karen Silkwood, who protested the exposure of plant workers to radiation and who died under mysterious circumstances. In 1985, Ephron adapted her roman à clef *Heartburn* into a screenplay that detailed the highly vitriolic breakup of her marriage to Washington journalist Carl Bernstein of Watergate fame. The film starred Meryl Streep and Jack Nicholson. Ephron also wrote the highly successful *When Harry Met Sally . . .* (1989), starring Billy Crystal and Meg Ryan, and cowrote *Cookie* with Alice Arlen. At the end of the 1980s, Ephron was a highly respected screenwriter, and she turned to directing as well. Both activities would bring her success in the 1990s.

In film editing in the 1980s, women defied any holdover views that only men can do justice to an action film. Thelma Schoonmaker, a longtime collaborator of Martin Scorsese, won the Academy Award for Film Editing for *Raging Bull* (1980), an often-violent movie about the career of boxer Jake LaMotta. In 1983, Lisa Fruchtman earned the film editing award for her work on *The Right Stuff* (1983), and Claire Simpson won the award for editing *Platoon* (1986). Women film editors also received Academy Award nominations in other types of films. Anne V. Coates was nominated for the film editing award for her work on *The Elephant Man* (1980), Dede Allen for *Reds* (1981), Carol Littleton for *E.T. The Extraterrestrial* (1982), and Nena Danevic for *Amadeus* (1984).

The 1980s held mixed success for actresses. Actress-singer Cher first appeared with former husband Sonny Bono in *Good Times* (1967), but her 1980s film roles were all nonsinging, dramatic roles. The former singer surprised both audiences and critics when she played a factory worker in *Silkwood* (1983). She won critical acclaim for her role as the mother of a boy whose face is disfigured by disease in *Mask* (1985). In *Suspect* (1987), critics observed that Cher turned in a "fine and utterly believable performance" as a public defender who battles against great odds to free her client, a deaf derelict accused of murder. She also received praise for her role in *The Witches of Eastwick* (1987). Her best performance of the decade was in the romantic comedy *Moonstruck* (1987). She won the Academy Award for Best Actress for her role as a young widow who falls hopelessly in love with the younger brother of her fiancé. Her success should have led to increased on-screen appearances, but Cher has remained out of films by choice since the late 1980s except for appearances in *The Player* (1992) and *Ready to Wear* (1995).

Not every actress, however, has had the choice. Rae Dawn Chong had a hot streak in film during the middle of the decade, starring in several successful films, including *Commando* (1985) and *Soul Man* (1986). Except for *Tales From the Dark Side* (1990), her 1990s roles have drawn little attention.

Actress Bo Derek became one of Hollywood's best-known commodities with the release of *10* (1980), and she gained eminence based on that one role. Her influence was brief, extending only shortly beyond the making of *Tarzan, the Ape Man* (1981), which she produced.

Broadway musical star Bernadette Peters had been lured to movies in the 1970s, playing comedy roles in several films, including *The Longest Yard* (1974). In the 1980s, however, she became the hope for a revival of film musicals, and she had the necessary screen presence to accomplish the task, had the starring vehicles been better. She earned critical acclaim for her role in the generally well-received movie *Pennies from Heaven* (1981), a period piece about a sheet music salesman set in the 1930s and costarring Steve Martin. Peters attracted attention in the film community for a time, but the interest in reviving musicals died out, and her brief period of ascendance soon ended.

In contrast, Jessica Lange emerged as one of the most influential actresses of the decade, despite the 1980 failure of *How to Beat the High Cost of Living*. In the 1981 remake of *The Postman Always Rings Twice* with Jack Nicholson, she showed audiences and the industry that she could handle steamy love scenes, and she projected a star quality that would continue to fascinate viewers throughout the decade. In 1982, Lange took on the diverse roles of an ingenue in *Tootsie*, for which she won the Academy Award for Best Supporting Actress, and that of actress Frances Farmer in *Frances*, in which she exhibited all of the demons that plagued the actress. Lange earned a Best Actress nomination for her roles in *Country* (1984) and *Sweet Dreams* (1985), a biography of country singer Patsy Cline. She was also lauded for her roles in *Crimes of the Heart* (1986), *Everybody's All-American* (1988), and *Music Box* (1989), for which she received another Best Actress nomination.

The 1980s were also a decade of major successes for Kathleen Turner, whose good looks and sultry voice made her a natural for the femme fatale roles she played to perfection. After a short stint on the daytime soap opera *The Doctors*, Turner appeared in *Body Heat* (1981) in a steamy role that captured the attention of both critics and audiences. Throughout the decade, she appeared in such commercially successful films as *The Man With Two Brains* (1983), *Crimes of Passion* (1984), *Romancing the Stone* (1984), *Jewel of the Nile* (1985), and *The War of the Roses* (1989). She received critical acclaim for her performances in *Prizzi's Honor* (1985), *Peggy Sue Got Married* (1986) which brought her a Best Actress Oscar nomination, and *The Accidental Tourist* (1988), then moved on to become the uncredited off-screen voice of the sultry animated sexpot Jessica Rabbit in *Who Framed Roger Rabbit*. Her box-office bottom line gave her substantial power in choosing her roles, which for the most part she did wisely.

To characterize any one period as being *the* period of greatest influence for a still-working actress is difficult, and the problem becomes especially difficult with Meryl Streep, who also did exceptional work in the 1970s and again in the 1990s. The 1980s, however, brought substantial recognition for her work. In *The French Lieutenant's Woman* (1981), for which Streep earned the Acadamy Award nomination for Best Actress, she played the dual role of an actress and of the character being played by that actress. She followed this challenging role with that of Sophie, the Polish immigrant, in *Sophie's Choice* (1981), for which she won the Academy Award for Best Actress, then portrayed the nuclear activist Karen Silkwood in *Silkwood* (1983), which brought another Academy Award for Best Actress. Unafraid to appear in nonglamorous roles, she starred as a time- and alcohol-ravaged woman in *Ironweed* (1987), gained an Academy Award nomination for Best Actress for *A Cry in the Dark* (1988), then joined Roseanne Barr as the home-wrecking romance novelist in the comedy *She-Devil* (1989). Several of her films, notably *Still of the Night* (1982), *Out of Africa* (1985), and *Heartburn* (1986) were commercial disappointments, but her other successes kept Meryl Streep among the select few actresses in this decade who could control the works in which they appeared.

Sexy actress Kim Basinger has made a career out of playing the pouting starlet, a guise that seduced her audiences into making her one of the most financially successful actresses of the 1980s. She starred in films with many of Hollywood's leading men: Robert Redford in *The Natural* (1984), Richard Gere in *No Mercy* (1986), Mickey Rourke in *9 1/2 Weeks* (1986), Jeff Bridges in *Nadine* (1987), Michael Keaton in *Batman* (1989), and Alec Baldwin in *The Marrying Man* (1991). Such movies as the 1992 *Cool World* and *Final Analysis* (1993) were not as successful as her films of the 1980s, although her cameo in *Wayne's World II* (1994) brought her to the attention of younger viewers. Basinger also attempted to take on the Hollywood establishment of the 1980s when she formed her own production company, Mighty Winds Productions, but it did not appear to be very active into the next decade.

Sally Field emerged from television in the 1960s to make a series of moderately successful films in the 1970s, including *Smokey and the Bandit* (1977), *Heroes* (1977), *The End* (1978), and *Beyond the Poseidon Adventure* (1979). Her portrayal of a poor working-class Southern woman in *Norma Rae* (1979) not only made critics and audiences take note of her acting ability, but it won for her the Academy Award for Best Actress. This film paved the way for increasingly more dramatic roles during the 1980s, and for increased opportunities to show her acting range. She made *Smokey and the Bandit II* (1980) with Burt Reynolds, then played a hard-nosed journalist opposite Paul Newman in *Absence of Malice* (1981). The 1984 *Places in the Heart* won Field another Academy Award for Best Actress. For the remainder of the 1980s, she made unwise choices in roles, aside from *Punchline* (1988) with Tom Hanks. Thus far her career has been marked by an unevenness that has limited her influence in the film industry.

The career of Goldie Hawn has also been relatively uneven, although the early 1980s made her an on-screen power to be reckoned with, and the end of the decade found her forming her own production company. After winning the Academy Award for Best Supporting Actress in *Cactus Flower* (1969), Hawn traded on her comedy image during the 1970s in such films as *There's a Girl in My Soup* (1970), *$* (1971), *Butterflies Are Free* (1972), *The Girl from Petrovka* (1974),

Goldie Hawn in Private Benjamin (1980) (National Film Archive)

Shampoo (1975), *The Duchess and the Dirtwater Fox* (1976), and *Foul Play* (1978). She briefly tried drama in *The Sugarland Express* (1974), an early Steven Spielberg film, playing a mother on the run who tries to regain her children, but returned quickly to comedy. She had a string of hit movies in the early 1980s, starting with *Private Benjamin* (1980), which grossed $100 million and made Hawn one of the top-earning female stars in the business. She followed with *Seems Like Old Times* (1980), *Best Friends* (1982), *Swing Shift* (1984), and the disappointing *Protocol* (1984). Her box-office appeal diminished in the last half of the decade, and *Overboard* (1987), filmed by her recently formed production company, failed to meet commercial expectations.

Many of the influential women of the 1980s continued to thrive in the film industry of the 1990s, a decade that became increasingly open to them in all capacities. Greater numbers of women assumed positions of power at all levels. The "old-boy" networks that had long nurtured the ambitions of young male directors, producers, studio executives, and others aiming for power roles underwent a slow but steady metamorphosis into a growing "old girl" network. The 1980s had begun the process, as Hollywood experienced a shift of power with women entering, and in some cases reentering, areas that had long been the exclusive domain of men. Marketing, producing, directing, developing projects, negotiating deals, and other decision-making facets of the business all became women's work during that vital and exciting decade.

The Limitless Decade: The 1990s

•

WOMEN IN THE 1980s had reason to feel that the only way to assume an element of control was to create a whole new enterprise, their own production company, but women in the 1990s chose to invade already existing enterprises. While the approach of creating new and separate enterprises served many actresses well in earlier decades, and their efforts provided opportunities for fledgling writers, directors, and producers, they remained outside of the mainstream of power. By the 1990s, women in the film industry had decided that separate but unequal operations, in terms of money and accessibility if not talent, were not serving them well. In the 1990s, women moved into the exclusive network relationships that men had long enjoyed, assuming decision-making roles at the major studios.

Industry deal-maker Sherry Lansing ended nine years as an independent producer in 1992 when she was named chairperson of the Paramount Motion Picture Group, with full power to give the green light to movie productions. With her sharp eye for what would succeed on screen, Lansing moved Paramount from last place among the six major studios in 1993 to third place by 1994, behind only Disney

Studios and Warner Bros. Although she made several expensive mis-judgments, her successes in film projects during her first three years at Paramount were solid. Among her major films were *Indecent Proposal* (1993), starring Demi Moore and Robert Redford, which grossed $106.6 million in the first year of its release, and *Clear and Present Danger* (1993), starring Harrison Ford, which approached $205 million in gross profits in little over a year. Lansing's greatest gamble, and para-doxically her greatest winner, was *Forrest Gump* (1994), starring Tom Hanks. The film had moved with producer Wendy Finerman from one studio to another for nine years before Lansing decided to take the risk. Once again, her business instincts were right. *Forrest Gump* earned three Golden Globe Awards, including the award for Best Motion Picture Drama and then earned four Academy Awards, for Best Picture, Best Actor, Best Director, and Film Editing. By April 1995, soon after the Academy Awards were announced, *Gump* became one of the top five profitable films of all time, surpassing $500 million in worldwide box-office receipts. Lansing also had more modest successes with *Drop Zone, Star Trek: Generations*, and *Nobody's Fool* (all 1994).

Women occupied top positions at other major studios as well. At thirty-three, Lisa Henson became the youngest studio head in Hollywood when she was appointed president of worldwide production at Columbia Pictures in 1994. An anomaly in the business, with her Harvard education and degree in ancient Greek and folklore mytholo-gy, Henson was also the first female president of *The Harvard Lampoon*. Daughter of the late Jim Henson, creator of the Muppets, she worked for Warner Bros. during the late 1980s and early 1990s and left as an executive vice president in 1992. While there, however, she was involved in the development of *Lethal Weapon* (1987), *Batman* (1989), *The Last Boy Scout* (1990), and other action films. In her posi-tion at Columbia, Henson was involved during her first year in the pro-duction of *Little Women* (1995), starring Winona Ryder and Susan Sarandon, and *First Knight* (1995), with Sean Connery and Richard Gere.

Laura Ziskin became the president of a new movie division at 20th

Century–Fox in 1994. She had been an independent producer for nearly ten years, during which time she produced *Murphy's Romance*
(1985), *No Way Out* (1987), *Everybody's All-American* (1988), and
Pretty Woman (1990), as well as other films. At Fox, Ziskin was given
authority over eight to ten films per year, beginning with *To Die For*
(1995).

Former Amblin Productions president Kathleen Kennedy left Steven
Spielberg's company in 1992 to set up her own production division at
Paramount. She played a major role in the production of the high-
grossing *Jurassic Park* (1993). After producing the mediocre *Milk
Money* (1994) for Paramount, she independently produced the long-
awaited *Bridges of Madison County* (1995), based on the novel by
Robert James Waller. With her husband, Frank Marshall, Kennedy pro-
duced the big-budget movie *Congo* (1995), based on Michael
Crichton's novel. In late 1995, she and Marshall departed Paramount
for Disney.

Other women producers gained the spotlight in the 1990s as their
accomplishments increased the influence of women in the industry. In
1995, Amy Pascal became president of production at Turner Pictures,
in charge of building a new studio. She had worked for British producer
Tony Garnett before becoming a studio executive. She was executive
vice president of production at Columbia in the early 1990s, where she
backed *A League of Their Own* (1992) and *Single White Female* (1993).

Denise Di Novi began as a producer in Canada, then worked as a
screenwriter before joining director Tim Burton in 1989. She produced
Edward Scissorhands (1990), *Batman Returns* (1991), and *The
Nightmare Before Christmas* (1992). She then left in 1992 to form her
own production company. In 1995, she was the executive producer of
Little Women.

Women produced some of the most successful films of the 1990s.
Barbara De Fina earned an Academy Award nomination for coproducing *GoodFellas* (1990), the same year that Lisa Weinstein earned the
same nomination for coproducing *Ghost* (1990). Producer Wendy
Finerman fought for nine years to make *Forrest Gump* (1994), moving

it from studio to studio. The film won the Academy Award for Best Picture and became a huge commercial success. Stacy Snider, head of production at TriStar Pictures, shepherded through the films *Philadelphia* (1993) and *Legends of the Fall* (1994). Independent producer Lauren Shuler-Donner produced *Dave* (1993) and *Free Willy* (1993). Linda Obst, who worked as a magazine editor in New York before entering the film industry, produced *This Is My Life* (1992) and *Sleepless in Seattle* (1993). B. J. Rack coproduced *Terminator 2: Judgment Day* (1991), and Gail Katz was the coproducer of Clint Eastwood's action thriller *In the Line of Fire* (1993). Michelle Rappaport produced the Nick Nolte/Shaquille O'Neal vehicle *Blue Chips* (1994), and Paula Weinstein produced *With Honors* (1994), starring Joe Pesci.

Producer Gale Hurd continued her success of the 1980s in making action/adventure films. She followed her earlier *Terminator* (1984) with *Terminator 2: Judgment Day* (1991) and fought with other decision makers to make it a woman's story as well. Hurd's instincts were correct and her choices were vindicated when the film grossed nearly $205 million in the United States. She made *No Escape* (1994), starring Ray Liotta, which opened number one at the box office. Hurd approached the middle of the 1990s, firmly established among the reigning women producers in the business.

The number of feature films directed by women in Hollywood also increased during the 1990s. Writer-director Jane Campion won the 1993 Academy Award for Best Original Screenplay for *The Piano*. She also won the Palme d'Or at the Cannes Film Festival, the first woman ever to take the top prize. She is also only the second woman to ever earn an Academy Award nomination for Best Director and, although she lost to Steven Spielberg for *Schindler's List* (1993), the recognition was not lost upon others in the film community. The New Zealand–born Campion had been severely criticized in some quarters for not permitting the mute central character, Ada, to show sufficient motivation for her choice to refrain from speaking, but adhering to her vision made Campion's film a critical and box office favorite. The

Nick Nolte and Barbra Streisand in The Prince of Tides *(1991)* (Movie Graphics)

planned followup project to *The Piano* was an adaptation of Henry James's novella *Portrait of a Lady*.

Penny Marshall was the first woman director whose films earned $100 million. She directed her first feature in 1988, and the success of *Big* fueled her efforts in bringing *A League of Their Own* (1992) to the screen. The film, which starred Geena Davis and Madonna, told the story of professional women baseball players during World War II and drew both male and female audiences of all ages.

Barbra Streisand coproduced and directed *The Prince of Tides* (1991) through her production company, Barwood Films. She told an interviewer in 1995 that she received more offers to direct than to act, and she was offered a number of roles with the stipulation that she must also direct: "It's like directors are frightened of me," she said. In 1996, Streisand returned to the big screen with the romantic movie *The Mirror Has Two Faces*, which earned two Academy Award nominations.

From Jodie Foster's first directorial effort, *Little Man Tate* (1991), she has realized that in order to obtain the needed budget she has had to appear as a star so that backers could feel secure. In *Little Man Tate*, she contrasts the street-savvy, nurturing Dede, who has only love to offer her son, with the woman whose intellect has obscured her capacity for nurturing but who can offer Dede's son the advantages of privi-

Jodie Foster in The Accused *(1988)* (National Film Archive)

lege. In 1994, PolyGram supplied Foster's production company, Egg Pictures, with $100 million to produce *Nell* (1994) and other projects. *Nell* is the story of a girl who has been locked away from civilization since birth. She is a wild creature who has created her own language, unintelligible to other humans. Foster then directed *Home for the Holidays* (1995), starring Holly Hunter.

In 1992, director Penelope Spheeris gained new prominence in Hollywood when *Wayne's World* grossed $122 million and became the biggest moneymaker of any film directed by a woman.

Screenwriter Nora Ephron began directing to preserve the integrity of her scripts. Her directorial debut was *This Is My Life* (1992), a film she cowrote with her sister Delia Ephron. The two continued the partnership with *Sleepless in Seattle* (1993), which Nora Ephron also directed. With her second success as director/writer, Ephron became one of the most powerful women in Hollywood.

Writer/Director Nora Ephron on the set of This is My Life *(1992)* (National Film Institue)

Although she had become disillusioned with Hollywood in the mid-1980s, director Martha Coolidge returned to feature films with *Rambling Rose* (1991), which starred Laura Dern in a story with an underlying feminist message. It concerns a poor girl in 1935 Georgia who confuses promiscuity with love. The surrogate father in her well-off, adoptive family agrees with an unscrupulous doctor that a hysterectomy is the only cure for her sexual behavior. The trick is that "Big Daddy" is fighting his own sexual attraction to Rose. His wife thwarts this classic if corrupt example of male bonding and threatens to ruin them both if they hurt Rose. The unusual subject matter made the film a risk for Coolidge, who acknowledged in a 1986 interview that being a woman meant that she took twenty years to get where a male would have been at the start of his career. She also directed *Crazy in Love* (1991), and the Neil Simon play adaptation *Lost in Yonkers* (1993).

Women filmmakers in the 1990s also made films about subjects not traditionally associated with women. They sought to prove wrong those who claimed that women cannot make the big-budget action movies that bring in the masses of teenage boys who support the industry. Such directors as Lili Zanuck with *Rush* (1991) and Kathryn Bigelow with *Blue Steel* (1990) adopted the blood-and-guts tactics of male directors and used directorial competence to beat the competition with a hearty dose of violence.

Screenwriter Callie Khouri gained prominence in this decade for her screenplay *Thelma & Louise* (1991), an action picture starring Geena Davis and Susan Sarandon that was quickly labeled a "female buddy movie." In essence, *Thelma & Louise* is a Cinderella story. Former rock video producer Khouri won the Academy Award for Best Original Screenplay with her first script. Khouri claimed that she made a conscious effort to counter the Hollywood tendency toward limiting women to playing "bimbos, whores and nagging wives." The film played an important part in helping to open the way for greater change in Hollywood by making it possible for studios to more readily accept movies carried by female leads.

After many years as a screenwriter, Ruth Prawer Jhabvala became a well-known figure in the film industry. The novelist and screenwriter had for many years written most of the films for American director James Ivory and Indian producer Ismail Merchant. In 1986, she won the Academy Award for her adaptation of E. M. Forster's novel *A Room With a View*. In the 1990s, her adaptation of another novel, *Mr. and Mrs. Bridge* (1990), drew high praise. She won her second Academy Award for *Howard's End* (1992), an adaptation of the E. M. Forster novel.

In most decades, the extent of an actress's influence in Hollywood has been in direct proportion to the success of her most recent films. Bankability translates into power, and only a limited number of actresses in the 1990s could generate the kind of box office revenues that would guarantee them first choice among scripts. Although Julia Roberts's personal life interested the media in the early 1990s more than her accomplishments on screen, she soon became one of the few truly bankable actresses of the decade and began to demand her worth. Her first major role was in the quirky and well-received *Mystic Pizza* (1988); then came *Steel Magnolias* (1989), for which she earned an Academy Award nomination for Best Supporting Actress. *Pretty Woman* (1990) made Roberts a household name. The romantic comedy with its artificially created upbeat ending replayed the familiar theme of the hooker with a heart of gold saved by Prince Charming. Her stock in the film industry soared with the success of that film, and she earned an Academy Award nomination for Best Actress. *Pretty Woman* was followed by *Flatliners* (1990), *Sleeping With the Enemy* (1991), *Dying Young* (1991), *Hook* (1991), *The Pelican Brief* (1993), for which she reportedly earned over $8 million, and *I Love Trouble* (1994). By mid-decade, Roberts had become a member of the very elite group of actresses who could command $12 million for a film. Although some of her films did not meet box office expectations, her foray into lighter fare in 1997, in such films as *My Best Friend's Wedding* and *Conspiracy Theory*, seems to have brought audiences back.

By 1995, the estimated box office-gross of Meg Ryan's films was conservatively estimated at $600 million. Not all of her films were hits, but she was lucky with many of her choices. Such films as *Top Gun*

Meg Ryan — Sleepless in Seattle *(1992)* (Movie Graphics)

(1986), *The Presidio* (1988), *The Promised Land* (1988), *When Harry Met Sally . . .* (1989), *The Doors* (1992), *Sleepless in Seattle* (1993), and *When a Man Loves a Woman* (1994) extended her acting range and audience and increased her financial worth to the industry. In common with many actresses in the 1980s and the 1990s, Ryan formed her own production company, Prufrock Productions, and worked to create her own starring vehicles, beginning with a movie about poet Sylvia Plath.

The highly dramatic *Courage Under Fire* (1996) added a new dimension to Ryan's acting, casting her as Medal of Honor nominee.

Winning the Academy Award for Best Actress and the Cannes Film Festival award in the same category in 1993 for her role as the deliberately mute Ada in *The Piano* permitted Holly Hunter great leverage in choosing and rejecting future scripts. Her performance in that movie focused attention on her work and revealed that what some had called "instant success" was more the result of years of perfecting her craft. Hunter electrified audiences in the 1987 *Raising Arizona* and then won an Academy Award nomination for Best Supporting Actress for her role in *Broadcast News* (1987). Although she almost hit a dead end with *Miss Firecracker* (1989) and *Always* (1991), her performance as the ditzy blond secretary in *The Firm* (1993) reminded critics and audiences of her prodigious talent. *The Piano* increased Hunter's influence in the film industry, both because of her fine performance and because of the overall success of the movie. In 1995, she starred in Jodie Foster's *Home for the Holidays*.

Demi Moore became the first actress during the 1990s to command $12 million per picture, and she pushed the limits in other areas as well. She was at first associated with Hollywood's "brat pack" in the early 1980s, and she appeared with many other "pack" members in *St. Elmo's Fire* (1985). She shook the image early, however, and appeared in an impressive list of commercially successful films, many of them controversial. In *Indecent Proposal* (1993), she and her screen husband, Woody Harrelson, are offered $1 million by wealthy businessman Robert Redford if Moore will spend the night with him. Moore accepts the money. The film came under heavy fire from feminists who saw the story line as demeaning to women. In *A Few Good Men* (1993), she played a Marine Corps lawyer, a woman forced to confront the misogynist commanding officer, played by Jack Nicholson, while also observing military decorum. In *Disclosure* (1994) she was at her steamy best as an ambitious corporate executive who sexually harasses a fellow executive, played by Michael Douglas. Moore was wicked and unyielding in the part. In real life, she also became unyielding in regard to the

Demi Moore (Movie Graphics)

film industry, staking out her territory and demanding better scripts and financial arrangements once she had proved her power at the box office. Moore formed her own production company and worked on several movies during the 1990s, including the poorly received *Striptease* (1996). In 1997, Moore took on the daring role of a trailblazer as the the first female Navy Seal in *G.I. Jane*.

Sharon Stone became famous with the release of *Basic Instinct* (1992). Although her seemingly rapid success in the 1990s made her appear to be a newcomer to the film business, Stone had served her time. Among other forgettable films, she appeared with Richard Chamberlain in *King Solomon's Mines* (1985) and its sequel, *Allan Quartermain and the Lost City of Gold* (1987). She followed these with *Action Jackson* (1988). Stone appeared with Richard Gere in *Intersection* (1993) and then with William Baldwin in *Sliver* (1993). All the while she was building her image as a tough negotiator and a woman who would not allow others to ignore her. She also appeared with Sylvester Stallone in *The Specialist* (1994), playing another tough and sexy role. Stone's role as a female gunslinger in *The Quick and the Dead* (1995) with Gene Hackman cemented her strong image, and she became a tough negotiator off screen as well. Her box office drawing power made her a hot film property, and she used that influence in her dealings with studio executives and producers. By the mid-1990s, with film like Martin Scorsese's *Casino*, she was among the few actresses who could call their own shots on the set without having formed their own production companies. Stone received an Academy Award nomination for Best Actress for *Casino* (1995), and she solidified her influence.

The 1990s include other actresses whose influence has been strong, if inconsistent. Whoopi Goldberg won the Academy Award for Best Supporting Actress in *Ghost* (1990), the first African-American woman so honored in fifty-one years, since Hattie MacDaniel won the award in 1939 for her role in *Gone With the Wind*. No newcomer to the screen, Goldberg had already appeared in *The Color Purple* (1985), *Jumpin' Jack Flash* (1986), and *Fatal Beauty* (1987). Following *Ghost*, she starred in *Sister Act* (1992), *Corinna, Corinna* (1993), and *Made in*

America. In 1993, Goldberg was offered $7 million for *Sister Act II*, the highest fee ever paid an actress until Julia Roberts matched the fee for *The Pelican Brief* and Demi Moore later surpassed it for *Disclosure*.

Rosie Perez, a former *Soul Train* dancer, "Fly Girl" choreographer on the television show *In Living Color*, and part-time choreographer for Bobby Brown, LL Cool J, and Heavy D and the Boyz, became a surprise winner at the box office. Feisty and outspoken, Perez had her first role in Spike Lee's *Do the Right Thing* (1989). She developed an audience following with *White Men Can't Jump* (1992), a film in which she played Woody Harrelson's *Jeopardy!*-obsessed girlfriend. She appeared in *Fearless* (1993), then opposite Nicolas Cage in *It Could Happen to You* (1994). Perez, of Puerto Rican heritage, claimed that the roles in *White Men Can't Jump* and *It Could Happen to You* were originally written for "white" actresses. When she auditioned and won the roles, she insisted that they be rewritten. The story may be apocryphal, but she played the roles and the movies were commercially successful. Her ethnic emphasis is a part of Perez's appeal, and that appeal translates into box office dollars. As she has told interviewers, the result of her success is a greater voice for actors of Hispanic background in Hollywood.

With her wisecracking manner and easygoing charm, Rosie O'Donnell has been compared to Joan Blondell, the talented comedy star of the 1940s. The standup comedienne–turned–actress first attracted attention in *A League of Their Own* (1992) as a foil for Madonna. She moved on to play appealing and funny characters in *Sleepless in Seattle* (1993), *Another Stakeout* (1993), *The Flintstones* (1994), and *Exit to Eden* (1994). While not the leading lady, O'Donnell established her reputation as a strong supporting actress, and one whose presence in a film could help influence box office success.

By the middle of the 1990s, Michelle Pfeiffer had made twenty movies and earned three Academy Award nominations, and her influence was strongly felt. She has appeared in such films as *Scarface* (1983), *The Witches of Eastwick* (1987), *Married to the Mob* (1988), *The Fabulous Baker Boys* (1989), and *Batman Returns* (1991). Her performance in *The Age of Innocence* (1993) brought critical acclaim and

Michelle Pfeiffer (Movie Graphicss)

the freedom to select what she would film next. Pfeiffer seemed to have found her niche in later romantic films, such as *One Fine Day* (1996) and *Up Close and Personal* (1996). Audiences enjoyed her chemistry with leading men George Clooney and Robert Redford, respectively.

There are other actresses who have shown substantial promise by the middle of the decade, although none is yet a strong enough presence to be able to "open" a film. Among them are Winona Ryder, Natasha Richardson, Uma Thurman, Emma Thompson, Sarah Jessica Parker, and Kate Winslet. To some extent, they are victims of the popularity of the films in which they have appeared. Kate Winslet has enjoyed recognition for her work in both *Sense and Sensibility* (1995) and *Titanic* (1997) as a nominee for the Academy Awards for Best Actress and Best Supporting Actress, respectively. For Emma Thompson, whose efforts have appeared in most facets of the filmaking art, winning the Academy Award for Best Actress for *Howard's End* (1992) and the award for Best Screenplay Based on Material from Another Medium for *Sense and Sensibility* (1995), as well as receiving a nomination for Best Actress for the same film, provided needed incentive to continue taking chances.

The middle of the decade also brought several well-established actresses back to prominence in the public eye. Susan Sarandon won the Academy Award for Best Actress for her role in *Dead Man Walking* (1995) and Kim Basinger received the award for Best Supporting Actress for *L.A. Confidential* (1997). Audiences also enjoyed a return to the movie screen by Lauren Bacall, nominated for Best Supporting Actress in *The Mirror Has Two Faces* (1996), and Barbara Hershey, who was nominated in the same category for *Portrait of a Lady* (1996).

Julie Christy, who won the Academy Award for Best Actress for *Darling* (1965) was nominated for Best Actress for *Afterglow* (1997). Meryl Streep, who already had an Academy Award for Best Actress for *Sophie's Choice* (1982) and an award for Best Supporting Actress for *Kramer vs. Kramer* (1979), received the nomination for Best Actress for *Bridges of Madison County* (1995).

Epilogue

•

N THE ONE HUNDRED YEARS of the film industry's growth in the
United States, women have exerted varying degrees of influence. At
the outset, actresses wrote, directed, and produced their own work.
The lack of large conglomerates and major industry organizations
meant that no rules existed to limit their power. Often the most
sought-after actress was the one who could be called upon to make
changes in the cast or to direct a scene. Script changes were ongoing,
especially since dialogue in the silent period was minimal; the actors
themselves often made impromptu changes.

With no rules to bind them, silent film stars Florence Lawrence, Mary
Pickford, and others could meet their male counterparts on equal
ground. Once formal structures were established to determine roles and
to set standards, women quickly lost whatever power they had created
for themselves. It has taken eight decades for women to once again
move into roles as studio heads, producers, directors, and other positions
that determine the focus and direction of the film industry. The women
in this book, in every facet of the film industry, have all contributed to
opening the doors to even greater opportunity for all women in film.

Academy Awards for Acting, 1928—1997

•

YEAR	BEST ACTRESS	BEST SUPPORTING ACTRESS
1927–1928	Janet Gaynor *Seventh Heaven*	
1929–1930	Mary Pickford *Coquette*	
1930–1931	Marie Dressler *Min and Bill*	
1931–1932	Helen Hayes *The Sin of Madelon Claudet*	
1932–1933	Katharine Hepburn *Morning Glory*	
1934	Claudette Colbert *It Happened One Night*	
1935	Bette Davis *Dangerous*	
1936	Luise Rainer *The Great Ziegfeld*	Gale Sondergaard *Anthony Adverse*

1937	Luise Rainer	Alice Brady
	The Good Earth	*In Old Chicago*
1938	Bette Davis	Fay Bainter
	Jezebel	*Jezebel*
1939	Vivien Leigh	Hattie McDaniel
	Gone With the Wind	*Gone With the Wind*
1940	Ginger Rogers	Jane Darwell
	Kitty Foyle	*The Grapes of Wrath*
1941	Joan Fontaine	Mary Astor
	Suspicion	*The Great Lie*
1942	Greer Garson	Teresa Wright
	Mrs. Miniver	*Mrs. Miniver*
1943	Jennifer Jones	Katina Paxinou
	The Song of Bernadette	*For Whom the Bell Tolls*
1944	Ingrid Bergman	Ethel Barrymore
	Gaslight	*None But the Lonely Heart*
1945	Joan Crawford	Anne Revere
	Mildred Pierce	*National Velvet*
1946	Olivia de Havilland	Anne Baxter
	To Each His Own	*The Razor's Edge*
1947	Loretta Young	Celeste Holm
	The Farmer's Daughter	*Gentleman's Agreement*
1948	Jane Wyman	Claire Trevor
	Johnny Belinda	*Key Largo*
1949	Olivia de Havilland	Mercedes McCambridge
	The Heiress	*All the King's Men*
1950	Judy Holliday	Josephine Hull
	Born Yesterday	*Harvey*
1951	Vivien Leigh	Kim Hunter
	A Streetcar Named Desire	*A Streetcar Named Desire*
1952	Shirley Booth	Gloria Grahame
	Come Back, Little Sheba	*The Bad and the Beautiful*
1953	Audrey Hepburn	Donna Reed
	Roman Holiday	*From Here to Eternity*

1954	Grace Kelly	Eva Marie Saint
	The Country Girl	*On the Waterfront*
1955	Anna Magnani	Jo Van Fleet
	The Rose Tattoo	*East of Eden*
1956	Ingrid Bergman	Dorothy Malone
	Anastasia	*Written on the Wind*
1957	Joanne Woodward	Miyoshi Umeki
	The Three Faces of Eve	*Sayonara*
1958	Susan Hayward	Wendy Hiller
	I Want to Live	*Separate Tables*
1959	Simone Signoret	Shelley Winters
	Room at the Top	*The Diary of Anne Frank*
1960	Elizabeth Taylor	Shirley Jones
	Butterfield 8	*Elmer Gantry*
1961	Sophia Loren	Rita Moreno
	Two Women	*West Side Story*
1962	Anne Bancroft	Patty Duke
	The Miracle Worker	*The Miracle Worker*
1963	Patricia Neal	Margaret Rutherford
	Hud	*The V.I.P.s*
1964	Julie Andrews	Lila Kedrova
	Mary Poppins	*Zorba the Greek*
1965	Julie Christie	Shelley Winters
	Darling	*A Patch of Blue*
1966	Elizabeth Taylor	Sandy Dennis
	Who's Afraid of Virginia Woolf?	*Who's Afraid of Virginia Woolf?*
1967	Katharine Hepburn	Estelle Parsons
	Guess Who's Coming to Dinner	*Bonnie and Clyde*
1968	Katharine Hepburn	Ruth Gordon
	The Lion in Winter	*Rosemary's Baby*
	tied with	

	Barbra Streisand *Funny Girl*	
1969	Maggie Smith *The Prime of Miss Jean Brodie*	Goldie Hawn *Cactus Flower*
1970	Glenda Jackson *Women in Love*	Helen Hayes *Airport*
1971	Jane Fonda *Klute*	Cloris Leachman *The Last Picture Show*
1972	Liza Minnelli *Cabaret*	Eileen Heckart *Butterflies Are Free*
1973	Glenda Jackson *A Touch of Class*	Tatum O'Neal *Paper Moon*
1974	Ellen Burstyn *Alice Doesn't Live Here Anymore*	Ingrid Bergman *Murder on the Orient Express*
1975	Louise Fletcher *One Flew Over the Cuckoo's Nest*	Lee Grant *Shampoo*
1976	Faye Dunaway *Network*	Beatrice Straight *Network*
1977	Diane Keaton *Annie Hall*	Vanessa Redgrave *Julia*
1978	Jane Fonda *Coming Home*	Maggie Smith *California Suite*
1979	Sally Field *Norma Rae*	Meryl Streep *Kramer vs. Kramer*
1980	Sissy Spacek *Coal Miner's Daughter*	Mary Steenburgen *Melvin & Howard*
1981	Katharine Hepburn *On Golden Pond*	Maureen Stapleton *Reds*
1982	Meryl Streep *Sophie's Choice*	Jessica Lange *Tootsie*

1983	Shirley MacLaine	Linda Hunt
	Terms of Endearment	*The Year of Living Dangerously*
1984	Sally Field	Peggy Ashcroft
	Places in the Heart	*A Passage to India*
1985	Geraldine Page	Anjelica Huston
	The Trip to Bountiful	*Prizzi's Honor*
1986	Marlee Matlin	Dianne Wiest
	Children of a Lesser God	*Hannah and Her Sisters*
1987	Cher	Olympia Dukakis
	Moonstruck	*Moonstruck*
1988	Jodie Foster	Geena Davis
	The Accused	*The Accidental Tourist*
1989	Jessica Tandy	Brenda Fricker
	Driving Miss Daisy	*My Left Foot*
1990	Kathy Bates	Whoopi Goldberg
	Misery	*Ghost*
1991	Jodie Foster	Mercedes Ruehl
	The Silence of the Lambs	*The Fisher King*
1992	Emma Thompson	Marisa Tomei
	Howards End	*My Cousin Vinny*
1993	Holly Hunter	Anna Paquin
	The Piano	*The Piano*
1994	Jessica Lange	Dianne Wiest
	Blue Sky	*Bullets Over Broadway*
1995	Susan Sarandon	Mira Sorvino
	Dead Man Walking	*Mighty Aphrodite*
1996	Frances McDormand	Juliette Binoche
	Fargo	*The English Patient*
1997	Helen Hunt	Kim Basinger
	As Good As It Gets	*L.A. Confidential*

Academy Awards in Other Categories

•

YEAR	WRITING[1]
1929–30	Achievement: Frances Marion, *The Big House*
1931–32	Original Story: Frances Marion, *The Champ*
1938	Original Story: Eleanore Griffin,[2] *Boys Town*
1942	Original Screenplay: Claudine West,[2] *Mrs. Miniver*
1946	Original Screenplay: Muriel Box,[2] *The Seventh Veil*
1950	Story and Screenplay: Edna Anhalt,[2] *Panic in the Streets*
1955	Story and Screenplay: Sonya Levien,[2] *Love Me or Leave Me*
1978	Screenplay, Written Directly for the Screen: Nancy Dowd, *Coming Home*
1985	Original Story: Pamela Wallace,[2] *Witness*
1986	Screenplay Adaptation: Ruth Prawer Jhabvala, *A Room With a View*
1991	Original Screenplay: Callie Khouri, *Thelma & Louise*
1992	Screenplay Adaptation: Ruth Prawer Jhabvala, *Howards End*
1993	Original Screenplay: Jane Campion, *The Piano*

| 1995 | Screenplay adaptation: Emma Thompson, *Sense and Sensibility* |

YEAR	FILM EDITING[3]
1940	Anne Bauchens, *North West Mounted Police*
1944	Barbara McLean, *Wilson*
1958	Adrienne Fazan, *Gigi*
1975	Verna Fields, *Jaws*
1977	Marcia Lucas,[2] *Star Wars*
1980	Thelma Schoonmaker, *Raging Bull*
1983	Lisa Fruchman,[2] *The Right Stuff*
1986	Claire Simpson, *Platoon*
1987	Gabriella Cristian, *The Last Emperor*

YEAR	COSTUME DESIGN[4]
1948	COLOR: Dorothy Jeakins and Karinska, *Joan of Arc*
1949	BLACK & WHITE: Edith Head,[2] *The Heiress*
	COLOR: Marjorie Best and Leah Rhodes,[2] *Adventures of Don Juan*
1950	BLACK & WHITE: Edith Head,[2] *All About Eve*
	COLOR: Edith Head, Dorothy Jeakins, Elois Jenssen, Gwen Wakeling,[2] *Samson and Delilah*
1951	BLACK & WHITE: Edith Head, A *Place in the Sun*
	COLOR: Irene Sharaff,[2] *An American in Paris*
1952	BLACK & WHITE: Helen Rose, *The Bad and the Beautiful*
1953	BLACK & WHITE: Edith Head, *Roman Holiday*
1954	BLACK & WHITE: Edith Head, *Sabrina*
1955	BLACK & WHITE: Helen Rose, *I'll Cry Tomorrow*
1956	COLOR: Irene Sharaff, *The King and I*
1959	COLOR: Elizabeth Haffenden, *Ben-Hur*
1960	BLACK & WHITE: Edith Head,[2] *The Facts of Life*
1961	COLOR: Irene Sharaff, *West Side Story*
1962	COLOR: Mary Wills, *The Wonderful World of the*

Brothers Grimm

1964   BLACK & WHITE: Dorothy Jeakins, *The Night of the Iguana*

1965   BLACK & WHITE: Julie Harris, *Darling*
        COLOR: Phyllis Dalton, *Doctor Zhivago*

1966   BLACK & WHITE: Irene Sharaff, *Who's Afraid of Virginia Woolf?*
        COLOR: Elizabeth Haffenden and Joan Bridge, *A Man for All Seasons*

1969   Margaret Furse, *Anne of a Thousand Days*

1971   Yvonne Blake,[2] *Nicholas and Alexandra*

1973   Edith Head, *The Sting*

1974   Theoni V. Aldredge, *The Great Gatsby*

1975   Ulla-Britt Soderlund and Milena Canonero, *Barry Lyndon*

1981   Milena Canonero, *Chariots of Fire*

1986   Jenny Beaven,[2] *A Room With a View*

1989   Phyllis Dalton, *Henry V*

1990   Franca Squaricapino, *Cyrano de Bergerac*

1993   Gabriella Pescucci, *The Age of Innocence*

1994   Lizzy Gardiner,[2] *The Adventures of Priscilla, Queen of the Desert*

1996   Ann Roth, *The English Patient*

1997   Deborah Lynn Scott, *Titanic*

YEAR	ART DIRECTION/SET DECORATION[5]
1960	Julia Heron,[2] *Spartacus*
1983	Anna Asp, Susanne Lingheim, *Fanny and Alexander*
1984	Patrizia von Bradenstein, Karel Cerny, *Amadeus*
1985	Josie MacAvin,[2] *Out of Africa*
1991	Nancy Haigh,[2] *Bugsy*
1992	Luciana Arrighi,[2] *Howards End*
1993	Ewa Braun,[2] *Schindler's List*
1994	Carolyn Scott,[2] *The Madness of King George*

1996   Stephanie Miller,[2] *The English Patient*

YEAR	PRODUCER, BEST PICTURE
1973	Julia Phillips,[2] *The Sting*
1989	Lili Fini Zanuck,[2] *Driving Miss Daisy*
1994	Wendy Finerman,[2] *Forrest Gump*

[1] The changing category titles reflect changes made by the Academy over the years.

[2] Indicates that the writer shared the award with one or more male collaborators.

[3] The Academy added the Film Editing category in 1934.

[4] The Academy added the Costume Design category in 1948.

[5] The Academy added the Interior Decoration category in 1937, then changed the designation to Art Direction/Set Decoration in 1947.

Top Moneymaking Female Stars, 1933—1992*

•

YEAR	THE RANK OF FEMALE STARS AMONG THE TOP TEN MONEYMAKERS
1933	Marie Dressler (1), Janet Gaynor (2), Jean Harlow (6), Mae West (8), Norma Shearer (9), Joan Crawford (10)
1934	Janet Gaynor (3), Mae West (5), Joan Crawford (7), Shirley Temple (8), Marie Dressler (9), Norma Shearer (10)
1935	Shirley Temple (1), Ginger Rogers (with Fred Astaire) (4), Joan Crawford (5), Claudette Colbert (6)
1936	Shirley Temple (1), Ginger Rogers (with Fred Astaire) (4), Joan Crawford (7), Claudette Colbert (8), Jeanette MacDonald (9)
1937	Shirley Temple (1), Jane Withers (6), Ginger Rogers (with Fred Astaire) (7), Sonja Henie (8), Myrna Loy (10)
1938	Shirley Temple (1), Sonja Henie (3), Myrna Loy (7), Jane Withers (8), Alice Faye (9)
1939	Shirley Temple (5), Bette Davis (6), Alice Faye (7), Sonja Henie (10)
1940	Bette Davis (9), Judy Garland (10)
1941	Bette Davis (8)

1942   Betty Grable (8), Greer Garson (9)

1943   Betty Grable (1), Greer Garson (6)

1944   Betty Grable (4), Greer Garson (6), Bette Davis (10)

1945   Greer Garson (3), Betty Grable (4), Margaret O'Brien (9)

1946   Ingrid Bergman (20), Greer Garson (7), Margaret O'Brien (8), Betty Grable (9)

1947   Betty Grable (2), Ingrid Bergman (3), Claudette Colbert (9)

1948   Betty Grable (2), Ingrid Bergman (10)

1949   Betty Grable (7), Esther Williams (8)

1950   Betty Grable (4), Esther Williams (8)

1951   Betty Grable (3), Doris Day (9)

1952   Doris Day (7), Susan Hayward (9)

1953   Marilyn Monroe (6), Susan Hayward (9)

1954   Marilyn Monroe (5), Jane Wyman (9)

1955   Grace Kelly (2), June Allyson (9)

1956   Marilyn Monroe (8), Kim Novak (9)

1957   None

1958   Elizabeth Taylor (2), Brigitte Bardot (7)

1959   Doris Day (4), Debbie Reynolds (5), Susan Hayward (10)

1960   Doris Day (1), Elizabeth Taylor (4), Debbie Reynolds (5), Sandra Dee (7)

1961   Elizabeth Taylor (1), Doris Day (3), Sandra Dee (6)

1962   Doris Day (1), Elizabeth Taylor (6), Sandra Dee (9)

1963   Doris Day (1), Elizabeth Taylor (6), Sandra Dee (8)

1964   Doris Day (1), Shirley MacLaine (7), Ann-Margret (8)

1965   Doris Day (3), Julie Andrews (4), Elizabeth Taylor (9)

1966   Julie Andrews (1), Elizabeth Taylor (3), Doris Day (8)

1967   Julie Andrews (1), Elizabeth Taylor (6)

1968   Julie Andrews (3), Elizabeth Taylor (10)

1969   Katharine Hepburn (9), Barbra Streisand (10)

1970   Barbra Streisand (9)

1971   Ali MacGraw (8)

1972   Barbra Streisand (5), Goldie Hawn (10)

1973   Barbra Streisand (6)

1974   Barbra Streisand (4)

1975   Barbra Streisand (2)

1976   Tatum O'Neal (8)

1977   Barbra Streisand (2), Diane Keaton (9)

1978   Diane Keaton (7), Jane Fonda (8), Barbra Streisand (10)

1979   Jane Fonda (4), Barbra Streisand (5), Jill Clayburgh (8)

1980   Jane Fonda (4), Sally Field (7), Sissy Spacek (8),
        Barbra Streisand (9)

1981   Dolly Parton (4), Jane Fonda (5), Bo Derek (8),
        Goldie Hawn (9)

1982   Dolly Parton (6), Jane Fonda (7)

1983   None

1984   Sally Field (5), Meryl Streep (10)

1985   Meryl Streep (10)

1986   Bette Midler (5)

1987   Glenn Close (7), Cher (9)

1988   Bette Midler (7)

1989   Kathleen Turner (10)

1990   Julia Roberts (2)

1991   Julia Roberts (4), Jodie Foster (6)

1992   Whoopi Goldberg (6)

*Years for which figures are currently available.

Select Bibliography

•

Acker, Ally. "Lois Weber." *Ms.*, February 1988, pp. 66–67.

Acker, A. *Reel Women: Pioneers of the Cinema*. New York: B. T. Batsford, 1991.

Allen, Robert C., and Dennis Gomery. *Film History: Theory and Practice*. New York: Alfred A. Knopf, 1985.

Anger, Kenneth. *Hollywood Babylon*. New York: Bell Publishing Co., 1975.

Ann-Margret with Todd Gold. *Ann-Margret: My Story*. New York: G. P. Putnam's Sons, 1994.

Arvidson, Linda. *When the Movies Were Young*. New York: Dover Publications, 1969.

Aylesworth, Thomas G. *Broadway to Hollywood*. New York: Gallery Books, 1975.

Balio, Tina, ed. *The American Film Industry*. Rev. ed. Madison: University of Wisconsin Press, 1985.

Balshofer, Fred J., and Arthur C. Miller. *One Reel a Week*. Berkeley: University of California Press, 1967.

Basinger, Jeanine. *A Woman's View: How Hollywood Spoke to Women, 1934–1960*. New York: Alfred A. Knopf, 1993.

Battrock, Gregory. *The New American Cinema*. New York: E. P. Dutton, 1967.

Baxter, John. *Hollywood in the Thirties*. New York: A. S. Barnes & Co., 1968.

_____. *Hollywood in the Sixties*. Cranbury, N.J.: A. S. Barnes & Co., 1971.

Behlmer, Rudy, ed. *Inside Warner Bros., 1935–1951*. New York: Simon & Schuster, 1987.

Behlmer, Rudy, and Tony Thomas. *Hollywood's Hollywood*. Secaucus, N.J.: Citadel Press, 1975.

Bellone, Julius, ed. *Renaissance of the Film*. New York: Macmillan, 1970.

Bluem, A. William. *The Movie Business: American Film Industry Practice*. New York: Hastings House Publishers, 1972.

Bookbinder, Robert. *The Films of the Seventies.* Secaucus, N.J.: Citadel Press, 1982.

Bordwell, David, Janet Staiger, and Kristin Thompson. *The Classical Hollywood Cinema: Film Style and Mode of Production to 1960.* London: Routledge & Kegan Paul, 1985.

Brode, Douglas. *The Films of the Sixties.* Secaucus, N.J.: Citadel Press, 1980.

Bruno, Michael. *Venus in Hollywood: The Continental Enchantress from Garbo to Loren.* New York: Lyle Stuart, 1970.

Cantwell, Mary. "Jane Campion's Lunatic Women." *New York Times Magazine,* September 19, 1993, pp. 40–45.

Card, James. *Seductive Cinema: The Art of the Silent Film.* New York: Alfred A. Knopf, 1994.

Ceplair, Larry, and Steven Englund. *The Inquisition in Hollywood: Politics in the Film Industry, 1930–1960.* Berkeley: University of California Press, 1979.

Chierichetti, David. *Hollywood Costume Design.* New York: Harmony Books, 1976.

Clark, Randall, ed. *Dictionary of Literary Biography.* Vol. 44. *American Screenwriters, Second Series.* Detroit: Gale Research Co., 1986.

Cohen, Daniel, and Susan Cohen. *Encyclopedia of Movie Stars.* New York: Gallery Books, 1984.

Corliss, Richard. *Greta Garbo.* New York: Pyramid Publications, 1974.

_____. *Talking Pictures: Screenwriters in the American Cinema.* New York: Penguin Books, 1974.

Coursodon, Jean-Pierre, with Pierre Sauvage. *American Directors.* Vol. 1. New York: McGraw-Hill, 1983.

_____. *American Directors.* Vol. 2. New York: McGraw-Hill, 1983.

Cross, Robin. *The Big Book of B Movies.* New York: St. Martin's Press, 1981.

Darin, Dodd. *Dreamlovers: The Magnificent Shattered Lives of Bobby Darin and Sandra Dee.* New York: Warner Books, 1994.

Davies, Marion. *The Times We Had: Life With William Randolph Hearst.* New York: Bobbs-Merrill, 1975.

Dick, Bernard. *The Star Spangled Screen: The American World War Two Film.* Lexington: University of Kentucky Press, 1985.

Dick, Bernard F. *Hellman in Hollywood.* Rutherford, N.J.: Fairleigh Dickinson University Press, 1982.

Doane, Mary Ann, Patricia Mellencamp, and Linda Williams, eds. *Re-Vision: Essays in Feminist Film Criticism.* Los Angeles: American Film Institute, 1984.

Dowdy, Andrew. *The Films of the Fifties: The American State of Mind.* New York: William Morrow and Company, 1973.

Drew, William M. *Speaking of Silents: First Ladies of the Screen.* Vestal, N.Y.: The Vestal Press, Ltd., 1989.

Durgnat, Raymond. *Films and Feelings.* Cambridge, Mass.: The MIT Press, 1971.

Dyer, Richard. *The Stars.* London: British Film Institute, 1979.

Eames, John Douglas. *The MGM Story.* New York: Crown Publishers, 1976.

_____. *The Paramount Story.* New York: Crown Publishers, 1985.

Ellis, Jack C. *A History of Film.* Englewood Cliffs, N.J.: Prentice-Hall, 1979.

Erens, Patricia, ed. *Sexual Strategies: The World of Women in Film.* New York: Horizon Press, 1979.

Everson, William K. *The American Movie.* New York: Atheneum Press, 1963.

_____. *American Silent Film.* New York: Oxford University Press, 1978.

Fell, John L. *Film Before Griffith.* Berkeley: University of California Press, 1983.

Fenton, J. R. *Women Writers: From Page to Screen*. New York: Garland Publishing, 1990.

Finler, Joel W. *The Hollywood Story*. New York: Crown Publishers, 1988.

Flora, Paul. *Vivat Vamp*. London: Dobson Books, Ltd., 1965.

Foreman, A. *Women in Motion*. Bowling Green, Ohio: Bowling Green University Popular Press, 1983.

Franklin, Joe. *Classics of the Silent Screen*. Secaucus, N.J.: Citadel Press, 1959.

French, Brandon. *On the Verge of Revolt: Women in American Films of the Fifties*. New York: Frederick Unger, 1978.

Gallico, Paul. *The Revealing Eye: Personalities of the 1920s*. New York: Atheneum, 1967.

Gehring, Wes D. *Screwball Comedy*. Westport, Conn.: Greenwood Press, 1986.

Giannetti, Louis. *Masters of the American Cinema*. Englewood Cliffs, N.J.: Prentice-Hall, 1987.

Gish, Lillian. *The Movies, Mr. Griffith, and Me*. Englewood Cliffs, N.J.: Prentice-Hall, 1969.

Gledhill, Christine, ed. *Stardom, Industry of Desire*. New York: Routledge, 1991.

Goldman, W. *Adventures in the Screen Trade*. New York: Warner Books, 1983.

Gomery, Douglas. *The Hollywood Studio System*. New York: Macmillan, 1986.

_____. *Shared Pleasures: A History of Movie Presentation in the United States*. Madison: University of Wisconsin Press, 1992.

Goodman, Ezra. *The Fifty Year Decline and Fall of Hollywood*. New York: Simon & Schuster, 1961.

Griffith, Richard. *The Movie Stars*. New York: Doubleday and Company, 1970.

Griffith, Richard, and Arthur Mayer. *The Movies*. New York: Simon & Schuster, 1970.

Hamilton, Ian. *Writers in Hollywood, 1915–1951*. New York: Harper & Row, 1990.

Hampton, Benjamin B. *History of the American Film Industry: From Its Beginnings to 1931*. New York: Dover Publications, 1970.

Haskell, Molly. *From Reverence to Rape: The Treatment of Women in the Movies*. New York: Holt, Rinehart and Winston, 1974.

Heck-Rabi, Louise. *Women Filmmakers: A Critical Reception*. Metuchen, N.J.: Scarecrow Press, 1984.

Hendricks, Gordon. *Origins of the American Film*. New York: Arno Press, 1972.

Higham, Charles. *The Art of the American Film, 1900–1971*. Garden City, N.Y.: Doubleday & Co., 1973.

Higham, Charles, and Joel Greenberg. *The Celluloid Muse: Hollywood Directors Speak*. New York: Signet Books, 1972.

_____. *Hollywood in the Forties*. New York: Paperback Library, 1970.

Hirsch, Foster. *The Hollywood Epic*. San Diego: A. S. Barnes & Co., 1978.

Hudson, Richard. *60 Years of Vamps and Camps*. New York: Drake, 1973.

Isenberg, Michael T. *War on Film: The American Cinema and World War I, 1914–1941*. Rutherford, N.J.: Associated University Presses, Fairleigh Dickinson University Press, 1981.

Israel, Lee. "Women in Film: Saving an Endangered Species." *Ms.* (February 1975), pp. 51–7, 104.

Izod, John. *Hollywood and the Box Office, 1895–1986*. New York: Macmillan, 1988.

Jacobs, Lewis. *The Emergence of Film Art*. New York: Hopkinson and Blake, 1969.

_____. *The Rise of the American Film: A Critical History*. New York: Teachers College Press, 1968.

Jewell, Richard B. *The RKO Story*. New York: Arlington House, 1982.

Johnson, Claire, ed. *Dorothy Arzner: Towards a Feminist Cinema*. London: British Film Institute, 1975.

_____. *Notes on Women's Cinema*. London: Society for Education in Film and Television, 1973.

Jowett, Garth. *Film: The Democratic Art*. Boston: Little, Brown and Company, 1976.

Kaplan, E. Ann. *Women and Film*. New York: Methuen and Company, Inc., 1983.

Katz, Ephraim. *The Film Encyclopedia*. New York: Perigee Press, 1982.

Kay, Karyn, and Gerald Peary, eds. *Women and the Cinema: A Critical Anthology*. New York: E. P. Dutton, 1977.

Klein, Carole. *Gramercy Park: An American Bloomsbury*. Athens: Ohio University Press, 1967.

Kolker, Robert Phillip. *A Cinema of Loneliness*. New York: Oxford University Press, 1980.

Koszarski, Richard. *Hollywood Directors, 1914–1940*. New York: Oxford University Press, 1976.

Kuhn, Annette. *Women's Pictures: Feminism and Cinema*. London: Routledge & Kegan Paul, 1982.

Kuhn, Annette, and Susannah Radstone, eds. *Women in Film: An International Guide*. New York: Fawcett Columbine, 1990.

Kuhns, William. *Movies in America*. Dayton, Ohio: Pflaum/Standard, 1972.

Langman, L. *A Guide to American Screenwriters: The Sound Era, 1929–82*. New York: Garland Publishing, 1984.

Lavine, W. Robert. *In a Glamorous Fashion: The Fabulous Years of Hollywood Costume Design*. New York: Charles Scribner's Sons, 1980.

Lawton, Richard. *A World of Movies: 70 Years of Film History*. New York: Dell, 1974.

Leary, Liam. *The Silent Cinema*. New York: E. P. Dutton, 1965.

Leese, Elizabeth. *Costume Design in the Movies*. New York: Frederick Ungar and Company, 1977.

Leff, L. J., and J. L. Simmons. *The Dame in the Kimono: Hollywood Censorship and the Production Code from the 1920s to 1960s*. London: Weidenfeld and Nicolson, 1990.

Lenburg, Jeff. *Peekaboo: The Story of Veronica Lake*. New York: St. Martin's Press, 1983.

Macgowan, Kenneth. *Behind the Screen*. New York: Delta Books, 1965.

Madsen, Axel. *The New Hollywood*. New York: Thomas Y. Crowell Company, 1975.

Maltin, Leonard. *Behind the Camera*. New York: Signet Books, 1971.

Manchel, Frank. *Women on the Hollywood Screen*. New York: Franklin Watts, 1977.

Mann, May, *Jayne Mansfield: A Biography*. New York: Drake Publishers, 1973.

Manvell, Roger. *Love Goddesses of the Movies*. New York: Paul Hamlyn Books, 1975.

_____. *New Cinema in the USA*. New York: E. P. Dutton, 1968.

Marion, Frances. *Off With Their Heads! A Serio-Comic Tale of Hollywood*. New York: Macmillan, 1972.

Martin, A., and V. Clark, eds. *What Women Wrote: Scenarios, 1912–1929*. University Publications of America–Cinema History Microfilm Series, 1987.

Mast, Gerald. *A Short History of the Movies*. 4th ed. New York: Macmillan, 1986.

Mayer, Michael F. *The Film Industries*. New York: Hastings House, 1978.

Mayne, Judith. *Directed by Dorothy Arzner*. Indianapolis: Indiana University Press, 1994.

McBride, Joseph, ed. *Film Makers on Film Making*. Vols. 1 & 2. New York: Jeremy P. Tarcher, Inc., 1983.

McClelland, Doug. *The Unkindest Cuts: Scissors and the Cinema*. New York: A. S. Barnes and Co., 1972.

McCreadie, Marsha. *Women on Film: The Critical Eye*. New York: Praeger Publishing, 1983.

McGilligan, P. *Backstory: Interviews with Screenwriters of Hollywood's Golden Age*. Berkeley and Los Angeles: University of California Press, 1986.

_____. *Backstory: Interviews with Screenwriters of the the 1940s and 1950s*. Berkeley and Los Angeles: University of California Press, 1991.

Mellen, Joan. *Women and Their Sexuality in the New Film*. New York: Horizon Press, 1973.

Michael, Paul. *The Academy Awards: A Pictorial History*. 5th ed. New York: Crown Publishers, 1982.

Monaco, James. *American Film Now: The People, the Power, the Money, the Movies*. New York: Oxford University Press, 1979.

Mordden, Ethan. *The Hollywood Musical*. New York: St. Martin's Press, 1981.

_____. *Movie Star: A Look at the Women Who Made Hollywood*. New York: St. Martin's Press, 1983.

Morris, Michael. *Madame Valentino: The Many Lives of Natacha Rambova*. New York: Abbeville Publishing, 1990.

Munden, Kenneth, ed. *The American Film Institute Catalog: Feature Films, 1921–1930*. 2 vols. New York: R. R. Bowker, 1971.

Musser, Charles. *The Emergence of Cinema, the American Screen to 1907*. Vol. 1 of *The History of the American Cinema*. Edited by Charles Harpole. New York: Charles Scribner's Sons, 1990.

Norman, Barry. *The Hollywood Greats*. New York: Franklin Watts, 1980.

O'Leary, Liam. *The Silent Cinema*. New York: E. P. Dutton, 1970.

Palmer, Robert. "Suddenly Julia." *American Film*, July 1990, pp. 21–25, 46.

Phillips, Gene D. *The Movie Makers*. Chicago: Nelson-Hall Company, 1973.

Phillips, Julia. *You'll Never Eat Lunch in This Town Again*. New York: Random House, 1991.

Platt, Frank C. *Great Stars of Hollywood's Golden Age*. New York: New American Library, 1966.

Pratt, George C. *Spellbound in Darkness: A History of the Silent Film*. Greenwich, Conn.: New York Graphic Society, Ltd., 1966.

Pye, Michael, and Linda Miles. *The Movie Brats: How the Film Generation Took Over Hollywood*. New York: Holt, Rinehart and Winston, 1979.

Rhode, Eric. *A History of the Cinema: From Its Origins to 1970*. New York: Hill and Wang, Publishers, 1976.

Robinson, David. *Hollywood in the Twenties*. London: Tantivy Press, in association with A. Zwemmer, Ltd., and A. S. Barnes & Co., 1968.

Rosen, Michael. *Popcorn Venus: Women, Movies and the American Dream*. New York: Coward, McCann and Geoghegan, 1973.

Sands, Pierre N. *A Historical Study of the Academy of Motion Picture Arts and Sciences (1927–1947)*. New York: Arno Press, 1973.

Sarris, Andrew. *The American Cinema: Directors and Direction 1929–1968*. New York: E. P. Dutton, 1968.

Schatz, Thomas. *The Genius of the System: Hollywood Filmmaking in the Studio Era*. New York: Pantheon Books, 1988.

Schwartz, Nancy Lynn. *The Hollywood Writers' Wars*. Completed by Sheila Schwartz. New York: Alfred A. Knopf, 1982.

Scott, E. F. *Hollywood: When the Silents Were Golden*. New York: McGraw-Hill, 1972.

Sennett, Ted. *Great Movie Directors*. New York: Harry N. Abrams, Inc., 1986.

Sessums, Kevin. "Jessica's Heart: Jessica Lange Talks About Beauty, Love and Madness." *Vanity Fair*, March 1995, pp. 146–52, 188+.

Shadoian, Jack. *Dreams and Dead Ends: The American Gangster/Crime Film*. Cambridge, Mass.: The MIT Press, 1977.

Shales, Tom. *Legends: Remembering America's Greatest Stars*. New York: Random House, 1989.

Sharistanian, Janet. "Tess Slesinger's Hollywood Sketches." *Michigan Quarterly Review*, 18 (Summer 1979): 433.

Shipman, David. *The Great Movie Stars*. New York: Bonanza Books, 1970.

Shnayerson, Michael. "Barbra Streisand: The Way She Is." *Vanity Fair*, November 1994, pp. 150–59, 190+.

Sikov, Ed. *Screwball: America's Madcap Romantic Comedy*. New York: Columbia University Press, 1989.

Silver, Alain, and Elizabeth Ward, eds. *Film Noir: An Encyclopedic Reference to the American Style*. Woodstock, N.Y.: Overlook Press, 1979.

Singer, Michael, ed. *Film Directors: A Complete Guide*. Beverly Hills, Calif.: Lone Eagle Publishing Co., 1988.

Sklar, Robert. *Movie-Made America: A Social History of Movies*. New York: Random House, 1975.

Slide, Anthony. *Early Women Directors*. Cranbury & Co., N.J.: A. S. Barnes & Co., 1977.

_____. *The Griffith Actresses*. New York: A. S. Barnes & Co., 1977.

Smith, Sharon. *Women Who Make Movies*. New York: Hopkinson and Blake, 1975.

Spehr, Paul C. *The Movies Begin: Making Movies in New Jersey, 1887–1920*. Newark, N.J.: The Newark Museum, 1977.

Stanley, Robert H. *The Celluloid Empire: A History of the American Movie Industry*. New York: Hastings House, 1978.

Stern, Lee Edward. *The Movie Musical*. New York: Pyramid Publications, 1974.

Stine, Whitney. *Star and Star Handlers*. Los Angeles: Roundtable Publishing, Inc., 1985.

Sullivan, Kaye, ed. *Films for, by, and About Women*. Metuchen, N.J.: Scarecrow Press, 1980.

Sumiko, Higashi. *Virgins, Vamps, and Flappers: The American Silent Movie Heroine*. Montreal: Eden Press, 1978.

Talbot, Donald, ed. *Film: An Anthology*. Berkeley: University of California Press, 1969.

Taylor, John Russell. *Strangers in Paradise: The Hollywood Emigrés, 1933–1950*. New York: Holt, Rinehart and Winston, 1983.

Todd, Janet, ed. *Women and Film*. New York: Holmes and Meier, 1988.

Trent, Paul. *Those Fabulous Movie Years: The 30s*. Barre, Mass.: Barre Publishing, 1975.

Tyler, Parker. *Magic and the Myth of the Movies*. New York: Simon & Schuster, 1970.

Udovitch, Mim. "Demi Moore = Sex." *Rolling Stone*, February 9, 1995, pp. 38–41, 67.

Van Meier, Jonathan. "Kim Up Close." *Vogue*, May 1991, pp. 256–60, 320+.

Wagenknecht, Edward. *Movies in the Age of Innocence*. Norman: Oklahoma University Press, 1962.

Wasko, Janet, ed. *Hollywood in the Age of Television*. Boston: Unwin Hyman, Inc., 1990.

Weinraub, Bernard. "She's Young and Smart, But Not Too Smart to Lead." *New York Times*, April 4, 1994, p. C13.

_____. "A Woman Making Movies for Men." *New York Times*, May 3, 1994, p. C15.

Weltman, Manuel, and Raymond Lee. *Pearl White: The Peerless, Fearless Girl*. New York: A. S. Barnes & Co., 1970.

Whittemore, Don, and Philip Alan Cecchettini. *Passport to Hollywood*. New York: McGraw-Hill, 1976.

Wiley, Mason, and Damien Bona. *Inside Oscar: The Unofficial History of the Academy Awards*. New York: Ballantine Books, 1986.

Windeler, Robert. *Sweetheart: The Story of Mary Pickford*. New York: Praeger Publishing, 1973.

Zehme, Bill. "Is Sharon Stone Scaring You Yet?" *Esquire*, March 1995, pp. 84–91.

●

Adams, Catlin, 174
Adrian, 57, 84
Akins, Zoë, 47-49
Aldredge, Theoni V., 158, 205
Aldrich, Robert, 94
Allen, Dede, xiii, 156, 175
Allen, Gracie, 145
Allen, Jay Presson, 154-155
Allen, Woody, 156, 161
Allyson, June, 121, 208
Andrews, Julie, 142, 148-149, 200, 208
Anhalt, Edna, 203
Ann-Margret, 137, 142, 145-146, 208
Arbuckle, Roscoe "Fatty," 17
Arlen, Alice, 175
Armstrong, Gillian, 173-174
Arnaz, Desi, 119-120
Arrighi, Luciana, 205
Arthur, Jean, 37
Arzner, Dorothy, xii, 34, 35, 39, 42, 48-49, 52, 54, 92, 109
Ashcroft, Peggy, 202
Asp, Anna, 205
Asseyev, Tamara, 153
Astaire, Fred, 98-100, 149, 207
Astor, Mary, 36, 37, 69-70, 199

Bacall, Lauren, 86, 91, 196
Bainter, Fay, 199
Baker, Carroll, 124, 128
Baldwin, Alec, 178
Baldwin, William, 193
Ball, Lucille, 105, 119-120
Bancroft, Anne, 154, 200
Bankhead, Tallulah, 4, 22
Bara, Theda, 4, 21-23, 26
Bardot, Brigitte, 208
Barr, Roseanne, 178
Barry, Phillip, 94
Barrymore, Ethel, 4, 22, 47, 199
Barrymore, John, 36, 62, 70, 71
Basinger, Kim, 178, 196, 202
Bates, Kathy, 202
Bauchens, Anne, xii, 11, 13, 84, 113, 204
Baxter, Anne, 199
Beardsley, Aubrey, 42
Beattie, Ann, 157
Beatty, Warren, 96, 156, 157, 162
Beaven, Jenny, 205
Belasco, David, 14
Bening, Annette, 96

Bennett, Constance, 108
Bennett, Joan, 86
Benson, Sally, 76, 83
Beranger, Clair, 7
Bergman, Ingrid, 101-103, 108, 199-201, 208
Berle, Milton, 90
Berlin, Irving, 72
Bern, Paul, 59-60
Bernstein, Carl, 175
Best, Marjorie, 85, 204
Bigelow, Kathryn, 188
Bill, Tony, 153
Binoche, Juliette, 202
Bixby, Bill, 144
Blaché, Alice Guy, 3-4
Blaché Herbert, 3-4
Black, Charles, 68
Blake, Yvonne, 158, 205
Blondell, Joan, 70-71, 194
Boardman, Eleanor, 28
Bogart, Humphrey, 91, 96, 97, 111, 149
Boland, Bridget, 139
Bologna, Joseph, 155
Bono, Sonny, 175
Boone, Pat, 57, 145
Booth, Margaret, 40-41, 54, 156
Booth, Shirley, 199
Bow, Clara, 25, 28, 30, 40
Box, Muriel, 84, 203
Brabin, Charles, 22
Brady, Alice, 199
Braun, Ewa, 205
Bridge, Joan, 141, 205
Bridges, Jeff, 178
Brook, Clive, 65
Brooks, Louise, 28-30
Brynner, Yul, 131, 140
Buck, Pearl S., 51
Burke, Billie, 4
Burns, George, 145
Burstyn, Ellen, 154, 201
Burton, Richard, 136, 137
Burton, Tim, 183

Caesar, Sid, 90
Cage, Nicolas, 173, 194
Cagney, James, 59, 71
Campbell, Alan, 51
Campion, Jane, 184-185, 203

Cannon, Dyan, 173
Canonero, Milena, 158, 205
Capote, Truman, 139
Capra, Frank, 59, 74, 86, 87
Carlisle, Belinda, 162
Carroll, Madeleine, 81
Carson, Robert, 51
Cassinelli, Dolores, 4
Cavett, Frank, 51
Cerny, Karel, 205
Chamberlain, Richard, 193
Chaplin, Charlie, 16, 26
Charisse, Cyd, 121
Chatterton, Ruth, 48
Cheever, John, 139
Cher, 175-176, 202
Chevalier, Maurice, 73
Chew, Richard, 156
Chong, Rae Dawn, 176
Christie, Julie, 196, 200
Cimber, Matt, 127
Clark, Chris, 155
Clayburgh, Jill, 209
Cline, Patsy, 177
Clooney, George, 196
Close, Glenn, 170
Coates, Anne V., 140, 175
Coffee, Lenore, 76, 77, 79
Cohn, Harry, 81, 86, 123, 129
Colbert, Claudette, 74, 84, 198, 207, 208
Colman, Ronald, 71
Comden, Betty, 109, 110
Connery, Sean, 150, 182
Coogan, Jackie, 82
Coolidge, Martha, 173, 188
Cooper, Gary, 65, 71, 130, 149
Corman, Roger, 172
Cornell, Pamela, 158
Cotten, Joseph, 123
Courtot, Marguerite, 7
Crawford, Broderick, 120
Crawford, Joan, 28, 54, 74, 77-79, 85, 92-94, 98, 199, 207
Crichton, Michael, 183
Cristian, Gabriella, 204
Crosby, Bing, 103
Cryer, Jon, 171
Crystal, Billy, 175
Culp, Robert, 148

Curtin, Valerie, 155
Curtis, Tony, 146

Dalton, Phyllis, 141, 205
Dandridge, Dorothy, 106, 134
Danevic, Nena, 175
Darin, Bobby, 144
Darwell, Jane, 199
Davenport, Dorothy, 4, 10
Davis, Bette, 49, 74, 76, 77, 79, 85, 92,
    94, 96-98, 111, 145, 198, 199, 207,
    208
Davis, Frank, 51, 52
Davis, Geena, 185, 202
Day, Doris, 107, 132, 133, 208
Dean, James, 147
Dee, Sandra, 137, 142, 144-145, 208
De Fina, Barbara, 183
De Havilland, Olivia, 103, 199
Deitch, Donna, 174
De Mille, Bibi, 39
De Mille, Cecil B., xii, 7, 11, 13, 32,
    37, 41, 44, 74, 77, 157
De Mille, William, 7
De Niro, Robert, 167
Dennis, Sandy, 200
De Passe, Suzanne, 155
Derek, Bo, 176, 209
Dern, Laura, 188
Descenna, Linda, 158
DeVoe, Daisy, 30
Dickinson, Angie, 137
Dietrich, Marlene, 34, 55, 64-67, 73
Dillinger, John, 69
Di Novi, Denise, 183
Dix, Beulah Marie, 39
Donahue, Troy, 144
Donner, Richard, 171
Dors, Diana, 124, 128-129
Douglas, Michael, 191
Dowd, Nancy, 155, 203
Dressler, Marie, 198, 207
Dukakis, Olympia, 202
Duke, Patty, 200
Du Maurier, Daphne, 80
Dunaway, Faye, 151, 160, 201
Dunne, Irene, 55, 101, 103
Duras, Marguerite, 139
Durbin, Deanna, 55, 68-69, 100
Duryea, Dan, 126

Dwan, Allan, 61

Eastman, Carole, 155
Eastwood, Clint, 150, 184
Eddy, Nelson, 73
Edison, Thomas A., 1, 2
Edwards, Blake, 148
Ephron, Delia, 187
Ephron, Nora, 174-175, 187
Ephron, Phoebe, 139
Estevez, Emilio, 171

Fairbanks, Douglas, 8, 16, 26, 27, 70
Farmer, Frances, 177
Farrell, Charles, 56
Faulkner, William, 140
Fay, Frank, 86
Faye, Alice, 72, 207
Fazan, Adrienne, 113, 204
Feithsham, Fred, 140
Ferrer, Mel, 149
Field, Sally, xiii, 178-179, 201, 202, 209
Fields, Verna, 156, 204
Fields, W.C., 59
Finerman, Wendy, 182, 183, 206
Fisher, Eddie, 134, 136
Fisher, Lucy, 171
Fitzgerald, F. Scott, 28
Flaherty, Frances, 84
Fletcher, Louise, 201
Flynn, Errol, 97
Fonda, Henry, 164, 170
Fonda, Jane, 137, 151, 154, 162-164,
    201, 209
Fontaine, Joan, 103, 199
Ford, Harrison, 182
Forst, Willy, 37
Forster, E.M., 189
Fortensky, Larry, 137
Fosse, Bob, 160, 166
Foster, Jodie, 167, 186-187, 191, 202,
    209
Fowler, Marjorie, 140
Frank, Harriet, Jr., 139, 140, 155
Franklin, Miles, 174
Fricker, Brenda, 202
Fruchman, Lisa, 156, 175, 204
Furse, Margaret, 142, 158, 205

Gable, Clark, 59, 62, 69, 73, 74, 76, 82,

83, 89, 116, 124, 130
Garbo, Greta, 26, 34, 37, 47-49, 54, 62-64, 85
Gardiner, Lizzy, 205
Gardner, Ava, 53, 115-118, 130
Garland, Judy, 74, 83, 98-99, 116, 121, 159, 207
Garnett, Tony, 183
Garson, Greer, 52, 76, 199, 208
Gaumont, Leon, 4
Gautier, Gene, 10-11
Gaynor, Janet, 37, 44, 55-57, 198, 207
Gaynor, Mitzi, 107
Gere, Richard, 178, 182, 193
Gibson, Mel, 174
Gilbert, John, 63
Gilliat, Penelope, 155
Gish, Dorothy, 4, 10, 17
Gish, Lillian, 4, 10, 17-19, 98
Glyn, Elinor, 30, 31, 39-41
Goldberg, Whoopi, 174, 193-194, 202, 209
Goldwyn, Samuel, 22
Goodman, David, 155
Goodrich, Frances, 27, 49-50, 76, 107-108
Gordon, Ruth, 76, 84, 108-109, 200
Gottlieb, Linda, 172
Gould, Elliott, 148
Gould, Lois, 157
Grable, Betty, 72, 103, 208
Grahame, Gloria, 199
Granger, Stewart, 88
Grant, Cary, 71, 92, 94, 149
Grant, Lee, 173, 201
Green, Adolph, 109
Green, Paul, 52
Gregory, Grace, 140
Griffin, Eleanore, 203
Griffith, D.W., xii, 7, 10, 11, 16, 17, 19, 26, 30, 46
Griffiths, Mildred, 85

Hackett, Albert, 27, 49-50, 107-108
Hackett, Raymond, 27
Hackman, Gene, 193
Haffenden, Elizabeth, 141, 204, 205
Haigh, Nancy, 205
Haines, Randa, 174
Hamilton, George, 144

Hammett, Dashiell, 49, 69, 76
Haney, Carol, 150
Hanks, Tom, 179, 182
Hargitay, Mickey, 127
Harlow, Jean, 46, 54, 59-61, 71, 72, 77, 116, 130, 207
Harris, Julie, 141, 205
Harrison, Joan, 76, 80
Harrison, Rex, 149
Hart, Arlene, 172
Hawks, Howard, 62, 87, 91, 137
Hawn, Goldie, xiii, 151-152, 179-180, 201, 208, 209
Hayes, Helen, 198, 201
Hayward, Susan, 115, 118, 119, 200, 208
Hayworth, Rita, 81-82, 86-89
Head, Edith, 55, 84, 85, 113-114, 141, 158, 204, 205
Heckart, Eileen, 201
Heckerling, Amy, 174
Heller, Rosilyn, 154
Hellman, Lillian, 76-77, 107, 170
Henie, Sonja, 207
Henkin, Hilary, 174
Henson, Jim, 182
Henson, Lisa, 182
Hepburn, Audrey, 107, 113, 129, 142, 143, 148-150, 199
Hepburn, Katharine, 54, 74, 85, 92, 94-96, 152, 198, 200, 201, 208
Herbert, Jocelyn, 141
Heron, Julia, 140, 205
Hershey, Barbara, 196
Heston, Charlton, 39
Hill, Gladys, 155
Hiller, Wendy, 200
Hilton, Nicky, 136
Hirsch, Paul, 156
Hitchcock, Alfred, 62, 80, 81, 102, 131, 150
Hoffman, Dustin, 165
Holliday, Judy, 118-121, 199
Holm, Celeste, 199
Hope, Bob, 49, 103, 118
Hopkins, Miriam, 49
Horne, Lena, 116
Hudson, Rock, 144
Hughes, Howard, 59, 116, 118
Hull, Josephine, 199

Hunt, Helen, 202
Hunt, Linda, 201
Hunter, Holly, 187, 191, 202
Hunter, Kim, 199
Hunter, Ross, 144
Hurd, Gale Ann, 172, 184
Huston, Anjelica, 202
Huston, John, 156
Hutton, Betty, 100, 103, 132
Hyams, Nessa, 154
Hyde, Johnny, 123

Ince, Thomas, 27
Irene, 84-85
Iribe, Paul, 44
Ivens, Joris, 76
Ivory, James, 189

Jackson, Glenda, 201
Jackson, Horace, 81
Jaffe, Stanley, 170
Jannings, Emil, 65
Jarrico, Paul, 111
Jaynes, Clare, 79
Jeakins, Dorothy, 85, 141, 158, 204, 205
Jenssen, Elois, 204
Jhabvala, Ruth Prawer, 188-189, 203
Jones, Jennifer, 199
Jones, Shirley, 200
Joy, Leatrice, 28
Joyce, Alice, 7

Kanin, Garson, 109
Karinska, 85, 204
Katz, Gail, 184
Katz, Gloria, 155
Kaufman, George S., 70
Kaye, Danny, 27
Keaton, Diane, 160-162, 173, 174, 201, 209
Keaton, Michael, 171, 178
Kedrova, Lila, 200
Kellogg, Virginia, 84
Kelly, Gene, 68, 89, 100
Kelly, Grace, 107, 115, 129-131, 200, 208
Kennedy, Joseph, 33
Kennedy, Kathleen, 171, 183
Kerr, Deborah, 129, 131-132

Khouri, Callie, 188, 203
Kilmer, Val, 173
Kingsley, Dorothy, 108
Klingman, Lynzee, 155
Kramer, Stanley, 130

Ladd, Alan, 89
Lake, Veronica, 86, 89-90
Lamarr, Hedy, 86, 89, 101-102
Lamour, Dorothy, 103
Lamprecht, Gerhard, 37
Lancaster, Burt, 131
Landi, Elissa, 40
Lange, Jessica, xiii, 165-167, 176-177, 201, 202
Lansing, Sherry, xiii, 168-170, 181-182
Laughton, Charles, 62
Lawrence, Florence, 2-4, 6, 197
Lawrence, Viola, 113, 140
Leachman, Cloris, 201
Leavitt, Ruby, 158
Lehman, Gladys, 84
Leigh, Vivien, 102-104, 199
Lemmon, Jack, 146
Lennart, Isobel, 108, 139
Lennon, John, 126
Levien, Sonya, 52-54, 76, 203
Levitt, Helen, 84
Lewis, Mildred, 171
Lingheim, Susanne, 205
Liotta, Ray, 184
Littleton, Carol, 175
Lloyd, Christopher, 173
Locke, Sondra, 173
Loeb, Janice, 84
Lollobrigida, Gina, 144
Lombard, Carole, 61-62, 81, 84, 121
Loos, Anita, xii, 7-8, 16, 37, 46, 76
Loren, Sophia, 142, 200
Love, Bessie, 4
Lovett, Josephine, 44
Lowe, Rob, 171
Loy, Myrna, 37, 69, 207
Lubitsch, Ernst, 35, 62
Lucas, Marcia, 156, 204
Luce, Claire Booth, 84
Ludwig, William, 54
Lumet, Sidney, 156
Lupino, Ida, xii, 79, 109-113
Lynley, Carol, 137, 142

MacAvin, Josie, 141, 205
MacDonald, Jeanette, 73, 207
MacGraw, Ali, 208
MacLaine, Shirley, 142, 150-151, 201, 208
Macpherson, Jeanne, xii, 11, 37, 157
Macrorie, Alma, 113
Madonna, 173, 185, 194
Magie, George, 4
Magnani, Anna, 200
Malone, Dorothy, 200
Mamoulian, Rouben, 63
Mansfield, Jayne, 124-128
Marion, Frances, 8-10, 37, 39, 40, 44-47, 76, 203
Marsh, Mae, 4
Marshall, Frank, 183
Marshall, Penny, 174, 185
Martin, Steve, 176
Mathis, June, 37, 39
Matlin, Marlee, 174, 202
Matthau, Walter, 146
May, Elaine, 157
Mayer, Louis B., 34, 84
McCambridge, Mercedes, 199
McCarthy, Andrew, 171
McCarthy, Joseph, 106
McCloy, Terence, 155
McCrea, Joel, 89
McDaniel, Hattie, 72-73, 199
McDormand, Frances, 202
McLean, Barbara, 84, 113, 204
McMurty, Larry, 140
McQueen, Steve, 147, 165
McVey, Lucille, 10
Merchant, Ismail, 189
Meredyth, Bess, 7, 39, 46
Midler, Bette, 209
Miller, Ann, 107, 121
Miller, Charlotte, 82
Miller, Stephanie, 206
Millette, Dorothy, 60
Mimieux, Yvette, 137
Minnelli, Liza, 159-160, 201
Minnelli, Vincente, 100, 159
Minter, Mary Miles, 4
Mitchum, Robert, 131
Mix, Tom, 40
Monroe, Marilyn, 8, 107, 118, 121-124, 128, 129, 134, 208

Montand, Yves, 124
Montgomery, Robert, 62
Moore, Colleen, 28, 30
Moore, Demi, 171, 182, 191-194
Moore, Dickie, 68
Moore, Owen, 6, 26
Moreno, Rita, 200
Morgan, Dennis, 101
Morse, Susan E., 156
Murphy, Brianne, 154

Nasatir, Marcia, 154
Nazimova, Alla, 4, 19-21, 43, 44, 51
Neal, Patricia, 200
Negri, Pola, 26, 34-35, 37
Neilan, Marshall, 17
Nelson, Judd, 171
Nelson, Kay, 85
Nelson, Lori, 126
Neuberger, Elsa, 101
Newman, Eve, 140, 155
Newman, Paul, 140, 144, 146-147, 156, 165, 178
Nichols, Mike, 146, 157, 174
Nicholson, Jack, 155, 175, 176, 191
Niven, David, 131
Nolte, Nick, 171, 184, 185
Normand, Mabel, 17
Novak, Kim, 53, 124, 129, 208
Novarro, Ramon, 33, 64

Oberon, Merle, 74, 103
O'Brien, Margaret, 208
Obst, Linda, 184
O'Donnell, Rosie, 194
O'Hara, Maureen, 51, 54, 103
Olivier, Lawrence, 124
O'Neal, Shaquille, 184
O'Neal, Tatum, 201, 209

Page, Geraldine, 151, 202
Paquin, Anna, 202
Park, Ida May, 10
Parker, Dorothy, 50-51, 76
Parker, Sarah Jessica, 196
Parsons, Estelle, 200
Parton, Dolly, 164, 209
Pascal, Amy, 183
Pasternak, Joe, 65
Paxinou, Katina, 199

Perez, Rosi, 194
Perry, Eleanor, 139-140
Pesci, Joe, 184
Pescucci, Gabriella, 205
Peters, Bernadette, 176
Petrova, Olga, 4
Pfeiffer, Michelle, 194-196
Phillips, Julia, 153, 206
Phillips, Michael, 153
Pickford, Mary, 2, 4, 6, 9, 14-17, 25-27, 34, 67, 168, 197, 198
Plunkett, Walter, 115
Poitier, Sidney, 165
Potts, Annie, 171
Powell, Frank J., 21
Powell, William, 61-62, 69, 89
Powers, Mala, 126
Presley, Elvis, 83, 87, 145

Quinn, Anthony, 144

Rack, B.J., 184
Rainer, Luise, 198, 199
Ralston, Esther, 34, 35
Rambova, Natacha, 42-44
Rapf, Harry, 93
Rappaport, Michelle, 184
Ravetch, Irving, 140
Reagan, Ronald, 101
Redford, Robert, 147, 148, 164, 165, 178, 182, 191, 196
Redgrave, Vanessa, 201
Reed, Donna, 199
Reed, Rex, 152
Revere, Anne, 199
Reville, Alma, 76, 80-81
Reynolds, Burt, 178
Reynolds, Debbie, 107, 126, 132-134, 136, 208
Rhodes, Leah, 85, 204
Richardson, Natasha, 196
Ringwald, Molly, 171
Roberts, Julia, 189, 194, 209
Roberts, Marguerite, 82-83
Rogers, Ginger, 74, 85, 89, 98-100, 199, 207
Roland, Ruth, 14
Rooney, Mickey, 100, 116
Roosevelt, Franklin D., 62
Rose, Alex, 153

Rose, Helen, 114-115, 204
Rosenberg, Mark, 170
Rossellini, Roberto, 103
Roth, Ann, 158, 205
Rourke, Mickey, 178
Ruehl, Mercedes, 202
Russell, Jane, 8, 115, 116, 118, 126
Russell, Rosalind, 92, 145
Rutherford, Margaret, 200
Ryan, Meg, 175, 189-191
Ryder, Winona, 182, 196

Saint, Eva Marie, 200
St. Johns, Adela Rogers, 39-40
Sanders, George, 123
Sarandon, Susan, 182, 196, 202
Schell, Maximilian, 67
Schenck, Joseph, 19, 123
Schoonmaker, Thelma, 155, 175, 204
Scorsese, Martin, 175, 193
Scott, Carolyn, 205
Scott, Deborah Lynn, 205
Segal, George, 164
Seidelman, Susan, 173
Selznick, David, 97, 98, 101, 102
Selznick, Lewis, 7
Selznick, Louis, 9
Sennett, Mack, 17, 30, 61
Sharaff, Irene, 115, 141, 204, 205
Shaw, Artie, 116
Shearer, Norma, 33-34, 207
Sheedy, Ally, 171
Sheehan, Winfield, 55
Sheridan, Ann, 86, 91-92, 101
Short, Martin, 171
Shuler-Donner, Lauren, 171, 184
Signoret, Simone, 200
Silver, Joan Micklin, 157
Simmons, Jean, 109
Simpson, Claire, 175, 204
Sinatra, Frank, 116, 150
Slater, Humphrey, 83
Slesinger, Tess, 51-52, 76
Smalley, Phillips, 5
Smith, Maggie, 201
Smith, Shirley W., 84
Snider, Stacy, 184
Snodgress, Carrie, 139
Soderlund, Ulla-Britt, 158, 205
Sondergaard, Gale, 198

Sorvino, Mira, 202
Spacek, Sissy, 160, 201, 209
Spencer, Dorothy, 113, 140
Spewack, Bella, 84
Spheeris, Penelope, 187
Spiegel, Arthur, 7
Spielberg, Steven, 171, 180, 183, 184
Squaricapino, Franca, 205
Stallone, Sylvester, 193
Stanwyck, Barbara, 74, 79-80, 85-87, 92
Stapleton, Maureen, 201
Steel, Dawn, xiii, 170-171
Steenburgen, Mary, 201
Stewart, James, 62, 65, 67, 94, 129
Stiller, Mauritz, 63
Stokowski, Leopold, 63
Stone, Sharon, 193
Stonehouse, Ruth, 10
Straight, Beatrice, 201
Strasberg, Lee, 123
Streep, Meryl, 166, 167, 175, 177-178, 196, 201, 209
Streisand, Barbra, 5, 151-152, 164-165, 168, 172, 185, 200, 208, 209
Sturges, Preston, 87
Sullivan, Ed, 69
Susann, Jacqueline, 108
Sutherland, Donald, 170, 174
Swanson, Gloria, 11, 12, 27, 30-34, 40, 44, 168
Swayze, Patrick, 174
Sweet, Blanche, 4, 16-17, 27

Talmadge, Norma, 4, 19
Tandy, Jessica, 202
Taylor, Elizabeth, 83, 114, 115, 121, 134-137, 200, 208
Taylor, Renee, 155
Taylor, Ruth, 8
Taylor, William Desmond, 17
Temple, Shirley, 56, 67-68, 100, 207
Thalberg, Irving, 33, 49, 51, 77, 79
Thompson, Emma, 196, 202, 204
Thurman, Uma, 196
Tierney, Gene, 103
Todd, Mike, 136
Tomei, Marisa, 202
Tomlin, Lily, 164
Tracy, Spencer, 89, 96, 109
Trevor, Claire, 103, 199

Turner, Kathleen, 177, 209
Turner, Lana, 52, 83, 86, 90-91, 114, 144
Turner, Ted, 164
Turney, Catherine, 79-80

Umeki, Miyoshi, 200

Vadim, Roger, 151
Valentino, Rudolph, 35, 37, 40, 42, 44
Van Doren, Mamie, 127
Van Dyke, W.S., 49
Van Fleet, Jo, 200
Van Upp, Virginia, 76, 81-82, 154
Verdon, Gwen, 107
Viertel, Salka, 47
Von Brandenstein, Patrizia, 158, 205
Von Cube, Irmgard, 84
Von Sternberg, Josef, 65

Wakeling, Gwen, 204
Wallace, Lew, 11
Wallace, Pamela, 203
Waller, Robert James, 183
Wallis, Hal, 150
Warner, Jack, 96, 98
Warner, John, 137
Warrenton, Lule, 4
Wayne, John, 67, 83, 96
Weaver, Sigourney, 172
Weber, Lois, xii, 4-6, 8-10, 41-42
Weinstein, Hannah, 170
Weinstein, Lisa, xiii, 183
Weinstein, Paula, 170, 184
Welch, Raquel, 159
Weld, Tuesday, 137, 142
Welles, Orson, 71, 87
Wells, George, 108
Wertmuller, Lina, xii, 157
West, Claire, 44
West, Claudine, 83, 203
West, Mae, 37, 38, 57-59, 73, 114, 120, 127, 207
West, Vera, 55
Wharton, Edith, 49
White, Pearl, 14
Whitney, Claire, 4
Wiest, Dianne, 202
Williams, Esther, 108, 128, 208
Williams, Kathlyn, 10

Williams, Paul, 165
Wills, Mary, 141, 204
Wilson, Margery, 10
Winchell, Walter, 127
Winslet, Kate, 196
Winters, Shelley, 200
Withers, Jane, 207
Wood, Natalie, 137, 142, 146-148
Woodward, Joanne, 137, 140, 142, 146-147, 200
Wright, Teresa, 109, 199

Wyman, Jane, 121, 199, 208

Young, Clara Kimball, 2, 7, 77
Young, Collier, 111, 113
Young, Loretta, 71-72, 84, 199

Zanuck, Darryl, 56
Zanuck, Lili Fini, 188, 206
Ziskin, Laura, xiii, 182-183
Zorina, Vera, 101